C000004157

Up from the Ashes

Up from the Ashes

A Syrian Christian Doctor's Story of
Sacrifice, Endurance and Hope

DR A
with
Samara Levy

HODDER &
STOUGHTON

First published in Great Britain in 2021 by Hodder & Stoughton
An Hachette UK company

I

Copyright © Dr A with Samara Levy, 2021

The right of Dr A with Samara Levy to be identified as the Author of the Work has been
asserted by them in accordance with the Copyright, Designs and Patents Act 1988.

Unless indicated otherwise, Scripture quotations are taken from the Holy Bible, New
International Version (Anglicised edition). Copyright © 1979, 1984, 2011
by Biblica Inc.® Used by permission. All rights reserved.

All rights reserved. No part of this publication may be reproduced, stored in
a retrieval system, or transmitted, in any form or by any means without the prior
written permission of the publisher, nor be otherwise circulated in any form of
binding or cover other than that in which it is published and without a
similar condition being imposed on the subsequent purchaser.

A CIP catalogue record for this title is available from the British Library

Hardback ISBN 978 1 529 35842 1
eBook ISBN 978 1 529 35844 5

Typeset in Bembo MT by Palimpsest Book Production Ltd, Falkirk, Stirlingshire

Printed and bound in Great Britain by Clays Ltd, Elcograf S.p.A.

Hodder & Stoughton policy is to use papers that are natural, renewable
and recyclable products and made from wood grown in sustainable forests.
The logging and manufacturing processes are expected to conform to the
environmental regulations of the country of origin.

Hodder & Stoughton Ltd
Carmelite House
50 Victoria Embankment
London EC4Y 0DZ

www.hodderfaith.com

*To my children, whom I hope and pray will
continue this vital work here in Syria,
and the multitude of people around the
world who have supported us in prayer as
well as with resources.*

Contents

Foreword

It is rare to meet such a unique and inspirational individual with the true, sacrificial faith I have seen demonstrated in Dr A.[1] There are many gifted speakers and pastors who are capable of stirring hearts and emotions, connecting on issues we all relate to, leading large churches and directing people in their spiritual journeys. However, there are few who truly 'walk the walk' – enduring life-changing trials and discomfort in service to humanity.

I was introduced to Dr A in 2015, and that moment marked the beginning of a remarkable friendship and partnership serving the Syrian people. He is a natural and captivating storyteller, and over the years I have been moved and personally challenged by his stories, from childhood all the way through to working as an ICU[2] doctor in the most savage of wars. I am grateful to him for sharing some of these stories in this book. Reliving many of the events described has been extraordinarily painful, yet he has done so with willingness and grace. His message is one that our world desperately needs to hear.

We have not been called to a comfortable life, but one of difficulties, challenges and persecution. Jesus asked us to share with him in drinking from his cup of suffering and pain, before joining him in eternal peace and joy.[3] Yet many Christians settle for what is comfortable, for a gospel of cheap grace, and they invest their resources in pleasure-seeking and storing up treasures in this world rather than in heaven. If anyone on earth is entitled to challenge us about this with genuine authority, it is Dr A.

My work with Syrian people has taught me that, so often, we have more to learn from the poor, broken and suffering than they need to learn from us. Ministering to any suffering people must come from a place of total humility, with a genuine, heartfelt love for and inclination to learn *from* and *with* those we minister to. I believe we need a willingness to make ourselves lower than the people we reach out to, with an attitude of service. True, sacrificial love is hard to impart in its fullness, even from a posture of perceived equality. Jesus demonstrated the required position to us as he knelt before his disciples, washing their feet, then being flogged, humiliated and crucified in place of them, and us.

I am grateful to have such a discerning, Spirit-led partner, whose strong faith and spiritual wisdom have strengthened and encouraged me significantly in my own life and walk in faith. On many occasions I have felt moved and humbled when faced with his readiness to give from his own pocket, to love those who have persecuted him, or to forgo his own safety and security for the sake of others. Despite everything he has endured, there is not a hint of bitterness in his heart. I have learnt so much from him.

In the past I thought the journey to 'correct' faith followed a certain pattern or ticked specific boxes. Yet I have learnt over time and through my communion with Dr A and his community that it is only we humans who create such criteria. The Holy Spirit instead looks straight to our hearts and our willingness to respond to the radical, challenging call of Jesus. Dr A and his way of living faith might make some Christians feel awkward, yet there is no shadow of a doubt that Dr A is one of the genuine disciples of Jesus. He has much to teach our slumbering church about walking the narrow and difficult road that Jesus Christ called us to.

I have met few people who openly profess their desire to die serving Jesus. Dr A's refusal to cut corners or overlook issues that many would compromise on for a quiet or easy life sets a sobering example. I am greatly honoured that he has agreed to work with me to serve the Syrian people. We both concur that God has called us to do this work, from different continents, yet side by side. We have simply said 'yes' to the invitation, which has taken us on the most incredible, life-changing journey since. We are excited to see what the future holds.

Love,

Samara Levy
Founder of Samara's Aid Appeal

Introduction

Up from the Ashes is the true story of a poor Christian boy, born and raised in Syria, who worked hard to become a successful doctor with a comfortable life. When one of the most brutal and complex wars of our generation struck his nation, he was presented with a life-changing decision. When given the opportunity to relocate his family to a safer country and to start a new life, with a dream job and generous package, he did the opposite of *millions* of other Syrians who went to extraordinary lengths to flee. He committed instead to serve his people, at an extraordinary cost to himself and to his family.

The Syrian war began in 2011 and continues at the time of writing. It has been one of the most brutal, ugly and unforgiving wars of our time, and has been described by the UNHCR as producing 'the biggest humanitarian and refugee crisis of our time'.[1] We have avoided discussion about politics, governments and the many groups involved in this war as far as possible, as there are many books about these subjects already and we don't serve any government or political agenda. Issues relating to these subjects have been touched on briefly, only where necessary to highlight challenges faced by Dr A during the war.

It has taken years of conversations, interviews, recordings, discussions and revisiting memories to write this book. There have been many hundreds of messages and calls in between to fill in the gaps, clarify dates and expound descriptions and details, as we were keen to paint vivid images. We wanted readers to be able to really engage with, see, hear, sense and experience some of the beautiful moments in Dr A's childhood and adult life, and have meticulously checked these details to ensure accuracy. The chronology of a couple of events were harder to establish as, in the intensity and chaos of war, a traumatised human's desire to forget the most painful events is often favoured over their wish to remember.

The experiences, ideas, themes, messages, illustrations, anecdotes, analogies and most of the words are Dr A's. The structure, arrangement and syntax were written by me (Samara). I have tried very hard not to flavour the book with my own accent, and to ensure that the voice that comes through belongs to Dr A. We have changed names and details and have withheld place names to protect the privacy and safety of people and our projects. There are undoubtedly similarities between *Up from the Ashes* and my own story, *Rebuilding the Ruins*, which reflect the similarly held thoughts, beliefs and visions of both authors.

It is our hope that the many experiences and insights we have shared will impact, challenge and inspire others to apply the same principles of costly grace in their own lives. We share a great love for Jesus, and for our brothers and sisters from every background, who display his face to us in their vulnerable moments. Everyone in Syria, from every side, from every faith and in every part of the country, has suffered immeasurably during this war. There are *no* winners, and the cost to humanity has been immense.

We pray this book will challenge and inspire people from every nation to stand and respond to the call that is placed on each of our lives, and to love one another, no matter what the cost.

I

The Carrot and the Stick

'If you return to Syria now, they will kill you.' His words hung between us like thick smog in the hotel foyer. His dry laugh broke through his dark stare. Over time, Dr Khalifa had become very open about his position within a powerful jihadist group. In recent months they had revealed their true mettle and the violent and bloodthirsty means they were using to achieve their objectives of establishing an Islamic government. A few months earlier, Dr Khalifa, like many others, had left Syria.

Many years before he had become a work colleague and, over time, a friend. We had worked on patients together, shared notes and celebrated when our critical patients improved and recovered. We had drunk tea together, had eaten bread and *za'atar* together and had entered into a partnership with a group of other doctors to establish a new hospital. I recalled how he always used to say to people, 'If you want your patient to live, just call Dr A!'

It cut my heart deeply when I saw the same sinister changes taking place in him that I had witnessed in so many others around me. Over time, he had become increasingly hostile and aggressive towards anyone who didn't share his jihadist ideology. He had become an Islamist and, along with the rest of his fundamentalist group, very outspoken and active in the months leading up to the war.

My mind drifted back to a day, early in the war, when we were still working together and he had asked me to take him to a Christian area in Syria. Not knowing his motive, I had been happy to take him. I was encouraged and desperately hoping there was some good left in his heart. As we sat drinking our coffee, I had shared my vision for raising the standards of hospitals in our city.

'I don't understand,' he said, looking at me, bewildered, 'how a *Christian* like you can have such energy, determination and self-respect? After everything that has been done to your people? You Christians don't deserve this area.'

People here have always been looked down upon by radical groups that have infiltrated our country. Dr Khalifa's enmity towards us was a result of his radicalisation. His extremist group, and others like it, have tried extremely hard to destroy humanity over the centuries. There have been countless casualties already in this war, and Christians are not the only ones to be targeted. Every Syrian who doesn't support jihad has suffered at their hands, whether Muslim, Yazidi or of no faith at all.

Dr Khalifa recounted how his armed group had killed a Christian man the week before. The dead man's brother, terrified and under immense pressure from the group, submitted to them. He took to the streets the very next day with the murderers of his brother, representing their cause. He was now counted among the people stirring up unrest. Fear was their weapon, both their attack and their defence, and they had begun to use it with full force to bolster their numbers and gain influence. On hearing this, my hope to uncover any remaining goodness in Dr Khalifa promptly dissipated.

As he listed the recent murders and kidnappings his group had perpetrated, it became increasingly obvious that he wanted to intimidate me. 'AK-47s are just children's toys,' he shrugged. 'PKCs are women's machine guns; us men use the *real* weapons.' He elaborated, telling me how they had killed more of the Sunni Muslim group they had deviated from for refusing to accept jihad than they had killed Christians or other Muslims. 'I can't understand how you are still standing so strong.' As I saw his gaze fixed intently on me, it was clear he was making a direct threat. His eyes shone, relishing the power he held over me as he tried to break my resolve. 'Where do you get your strength?'

As I sat in that Christian town, listening to Dr Khalifa's hate-filled talk together with the catalogue of crimes he and his group had committed over the last few weeks, my heart ached for my old friend. The realisation that my colleague and fellow Syrian had been corrupted and deceived into harbouring such a dangerous ideology, which now made me a target for him rather than a friend, was overwhelming.

Back in the hotel foyer, Dr Khalifa sat watching my reaction, no longer hiding the satisfaction radiating from his face. Savouring my vulnerability, he lifted his glass and slowly took a sip of his orange juice while keeping his eyes fixed firmly on me. We sat in silence for a while. This high-end residence had been my base for the six-week contract I had been working on outside Syria. It was part of a very attractive package that paid for me to run enhanced first aid and disaster response training courses for an international corporation.

But I had begun to feel concerned that Dr Khalifa's group had connections to people working for this corporation and were using these connections to entice me to stay here. Days before, I had received an incredibly generous proposal from the company: $20,000 per month, including accommodation, to relocate from Syria and resettle in this country with my family. At that time, watching the war unfold, it was an extremely tempting offer.

'Look at this beautiful place,' Dr Khalifa was still smiling. 'You can start a new life here that you won't be able to have in Syria now. The war *will* get worse. Bring your wife and children – they will be safer.' He almost sounded as though he cared. My thoughts centred on Miriam and our precious little boys for a moment. Somehow, we had all survived until now, but we had seen so much monstrous killing since the war had begun. Their safety was an ever-constant concern in my mind.

As I scrutinised his gaze, I feared that one wrong word or gesture could cost me my life. He knew I had extensive know-ledge of the Syrian desert, and the ability to plan and see large, strategic projects through. In recent years, I had run numerous projects and evacuation scenarios in those areas, providing private medical, first aid responses and disaster management contracts, alongside my hospital work. This knowledge, together with my committed work ethic, made me a very valuable asset to my community, but a significant threat to his.

The exhortation to be 'as shrewd as snakes and as innocent as doves'[1] echoed through my mind. I had avoided Dr Khalifa's insistent phone calls for the six weeks I had been working here. His agenda had become crystal clear shortly before the war had begun as he, his group and many others had become much more overt and coordinated about their plan to establish an Islamic government in Syria.

Sitting in front of my old friend, I began to wonder if there was a link between his presence here now and other odd recent events. Could he be connected with the very attractive woman at the hotel who had been uncomfortably attentive? When I returned at the end of my working day, sometimes my key card didn't work, and I was forced to return to the reception desk. This woman took it upon herself to escort me to my room, not only opening the door but also entering the room with me. She was brimming over with smiles and gave excessive eye contact, always asking how else she could help. Typically, this isn't the way females behave around men in my culture. She knew that too. My suspicions were raised and, regardless of her motives, I ignored her openness.

Watching Dr Khalifa now, I joined the dots. My encounters at this hotel brought to mind events that had taken place in our hospital just as the hostilities were beginning to unfold in Syria. The manager brought a new employee to the team and asked me to train her in the ICU. She was stunningly beautiful and around ten years my junior. I later learnt she was one of their group. But she did not cover herself with the hijab that modest Sunni girls and women usually wear. The reason I was given for her being under my care had seemed tenuous. She was overly friendly and regularly asked me to help her with various tasks, show her somewhere in the hospital or go for coffee. I recoiled when she stood closer to me than I would expect a woman to. This was not the accepted way between men and women in my community, or hers.

Some weeks later I had been confronted by an exasperated Dr Khalifa, exposing his interest in the design of this strange set-up. 'What is wrong with you?' he spat at me. 'Why don't you see our women?!'

In his frustration, Dr Khalifa had revealed himself to be a man under pressure. He was accountable to someone and had a target he was failing to meet.

'I don't have any problem with your women,' I replied, meeting his eyes directly. 'But I am faithful to my family and beliefs.'

His black eyes pierced my gaze, then clouded over, before he silently left the room.

Perhaps Dr Khalifa had hoped that here, outside Syria, I could be caught off guard. The hotel I was staying at was a seemingly neutral environment, far away from my friends, family and workplace. Here, I was anonymous. Even so, I rebuffed the attempts of the hotel employee – I cared deeply about Miriam and our family. Even before I was married, I didn't have relationships with women like many men around me did. In some of the hospitals I worked in, extramarital relationships between staff were rife. Some of the people who worked with me couldn't understand why I didn't get involved with anyone else, especially when my position gave me so many opportunities. But that was simply not the way my family had been raised.

During the weeks I had been working on the contract outside Syria, a serious explosion had taken place in Damascus, killing three of the most senior government officials under the president. The situation was deteriorating daily, with increasing numbers of explosions and injuries. After this attack, all flights between Syria and this location ceased and my return air ticket became void. Since my contract had finished, the company had kept me as a guest in the hotel while I waited for the logistics to be resolved for my return to Syria. No progress had been made in this. I couldn't help wondering whether the people who had been instrumental in bringing me here may have done so for a different reason than simply providing training. No doubt they had planned many strategic events, both large and small, around the significant attacks that had been taking place in Syria.

Here and now, in this opulent hotel, it was clear I was being shown both the carrot and the stick. They had tried to use women, money and perceived security – but now Dr Khalifa had lost all pretence and patience with me. I could stay here willingly and be well compensated for doing so, or he and his group would kill me. My heart was thumping, but I fought to keep my composure.

'You are right.' I looked him directly in the eye. 'It is safer here. They have made a very attractive offer.' I had to sound interested, but not desperate, if he were to let me walk away from him today. 'I would be foolish not to consider it carefully.'

He reclined slowly back into his chair, smiling, as he placed one ankle across his other knee. He was the picture of confidence itself. Taking obvious pleasure from my powerlessness, his satisfied smile still lingered. I tried to regulate my breathing and battle the indignity rising within me. I could not scream or get out of his grip. I had no choice but to follow the path laid before me.

Before we said goodbye, he paused to take some selfies on his phone in the prestigious surroundings. I waited uncomfortably, watching in disbelief as he snapped a variety of shots from different angles. He was grinning broadly for each one, as if celebrating another notch on his belt.

Now I would have to calculate every move carefully if I wanted to get out alive. There was only one person I could trust with my life in this foreign country. It would be too risky to call him now, in case my calls were being monitored. I simply had to wait for Joseph's spontaneous visit, which usually came every couple of days.

The choices I made over the following days guaranteed that my life would never be the same again. These decisions were life-changing, and I did not choose the easy road. I chose the path of suffering and pain. But on this journey, I have found the true meaning of sacrifice, forgiveness and faith refined by fire. I have found the meaning of life.

2

Early Years in the Promised Land

The glowing orange sun slipped silently through the pink-streaked sky and edged slowly behind the hill. Long, dark shadows stretched lazily into the twilight, while a chorus of cicadas repeated their pulsating refrain in the evening air. Running up again to the brow of the hill, I paused at the top for a moment to catch my breath. Surveying the panoramic scene, my eyes scanned the grove of olive trees that extended into the distance on one side. On the other, the forest cast a shaded, uneven silhouette across the horizon.

I dropped to my knees and shuffled into position, then shoved with all the strength I could muster, sending my tiny frame shooting down the natural slide that our bottoms and knees had worn into the hillside over time. A cloud of dust billowed on either side of my body as it gathered momentum. Peals of laughter bubbled up from my stomach. As the cool evening air whistled past my ears, a whoop of sheer delight escaped my lips as the tear in my trouser leg ripped further into a gaping hole. I felt like a bird, flying. This was true freedom!

My knees were scuffed, my clothes were torn, I was covered in dust and nightfall was upon us. It was time to return home. Mother would not be happy, but I hadn't eaten since breakfast and my stomach grumbled insistently. I would be in trouble for ruining another pair of trousers we couldn't afford.

I was four years old and had spent the day, like every other, running through the village and countryside with our neighbours. They were a little older than me, and we ran ourselves ragged, exploring the hills, trees, river, waterfall and fields. We had our little group, and we were wild and free in our little piece of heaven.

When I burst through the front door, breathless and pink-cheeked, my mother gasped as her wide eyes scanned the contours of my shape. Every emotion flickered across her face as she stared at me.

'What on earth happened to you! And where have you been all day, *habibi*?'

She never waited for me to answer, but I never needed to – she always knew.

Ushering me quickly into the dark kitchen we shared with another family, my mother stooped to light the single-ring gas burner on the floor. The kitchen doubled up as our washroom in our tiny, one-roomed home. The match fizzled before surging into an orange flame, which then settled into a dreamy dance on the end of the tiny wooden stick. The smell of the burning match and the gas filled the air as a ring of blue flames burst into life, rushing and flickering. A large iron pot was put over the burning ring to heat the water that would be used to wash me.

Every item of filthy clothing was removed, and then the warning came: 'Close your eyes and mouth and don't move!' A jug of water was tipped straight over my head, drenching me from top to toe as I held my breath and squeezed my eyes tightly shut. 'You will never be clean again! Where did you manage to find all this dirt?'

I don't know how she expected me to answer while my mouth was closed, but her questions in these moments always seemed more by way of protest than demands for real answers. Jug after jug of water was poured over me as she scrubbed me from head to foot. Once the warm water had run out, I stood dripping in the middle of the room as she pushed the water off the floor with the squeegee.

My mother comes from a Syrian Orthodox family, while my father's family is Catholic. This is very unusual here, as people didn't normally intermarry in this way back then. When my mother and father wanted to marry, my mother's church wouldn't allow them to have the ceremony in their church. They were forced to gain special permission from the bishop of my father's church, which my mother liked, so we were raised as Catholics.

My whole family line is descended from Christians, as far back as any of us have memory and knowledge. Our family, our villages and our Christian communities are very likely to have descended from some of the first Christian converts from Judaism. We are living in places that the apostle Paul visited 2,000 years ago, bringing the message of Jesus. For my family and my community, Christianity is our identity and our heritage. Unless they convert to another religion, anyone born to a Christian family here in Syria will be a Christian, and most people are proud of this identity in Jesus, regardless of how much of the Bible they read, believe or live by. Our family grew up with a strong Christian faith and my parents taught us to trust God with everything.

My brother was the youngest in our family, so I felt a strong sense of responsibility for him when we were growing up. I did more with my sister, as we were closer in age, but as we got older I felt her frustration with me because she wanted a brother who would give her freedom. A girl cannot go anywhere alone in our community, so for her to go to parties and social events, she needed an older brother to go with her. To me, those parties were a waste of time – both mine and hers. If I was going to be her escort, I would have preferred it to be for something useful. As with most things I feel to be a waste of time, I was uncompromising, and she was often disappointed.

My father's career meant we moved often, sometimes from city to city. The most remarkable place for me was a little village we lived in, just outside a smaller city. It was very beautiful, and I would leave the house in the early morning to play in the countryside all day until it got dark. Often, I didn't eat between breakfast and nightfall, but I was happy. I loved running around in the fresh air with friends, playing in nature and making contraptions to catch birds.

When my father returned from his work absences, he was usually tired. Once, when I was small, my mother had promised to take us out for the day, and I was really looking forward to it. Suddenly my father appeared after a long absence and my mother cancelled the trip. Disappointed, I asked her, 'Is this an appropriate time for him to come home?' He felt more like a visitor than part of the family, we saw so little of him. My mother was the parent we relied on.

In later years, my father explained how he had tried to distance himself from us children, as he knew he would soon be leaving again. He didn't want us to become too attached and then be upset each time he left or to miss him when he was gone. He was keen to maintain the balance and routine we had with our mother. She was the one we relied on, but raising us alone was hard work for her.

I often suffered abdominal pain, and sometimes called out for her at night as I lay in bed. She was tired and didn't come, so I prayed instead – simply, with no knowledge of any specific ways of praying, Bible passages or anything else. I just spoke to God directly with the heart of a little boy, saying, 'My tummy hurts. Can you help?' Within seconds the pain would vanish. It felt warm in my stomach where it had been hurting before, and I went back to sleep.

In the early morning when I would tell my mother what had happened, she would just say, 'Yes, dear, that's nice,' with a smile.

When I was older and after my brother and sister were born, my father rented a two-roomed house. This contained just one bedroom and a sitting room (which we had to keep clean for visitors), with a kitchen and corridor in between. My brother and sister shared a single bed and I slept in the hallway. I spent much of my childhood in that corridor.

In the summer we used to play outside, but in winter, when it was cold, this corridor was the place we gathered to keep warm. It was freezing going to the outdoor toilet. There was a rug on the floor in that hall which I used to sit on, happily doing my homework, to the background noise of everyone else sitting around and talking. It was the only part of the house we could afford to heat in winter, so we all huddled together there around the *sobia*, the diesel heater used by every Syrian family to keep warm. We couldn't always afford enough fuel, so sometimes even the *sobia* didn't keep us warm. But as the corridor was very small, we all congregated there to sit.

We always had visitors staying in our lounge, so we put an extra small bed in the corridor which my sister and I would take turns to sleep in, but we never felt we didn't have enough space. My maternal grandfather often stayed in our sitting room, and we regularly stayed in his house, too, when my father was away. My aunt stayed with us frequently while she studied nearby; in fact, she stayed with us for most of the two years she was studying. After her, a cousin came to stay while studying close by.

I loved sitting on that floor doing my homework, with my sister beside me, listening to the adults chattering around me about something or other that had happened in the village. They were happy days, and life was simple. We had our struggles and very little money, but we were part of a community with its own customs and ways, and people really took time for each other. We knew we could depend on one another and we all took care of each other. We may have had little, but we were content.

My childhood was a genuinely happy time. Yet, looking back, it is clear my life has been a fight for survival from the beginning. Just before I was born, my father was put in prison. He hadn't broken the law. On the contrary, he was jailed for refusing to use his position as an army officer to exploit the soldiers below him to make a profit for his corrupt superior. For standing his ground and speaking out in the name of truth and justice, he was incarcerated.

On top of all the other challenges my mother was facing at the time, I became very sick as a newborn. The hospital staff told her that if I didn't have a blood transfusion quickly, I would die. To complicate matters further, my mother struggled to find a suitable donor, and time was running out.

The day I was born, another family had a baby girl in the same hospital; she was called Hope. She also became very sick, then died when she was only a few days old. Her grieving father heard the nurses talking about my life-or-death situation, and he was so moved that he donated some of his blood to save me. This Muslim man was so generous to my family. He not only gave me his blood but also showered me with gifts, and he asked my parents to consider me as his son from thereon. He gave our family the precious gift of my life, having just lost his daughter's. We will always be grateful to him. I feel like that event in my life is symbolic of what Jesus also did for me, for all of us – giving his blood so that we might live.

After some time, my father was released from prison and punished in a different way. He was demoted from his position as an army officer and instead given an unfavourable position, then he was transferred to a different area. He was never one to keep quiet about issues and practices he felt were wrong or unethical, and we faced the repercussions that went hand in hand with this, many times.

I inherited and learnt his unwillingness to compromise on important issues. I still believe that this life is too short to sacrifice our integrity or jeopardise who God wants us to be. Wherever we are in the world, and especially in a place like Syria, people's lives and whole families depend on individuals making the right decisions. My father taught me that the way in which we live our life is more important than living a 'successful' life that is full of compromise. We should behave rightly, even if this means we lose our life in the process. Jesus said we should not be afraid of those who want to kill our bodies but cannot kill our soul. We should instead feel afraid of 'the One who can kill both body and soul in hell'.[1]

My father is a very spiritual man and throughout his life he has periodically had dreams and visions from God. From him, I learnt what it looks like in practice to apply some of the toughest teachings of Jesus to our lives.

Later, the corrupt superior who had been responsible for placing my father in prison was exposed. Eventually my father was cleared and the guilty parties were removed. My father was given a better position, but that would not be the last time my father would be imprisoned for being a man of integrity and honour. It was not an easy mission to be a senior army officer and a faithful Christian at the same time. There were few Christian officers who had reached the same level as my father in those days.

There have been many occasions in my life when I have faced dangerous situations, but I did not run away when I felt there was something important that I should do. If God had wanted to let me die, he could have let me die back then as a baby. But he didn't. He intervened and let me live.

3

Growing up in Syria as a Christian

The blazing August sun scorched my shoulders as I heaved another cardboard box into our small supermarket. Sweat trickled down my back as I stooped to stack the box in our dark stockroom. There was hardly space to move between the goods, which on this day were stacked higher than my head. Walking back out to the tower of cartons still standing on the pavement, the noises of the car engines and tooting horns announced the special occasion taking place to the wide and dusty street as people bustled by.

It was Saint Mary's Day, and everyone was cheerful in our Christian district of the city as they prepared for the festivities in their churches and homes. We sold lots of sweets, which people gave to each other as gifts for this celebration.

We had started work early in anticipation of the extra customers who would be passing through the shop on this special day. The influx of people arriving so far had been promising.

We were still very poor and had to work day and night, especially on days like this, just to cover the basics for living. We just about managed to get by, but I never felt poor at the time; I felt happy and at peace. It was only when I compared our living situation to others that I realised how poor we were.

Hoping to capitalise on the good atmosphere, I stacked yet another carton on top of a pile, then asked my father once again for the watch I was hoping for. I was thirteen. Lots of my friends now had a watch and I had been asking him for months.

He looked up from the bag of rice in his hand and his eyes met mine. With his characteristic patient and accepting manner, he replied, once again, that I didn't need one.

I wanted a watch with all my heart, but I knew my father

had to be careful with money. I replied that it was okay because God would find a way to give me one.

He smiled lovingly at me as I turned, undeterred, to walk back into the street. Hauling the next cardboard box up to hip height and clutching it closely, I prayed with all my heart, with childlike faith and expectation, that God would give me a watch.

We worked so hard that day, moving boxes, refilling the shelves and serving customers. By nightfall we were aching, dusty and exhausted. I found a spot outside and sat on a concrete step to take a short rest. A warm breeze caressed my face as I sat listening to the evening sounds. The black sky was sprinkled with glittering stars, and seemed to act as a giant amphitheatre as it magnified the sounds of the people and cars. My eyes dropped to the steady passing vehicles. One whizzed past, its headlamps reflecting on something that glinted on the ground just a few steps in front of me. Curious, I lifted myself up from the step and stooped to pick up the shining object in the road. Fingering the metal and glass, I marvelled – I was cradling a watch in my hand.

There were a couple of small scratches on the glass face, and a metal joint had popped out, but I pushed it carefully with my fingers and fixed the joint back into place. I studied the silvery-grey metal that had a gold-coloured rim around the face. As I held it closer to the light from the shop window, I could see the words 'QUARTZ' written across the top of the face and 'WATER RESISTANT' written across the bottom. The pale colouring on the otherwise gold hands indicated they would glow in the dark. The red second hand made a gentle ticking sound as it flicked around each of the numbers on the face. It was perfect!

Barely able to conceal my excitement, I rushed back into the shop, asking every customer whether they had lost a watch. No one knew anything about it. Carrying it carefully in my hand, I took it to my father and showed him what God had given me. He smiled simply and nodded. I beamed with pride at this exciting and miraculous gift from heaven.

★

My father had been released from prison two years earlier, having been wrongly incarcerated for a second time. His imprisonment had been a huge and life-changing event for all of us. It felt like we were losing him, and I was terrified that he would be gone forever. At the age of eleven I suddenly found myself as the man of the family. My mother and younger siblings cried a lot, but I didn't feel I could cry in front of them. I felt they should be able to depend on me and that I must be strong for them. We lived in a very small house that had a little room with a ceiling so low we couldn't stand up in it, which I used to go into and sit in alone. When no one else could see, I would cry in there, pleading with God to save my father.

One day my father's closest friend came to our house. We had spent a lot of time with him and his family over the years. As a subordinate army officer, he said we should consider my father dead, as my father was nothing in the eyes of the people detaining him, and his life was worthless to them. He kept repeating that my father was worthless, as he stubbed out his cigarette. I felt his words and behaviour were totally inappropriate for our situation. He was disrespectful to our family and dishonoured my father. Neither I nor my mother or siblings could consider my father to be dead or worthless, and we could not give up hope for him. I challenged this man, young as I was, telling him that perhaps he was right, but he was equally as worthless. He was offended and didn't come to visit us again.

The encounter showed how attitudes of others changed towards us when my father was sent to prison. People stopped visiting us and even talking with us. We became nobodies in our community. Without knowing anything about the situation, they had already judged us all as being guilty. It was an isolating and difficult time for us all, and we longed for our father to return. Additionally, his salary was stopped, leaving us with only our mother's income to survive on. Financially, we were in an extremely precarious situation, and we could not afford to live or eat in the way we had previously.

Mercifully, God answered the cries of our hearts – after six months in prison my father was suddenly released. This was a miraculously short amount of time, as usually these situations take years to resolve. Although my father was innocent, upon his release he was also discharged from the army. When he found out what I had said to his friend, he told me I was right about him.

Few Christian men would reach high positions in the military in those days. My father was not a man who could be manipulated or coerced into doing the wrong thing for power or profit – neither his nor anyone else's. Over time, he became aware of individuals around him who could not tolerate him in a position of authority because he was unwilling to accept bribes and would not be bought. In particular, there was a man connected with the Muslim Brotherhood who plotted to murder him and planned to take his position. Instead of simply arresting the man who was planning to assassinate my father, my father was also arrested and locked up while they carried out their investigation.

With my father no longer in the military, we opened a small supermarket. This was a huge lifestyle change for all of us, particularly as I now had unlimited access to my father for the first time, and I couldn't get enough of him. My father is a wonderful man, and with this new time together we developed a very close relationship. This marked a different period in our lives, one where we would sit for hours together every day in the supermarket, and I learnt from him and his experience of life. My father shaped who I am now.

Until then, our family hadn't had much contact with the wider community. Overnight, we became exposed to everyone. People from every background came into our supermarket and we served them all. Initially, being so young, I didn't quite understand who they all were, but I started to suss out different groups of people and, in turn, their differing mentalities. They all came with stories, and I learnt that situations aren't always how they appear on the outside. I learnt that there are many different angles to the truth, and that people often show only particular aspects of themselves to the public, while other aspects remain hidden.

In a small community, people quickly form opinions about others, namely their status and standing in the community, and whether they are good or bad. I learnt even at this young age that people are not always as they seem on the outside. Sometimes, women who were known prostitutes would come into the shop. The community considered them to be bad and disgraceful. But those women were honest, good customers who paid for everything. They didn't do us any wrong. On the other hand, other people, perhaps friends or those who were well respected in the community, took products that they couldn't pay for, promising to come and pay the next day, but never giving what they owed. As a family we had so little and we depended on that money just to be able to eat.

These were hard lessons to learn about who is right and wrong, good and bad. But they were fascinating lessons to learn at such a young age about honour, pride, self-righteousness and hypocrisy.

On one occasion when I was older, I was given a job to deliver some items for the supermarket. It was too far to walk, and even taking the bus would still involve carrying a lot of heavy bags. I asked my father if I could get a taxi to deliver them but he said no. I didn't want to carry these heavy bags such a long way, so I said to him, 'It's okay, Jesus will help me.' Within a few minutes, someone we knew pulled up in a car next to me to offer me a lift. I looked up to see my father smiling at me as I loaded the heavy bags into the car.

My father never made anything easy for me, but he taught me resilience and a special faith which has served me well in life. One example was when he gave me a construction toy (similar to Lego®), but before he gave it to me, he took the instructions out of the box. It took me a long time to make that car! When I had finished it, my father congratulated me, then gave me the instructions. I couldn't believe he had had them all along yet hadn't given them to me beforehand. When I asked him why he did it, he explained that he wanted me to learn patience and problem solving.

Looking back over my life, I believe he achieved his goal.

His methods were unconventional, but I wonder whether I would have survived in Syria for so long or achieved so much if it hadn't been for his unusual ways of teaching me to depend on God. In life, no one gives us the instructions for most of the things we want to achieve. We have to figure them out for ourselves.

Perhaps because of our own experiences of having so little, my mother taught me a great deal about compassion and sacrifice, which I naturally began to live out in my own behaviour. One example was when I was around seven or eight years old and was on a long bus journey. While I was sitting on the bus, I noticed an older man who was standing. He looked tired, but there was no space for him to sit. His slumped shoulders and weary face touched my heart and I offered him my place.

Yet I had moments of mischief too. One day my mother took me to the city to see the doctor to have my tonsils removed as I suffered recurrent bouts of tonsillitis. I remember waiting in the doctor's room alone, with an elastic band in my hand. I spotted an ashtray full of cigarette butts (a common occurrence in those days). I picked them up one by one and, using the elastic band as a catapult, fired each cigarette butt through the window at people in the street as they walked past. There was no doubt that as well as being a loving boy, I was challenging!

I had so much energy and did not accept anything easily. It would always take my mother a long time and a lot of effort to convince me to do anything. She used to ask me to finish my dinner, but I argued and asked her why I had to eat it. When she said I had to eat this food to grow bigger, I argued that she kept putting food in the same dish every day, but the dish didn't grow any bigger – it stayed the same! Even now, it is not easy for anyone to convince me of anything, and I don't compromise on things I feel are important.

I also had strong opinions from an early age, one of which concerned the leaders of the churches that surrounded our communities. I didn't consider that their actions reflected the teachings of Jesus that I had heard and read about in the Bible. To me they seemed more like the Pharisees – the same people still crucifying Jesus rather than those sent by God to represent him. They walked around in long robes with an air of importance, but I didn't see them helping the poor. They didn't look like Jesus to me.

One day the bishop came to visit our house. He wore flowing robes and looked very stuffy and self-important. I was young and didn't warm to him. I asked him whether the solid gold cross he wore around his neck was the same cross that Jesus had asked him to carry. He was perplexed by my question, so I elaborated, asking why he wore a gold cross when Jesus asked us to sell our possessions and give to the poor. Quickly, my parents ushered me out, apologising and explaining that I was working through understanding my faith. But even now I would stand by this question to those religious men. I didn't feel they had anything to offer me in my journey in faith. They were dry and dull, and I didn't see any light or love coming from them. I could not feel Jesus in their hearts and I wondered whether they knew the same Jesus I did.

When I was a teenager, a young Bedouin man from a very large tribe came into our supermarket. He was very dark skinned and wore the customary white *abaya*[1] and the red-and-white *shmakh*[2] covering on his head, secured with a black *eakal*.[3] Our family knew their family. I watched as the man told my father he needed some things from the supermarket but said he couldn't pay as he didn't have any money. He promised that if my father allowed him to take what he needed he would return and pay him back.

My father replied that he couldn't take the items unless he paid for them. But the man was insistent, saying that he would put God as his guarantee that he would pay. My father paused thoughtfully before saying, 'I can't refuse if God is your guarantee. But you should be careful.' He continued, warning the man, 'God is real, and no one should play with him. No one should use him as a guarantee, thinking that nothing will happen if you don't honour the promise you made.'

The man insisted that he would return my father's money and that God was his guarantee. My father accepted, and allowed the man to take what he had asked for without him paying. We struggled financially, and when the time came for the man to pay, he did not. My father chased him for weeks, yet the man kept telling him he didn't have any money and he wouldn't pay. My father went to the man's parents, which is customary in our culture when there is a dispute. They in turn said they were not responsible for his behaviour and that he should pay himself, as they would not pay for him. We desperately needed that money.

One day, my father saw the man on his motorcycle and asked him again when he would pay his debt. The man replied that he would not pay and told my father to go to hell. In a loud voice, my father said to him in the street, 'You used God as your guarantee and now I am asking God to get my money from you. Go, but you can't escape from God.'

The man was engaged to be married. A week later, he was riding his motorcycle and had an accident just a few metres from our supermarket. It was the night before his wedding. He was taken to the hospital but died before he arrived.

My father went to the funeral, as he knew the family. Filled with compassion, he wanted to pay his respects to this grieving family. As he walked into the hall, the father of the man saw him. He rose to his feet, looked my father in the eye and said, 'God is bigger than anyone and He kept your money. We will pay the money our son took from you. We just want you to forgive him.'

My father accepted the money. When he returned home, he sat in the chair he always sat in and said, 'God is my guarantee.' I still remember both his smile and the fear in his eyes as he digested all the events that had taken place.

4

Medical School

The desk in the professor's clinic was discoloured and the edges were eroded. Papers were arranged neatly in files, next to the faint rings of worn varnish from hot coffee cups that had been placed on the otherwise tidy table. The faded furniture in the clinic was sparse. It was hard to tell which had been there longer, the furniture or the equipment, with its dated designs and yellowing plastic. Even the professor himself displayed a reasonable set of wrinkles.

Shelves filled with books lined the walls. His library was part of the attraction of his otherwise redundant clinic. The main attraction was his company. The professor was a wise man and a great conversationalist, offering in-depth analysis across many different subjects. The clinic was more of an office, really, and a place for meeting with friends, as no patients ever went there. He was a learned and experienced teacher who had completed his masters in the US, before accomplishing his doctorate here in Syria.

This was my second year of medical school. I had told the professor I was reading Guyton and Hall's textbook.

'Brilliant!' he replied. 'Can I borrow it?'

After I had lent him my book, our friendship had grown. I would visit him in his clinic where we discussed all manner of subjects. On that day, we had been talking about the novel he had been writing about the East and West, which he was now trying to get published.

As my eyes glanced up to the shelf, the spine of a thick hardback caught my eye. Curious, I leaned forward and plucked the faded green book carefully from its resting place. I blew the fine layer of dust from the top and fanned through the sheets of cream paper with my thumb and fingers. The sweet, musky scent of the yellowing pages wafted into the air as it fell open on a new chapter. As my eyes scanned the text, I spotted a description of a famous historical conqueror. I knew about him but had never studied him in detail. Intrigued, I read on. The date he died caught my eye.

'Wow,' I breathed.

Peering over the rim of his glasses, the professor studied me through the crow's feet around the corners of his eyes. His appearance and demeanour resembled the archetypal ageing and eccentric professor almost perfectly, except for his full head of salt-and-pepper hair. 'What is wow?' he probed.

The man's name was the same as mine, and the day and month of his death was my birthday.

'So, young Dr A,' his eyes were fixed on mine, deadly serious now, 'at your age, this man was ruling the world. What have you achieved so far in your life?' His gentle voice and soft expression coaxed a considered response.

'Well, Professor,' I smiled, taking my time, 'so far, I haven't killed anyone!'

His head tilted thoughtfully to the side as he waited for me to elaborate.

'That man killed many people to reach his position, but I have not taken anyone's life. I am training to be a doctor, and I hope I will save more people in my lifetime than he killed in his.'

His chair creaked as he shifted position and his face broke into a smile. 'Nice answer,' he replied.

This was an event in my life I will always remember. It was a defining moment. It seemed as if that book had been waiting there for me for that very purpose, to reveal my life's manifesto: to serve and heal my community. My heart was set and the concept implanted in that moment. I felt as if God was showing me that what is viewed as great in the world's eyes isn't great in his. This leader became world famous and powerful through killing others. He was rich and his name is in many history books. Yet his life came to an end, just like all the other rulers in this world. What was his legacy? Could anything he brought to the world justify the destruction and suffering he caused?

Many people like the idea of being someone important. However, sitting in the professor's office, I felt my eyes open. If I wanted to be someone important, then I should be important to my community through healing and serving people.

From as early as I can remember I wanted to be a doctor, and it was well known in my community. The people in our village started calling me 'Dr A' when I was a very young child. They humoured me when I said I would be a doctor, and would ask me about their aches and pains, some of which they undoubtedly made up to see what I would say. They sat still as I 'examined' them, and many people from our village came to visit 'Dr A'.

Some of the 'prescriptions' I gave for the problems they told me about were very bizarre indeed! One family friend came to visit when I was very small and told me he had abdominal pain. I replied that it was because he kept eating donkey meat! It became a standing joke among his friends and our family after this, and people regularly teased him about his alleged eating habits.

When I was a little older, I remembered hearing about Jesus healing people. I listened closely and began asking Jesus to help me when I was in pain, which he did. One day a man came to visit me. He was joking, saying, 'Oh, Dr A, my stomach hurts!'

This time I replied, 'Maybe you need to pray to Jesus, and he will heal you.'

He seemed surprised. Yet I in turn was amazed by his bewilderment. This seemed to me like the obvious solution. I knew Jesus had healed me when I had stomach pain. I couldn't understand why this man didn't warm to my advice.

Later, when I was an adult, these events stayed at the back of my mind. I really meant it when I gave that advice. I always believed, even when I went on to specialise in ICU, that we should ask God for healing, not just rely on medicine. If we want to work on the body God created, we should pray to him as we do so.

The only hope for a penniless boy like me to reach medical

school was to be the best at school. I worked hard and was the top student in my class, in both elementary and secondary school. For the first few years I was at the elementary school my mother taught there, but after four years the government moved me to another school, as it was running a pilot programme to teach English. Previously, English was not normally taught at elementary school. We had two English classes a week, which I enjoyed, even though my teacher wasn't brilliant.

When I made this jump from school to school, it was like moving home and family. I went from being with my mother all the time to suddenly being in an alien environment where I didn't know anyone. In the two years I was at this school, I had to learn how to fend for myself and survive alone.

The move was a culture shock. Previously I had always lived in a Christian community, but at this new school I was the only Christian. There was no teaching about Christianity there, only Islam. Ironically, although I was the only Christian, being the top student I also held the highest marks in Islamic studies. The teacher asked me to read from the Quran and explain to the other Muslim students how we should live. In spite of being top of the class, it was challenging studying the Quran, as the type of Arabic used is very complex. However, I enjoyed studying the etymology of the text, and studying it also helped me to understand the mentality of my Muslim brothers, which assisted me a great deal later on in life.

A group of Muslim students were unhappy, however, that a Christian exceeded their performance, not just in Islamic studies but across all subjects. Each year, that group of children attacked me when the exam results were released, saying I didn't deserve this position, being a Christian. Even though my friends at that school were all Muslim, they tried to defend me when I was attacked. My best friend, Munzer, was a Muslim and stood beside me as we both fought back, and he took some of the punches and kicks that were intended for me. I looked at him afterwards, concerned by a wound on his face. He glanced back at me, commenting that I had one too. We smiled at each other, proud that we had put up a good fight that day.

I gained my place at medical school through a scholarship, so I studied for free to become a doctor. Such scholarships are given to the students who attain the highest grades at school, and the medical school I went to was extremely selective. Coming from a poor family, it would have been impossible for me to study medicine if I hadn't gained this scholarship.

Students from wealthy families all studied abroad. For me that wasn't an option, but the medical school I attended was new and there were only about fifty students there at that time. The doctors teaching us were mostly younger and closer to our age as students – many were only ten years older than us, and they were also new to the school. They were people we could relate to, especially because ours were some of the first classes they ever taught. It was very intimate, and we developed a close relationship with our professors and teachers. We became good friends and went to visit them in their homes and medical clinics. There was plenty of time to sit talking with them, hearing their opinions and in turn sharing ours with them. It felt like a private medical school as our classes were so small.

We had a general hospital in the city that was linked to our medical school. This was really helpful because we were able to spend a lot of time in the same working environment as quali-fied doctors. It wasn't just a place where we studied; we spent a lot of our time as students in this hospital dealing with sick patients, working across every department. Because we didn't have our own building, we spent more time in the general hospital than we might have done at a well-resourced university with a medical faculty.

One of my fellow students in medical school was an old friend and neighbour. We had grown up together, and our mothers had taught together at the same school. In our first year at medical school we started dreaming of building a new hospital for our city. We spent many hours fantasising about it. He was very gifted in using computer-aided design packages, and we soon started to put together drawings and plans for what we thought our dream hospital should be like. Every day, after learning something new, we would revisit the designs, adding extra details to our creation. There was a TV programme at the time called *Chicago Hope*, set in a very beautiful and modern hospital. We started calling our dream hospital 'Hope' after being inspired by that hospital.

I made lots of new friends during my first year at medical school and each subsequent year as the new cohorts joined, but some familiar faces joined too. One of these was an old secondary school friend whom I had formerly sat next to in class. Once we got to university, the history we shared meant we got to know each other better and our friendship deepened.

We often visited each other in our homes, and one day in our third or fourth year I was invited to dinner with his family. His father had been a prosperous businessman and was very wealthy. In the days and weeks after this dinner, my friend told me that his sister kept asking him about me. I didn't say anything and eventually he went off to finish his medical training abroad.

When he returned, he reminded me of his sister's interest and tried to persuade me to become part of their family. When I didn't respond, he came to my house. He brought with him designs and plans for a new hospital in our city. It looked amazing and had been designed by an architect outside Syria for a piece of land in a nice Christian area. After showing me all the plans, he stopped, looked me directly in the eye and said, 'This hospital will be yours.'

Although they were a nice family, I felt I would be selling myself for this hospital. It felt uncomfortable. When I looked at the plans for the hospital, impressive as they were, it didn't feel like my dream or vision. I felt God say to me, 'This is not my way.' As much as it was my dream to have a hospital in the city, it would have to come another way; I didn't feel I could marry with the hospital essentially being used as bait. When I got married, it would be to the woman of my choice, and for the right reasons.

It was while I was at medical school that I met Miriam. We became good friends and later married.

★

Early in my studies I felt it was unwise to just study medicine in Arabic textbooks. They were limited compared with what I could learn if I were to study in English. I started reading English medical textbooks too. My father encouraged me and helped me to buy them, which was very precious to me. But it also caused me significant problems; as I focused so much on learning in English, I didn't have such a strong ability to communicate everything I needed to (relating to medical scenarios) in Arabic.

On one hand, I knew it was important to learn all the English terminology so I could look at research papers, which would detail a wider variety of current practice. On the other hand, my exams were all in Arabic, so I was at a disadvantage to my peers in our cohort. It was harder to give comprehensive answers in Arabic. The teachers tried to help me as much as they could to prepare for the Arabic exams. They said it was a good idea to continue studying in English, but they warned me that I wouldn't get as high a mark in my degree as many of my fellow students. However, the doctors and professors at medical school marvelled that I was doing this, as no one else was. They considered me to be one of the best students in the cohort. They encouraged me to continue focusing on my studies in English because of the greater understanding I would gain.

*

While I was at medical school, my father went to work in the US. He was earning very good money there and we were all preparing to emigrate there as a family. The plan was for me to finish my medical training, then go and specialise in the US.

One day, while my father was working on a building site, he had a serious accident and was taken to hospital. He was unable to move or do anything for months.

With my father absent, the responsibility for my family fell to me, as the oldest son. This was a big responsibility; I had to run all the family affairs (including the family business) and be the main representative of the family for everything. If there was a funeral or any other event where our family should be represented, it was up to me to go. During this time, my sister got engaged and her fiancé had to ask me for her hand in marriage, even though I was of a similar age to her.

I was studying one day, when my father called me. He was still convalescing from his accident. As we talked, he described what life was like in the US, specifically with regard to how advanced things were compared to at home. I asked him if he liked it. He didn't.

He said that, in America, people lacked a true sense of community. People were like independent numbers rather than being really connected to each other. He described how no one cared who your family were or who your father was, and how people struggled to have meaningful relationships with each other, jumping from one partner to the next. He described how an old man would be left on his own in a home while his adult children would be off on holidays and trips and living their lives independently, all the while neglecting their father. He went on to analyse how the system in America seemed to push people towards that kind of individualistic lifestyle, away from a true sense of community and belonging. He was amazed how no one seemed to feel any shame when they did the wrong thing. Instead they were more focused on their own pleasures, desires and needs – setting their priorities on things like a new house, a new car, more holidays or more things to fill their house with. Because they felt they needed all these things, they would work more hours in order to buy more of everything.

He asked me what the benefit of having money is if you don't have the time to spend it. And if you have the money and the time, then you don't have the people to spend it with. He told me that if I were to go and work in the US, I would be very busy in my work in the hospital, but I wouldn't have time to spend with him. He said living in America was like a film: it was nice to watch it, but living in that world is a totally different matter.

As I talked with him, I felt God put it in my heart to tell him to come home. But I resisted saying anything, as our entire family had been planning this for years, and my father had spent two years working there to set everything up for us. How could I make a statement like that when all our family had invested so much time, energy and hope into the plan?

However, I decided to be obedient no matter the consequences, so I took a deep breath and told him what I felt. I asked him to come back because I felt God wanted us to be in Syria and that our mission was here, not in the US. I explained that I felt God had allowed him to have this accident, and that he should come home, as the US was not where we were meant to be. He replied simply that he felt the same and would return. He informed my mother of his decision and within a few weeks he was back with us in Syria. My father has always been a rock for me and I built my decisions and responses on his wisdom during the war years. I was glad that God sent him back.

*

When I was in the fourth year of medical school, I started going to the main city hospital regularly. I spent a lot of time there and went to work with the doctors. Sometimes I worked with the doctors all night even though I was still a student. After a while they started allowing me to do more work with them. Seeing my work, several doctors remarked that I was more able to run their ICU than the new resident doctors coming straight from medical school. I discovered how much I liked ICU, and I felt it was where I was meant to work. It was a high-pressure, fast-paced environment, caring for extremely sick patients and handling many complicated cases. I was happy and enjoyed the challenges that I faced there, as I worked better under pressure. Although I was keen to look at other disciplines, such as surgery, I always gravitated back to ICU.

When I finished medical school, I began to specialise in emergency care (Accident and Emergency). At the time I was newly married, and Miriam was pregnant with our first child. My residency didn't pay enough, especially bearing in mind we were expecting our first baby. I took a part-time job working as a medical supervisor for a pharmaceutical company. This was a fascinating experience, particularly as a large part of the job was to tell doctors about various products, so it gave me a good reason to go into their clinics and speak with them. Here I gained invaluable insight into the challenges doctors faced with medications and with patients. I began to understand the different medical settings and I also learnt how different medical environments worked.

Despite these positives, I didn't like the job, and the longer I was there, the more I felt it was a wholly inappropriate job for a doctor. I didn't feel any doctor should spend time convincing people to take medications that may not even help. Doctors should give the treatments they believe are best for their patients. I noticed some doctors were easily persuaded to prescribe one medication over another if the company was offering a trip abroad or another incentive. If there were two or three products, the doctors would always prescribe the one with the biggest incentive for them. This convinced me early on that there are two things that should never be done together: trading and practising medicine. The focus should be on whether your treatment is effective and good, not on who will reward you for prescribing their medication.

It opened my eyes to the huge responsibility of being a doctor. Having someone's life in your hands is clearly the biggest responsibility anyone could have. But the ethical issues are enormous. It's easy for doctors to deceive patients, because they come willing to do anything you say. Doctors must respect and value patients as human beings and not see them as products, or as people who can help them in their career or could be a selling point for them. When treating patients, all doctors should work as if they were treating themselves. This understanding helped me as my career developed, especially where I saw unethical practices taking place.

Unsurprisingly, the pharmaceutical company didn't like this mentality at all. When people asked me if the drug was good, I gave an honest answer. When the company found out I wasn't saying their product was brilliant, they fired me! I wasn't sorry to leave that job behind, and it worked out for the best because I soon had to move to another area.

5

Becoming a Doctor

When I was a newly qualified doctor completing my residency in emergency care, I had the chance to attend a specialised intensive care course. It was being run in English, so suddenly all my studying in English paid off and I was at a great advantage compared to everyone else doing the course. There were around a hundred medical students and nurses on the course, yet I was the only one who passed at the end. It wasn't because I was better, but because I could understand the teaching and terminology and could communicate with the instructor. I still have the badge I gained from this course as it proved to be an essential stepping stone in my career.

On the way home from the course I overheard some people chatting with the bus driver, one of whom was a senior doctor. They were discussing cardiac surgery and how to get into this specialism. My ears pricked up as I hadn't known much about it before; they were talking about a specialist cardiac hospital in another city but that it wouldn't be interested in people at our level.

The next day I went straight to the health division in my area and asked to train in cardiac surgery at this specialist hospital. Usually they would say no, yet to my shock the health division chief agreed, saying, 'Why not?' I completed a form, which he sent to the head of medical students. Normally they would refuse any request deemed inessential for our training, regardless of the backing of the health division chief. But the health division chief's secretary didn't wait for the head of medical students to reply, and signed the approval by mistake. I took it straight to the health division office in the other city on the same day. They protested, as I didn't have permission from the head of medical students, but as I had travelled all the way there, I persuaded them to let me go ahead.

The head of the emergency department in my city, where I had been doing my residency, told me they needed students so I couldn't be seconded to the cardiac hospital for long. He agreed to release me for three months only, after which he wanted me to train in orthopaedics as they needed doctors there. I told myself that three months would be more than enough. Normally, to be accepted in this particular hospital you must have finished your four-year residency. After completing your specialism, you can then progress to doing a further specialism, even more focused, so for me to gain a place there at that stage in my career was a real miracle. I felt as if an angel had taken my papers for approval that day.

When I arrived at the hospital, they asked when I wanted to start work. They were surprised when I said, 'Right now!' They took me straight to the specialist cardiac ICU in their hospital. Most of the doctors there had completed their specialist training abroad, in France, England or the US. It was rare to find anyone employed there who had completed their specialist training in Syria because cardiac surgery is such a prestigious field demanding only the best doctors.

I hadn't even had the chance to get changed when I entered the ICU; I was still wearing my own clothes with a gown thrown hastily over the top. The ICU doctor began to question me about one of the complicated patients they were treating, so I asked for his history and took the details while simultaneously checking his lab results. I said he had disseminated intravascular coagulation (DIC). The doctor looked at me curiously, asking if I was sure. I was. He looked at the doctor working under him who had specialised in cardiology and had begun a further specialism within that field, and asked whether he had considered this diagnosis. He hadn't. They investigated further and confirmed the patient did indeed have DIC. He would have died from this life-threatening condition (which has a very bad prognosis, especially after cardiac surgery), but we gave him the correct treatment and he miraculously recovered and was discharged.

They were surprised, especially as I came from a city not as esteemed as that one and I had come to them only part way through my residency. They gave me a room and told me I could stay there, but this room was shared by seven doctors and only had two beds! We had to take it in turns to sleep for a few hours so that all the doctors could rest, and I worked seven days a week with just a few hours' sleep each day. Fortunately, I don't need much sleep and I functioned well with so little, meaning I could cram a lot of work and learning into my waking hours. I worked hard and I loved it.

After I had started to work there, the head of medical students in my own city instructed me to return as I didn't have permission, but the manager of the specialist hospital liked me by then, so he gained a special permission from the Health Minister,[1] which overrode the authority of the head of medical students.

After I had been working there for a month, a patient had a cardiac arrest, then was pronounced dead after the team carried out CPR.[2] I noticed there was no resuscitation team in this hospital, or in any other hospital I had heard of in Syria, and therefore a mistake had been made in handling his resuscitation. I went to the General Manager, concerned about the loss of this patient, and others, because we didn't have a resuscitation or 'crash' team. I told him his team was good, but they were not trained to work together in emergency situations. One nurse would start CPR then another would intubate the patient,[3] but there was no structured coordination and no one leading the resuscitation. I told him it should be a more focused operation, with a team leader giving the orders and managing the resuscitation.

He asked if I knew how to do this. I replied that I could read and would learn, so he gave me eight newly qualified anaesthetic assistants to train, as an anaesthetist should be present at every resuscitation, and we started a resuscitation team. I was still only in the second year of my residency in emergency care in my original city, but I quickly progressed to become the manager of emergency care at this more prominent hospital before I even finished my residency.

When I started leading resuscitation training, I met Resusci

Anne, a training dummy which has helped millions of people learn CPR. I completed training courses accredited by the UK Resuscitation Council and the European Resuscitation Council and started watching videos and lectures.

Our resuscitation team worked hard and, as a result, improved the survival rate in the hospital. We became the team everyone called if any patient was about to suffer or suffered a cardiac arrest, and we were a little proud of ourselves.

When my three months was up, the head of the ICU asked me to stay and complete my residency at this specialist hospital, which was a great honour. I managed its emergency department as well as working in the cardiac ICU during this time.

When the management asked me to train more doctors, we branched out from our hospital and then across the country. We began to make plans for long-term medical training in Syria, and I felt we needed to set up a separate company to do this work. Our first private medical training company was established, and we began to train doctors from many different backgrounds. Our building was next to the hospital, and a large international corporation was based on the other side.

This international corporation needed to implement a policy to respond to any medical problems for its staff. It had been asking the manager of the cardiac hospital to provide an emergency response service for the company for some time, but the manager had been unsure whether the hospital could deliver this service. However, with our new training team established, he felt more confident.

The international corporation already had doctors working for it in the building next door as well as in other locations. To test both them and us, its managers created an exam scenario then set off an alarm. They said there was someone with a cardiac problem on the twelfth floor of their building. My team got to the patient from outside the building within seven minutes. Their team working inside the building took twenty minutes to get to the person in need! The doctors who came from outside, but who were employees of the company (receiving huge salaries from them), arrived an hour later!

As soon as my team arrived, I started caring for the patient and prioritised taking him to the hospital for treatment. As we were leaving, we passed the team who arrived late. They told me I had done something wrong, but I apologised and said I was the team leader and couldn't speak with them, and they should instead speak with their manager as I needed to focus on saving the life of this patient.

The whole exercise was filmed and sent to the managers outside Syria to be analysed. After two weeks they called me. They apologised for the doctor who had criticised the way I had handled the situation and told me they had fired him because he had undermined me when, in fact, I had done everything correctly. They said I had been right not to allow him to interfere with the treatment of the patient. After this exercise they sent a request to the Health Minister[4] to ask for me to take responsibility for the emergency systems for their corporation inside Syria. This gave a significant boost to my career at the very start, and I was earning a considerable salary before I even completed my residency.

My work with this company gave me access to lots of resources. I knew the organisation had a programme and fund for training and developing people in Syria, yet no one had asked for any money. I told the managers I needed some money to establish a disaster-management protocol and a set of courses for how to respond to a significant event, such as a natural disaster or other adverse event that could affect an entire area or result in many injuries at the same time. They agreed the funding, so we brought instructors from abroad to train us in Syria, with each course costing about $30,000. After the second course they wanted to establish an instructor inside Syria, so they appointed me. I became the trainer for new trainers, and this was when my career branched out into disaster management consultancy and training.

We invested a lot of time and energy in training the resuscitation team over many weeks and months. We did CPR training on Resusci Anne for at least an hour every day, to ensure that everyone was really confident that their resuscitation skills were of a high enough standard. We spent hours training, doing CPR, reviewing what medication to give and how to communicate in emergency situations. I wanted the hands and muscles of the team to be strong enough to be able to physically perform CPR for long periods every day for an extended time, not just occasionally for a short time, as it is a physically exhausting action to carry out. We were a specialist cardiac hospital where cardiac arrests were a common occurrence. The problem is that if you only perform chest compressions occasionally, you will not have the physical strength or stamina to continue for long, and will not feel confident enough to persist and follow the process through for as long as needed.

The result was that we had a very well-trained team specialised in CPR, and the cardiac arrest survival rate increased from about 20 per cent to 90 per cent, without any neurological complications. At first the heads of department struggled to believe that this was possible, but I had kept accurate records and reports about every resuscitation and had asked the appropriate department manager to sign afterwards, proving the success of this project.

One day we were called to a cardiac arrest. A sixty-year-old man, hospitalised with angina, had suddenly died. We carried out CPR for one and a half hours, continuing long after others would have given up. Eventually he was resuscitated, and we kept him sedated and ventilated. When I went to see him the next day, I introduced myself as the resuscitation team leader. He had no idea what I was talking about, so I explained that we had spent an hour and a half working on him and trying different things to bring him back to life, and that he was very blessed to have survived.

He was shocked that a big group of people would have devoted an hour and a half to trying to bring someone back to life. 'If that had happened in my village,' he told me, 'they would have buried me in my grave within an hour and a half of me dying!' In Islam, it is considered disrespectful to delay burying someone when they die, so his comment was absolutely true. He made a good recovery and was discharged shortly after.

I worked hard for my patients, and the hopeless cases were brought to me when all else had failed. I set up a specialist team to analyse the cases that doctors across other hospitals were struggling to treat. For me, the words, 'It's impossible,' were like the starting gun at the beginning of a race. Those cases were like a puzzle waiting to be solved, each one needing a different approach. Too many doctors view patients as cases that should fit into a box, but each one is an individual who needs a special, unique and persistent approach. I refused to give up on them and would study their cases carefully, reviewing research papers and looking for solutions. Every 'hopeless case' had a family who loved them and wanted them to live. At times I felt frustrated by the defeatist, sometimes even lazy, attitude I saw in many doctors.

One day I was talking with another doctor, explaining how our resuscitation team worked. He was intrigued and asked how we had such an impressive survival rate.

'Well,' I replied, half serious and half joking, 'I am very persistent. We are determined and don't give up. Do you know Azrael?[5] Maybe he gets tired of waiting and after a while decides to come back another time when it will be easier and quicker for him!'

For us it really was a matter of life or death and I often had an image in my mind of an angel of death standing beside these patients, holding their hand, trying to drag them off and claim them for death. While he did that, we stood holding the other hand and refused to let go. We fought hard for those patients and I always felt that if we kept going and didn't give up, we could win that battle to keep these people here in our world. It was a true battle. We didn't do CPR so we could simply tick a box on a protocol or say that we'd done it for ten or fifteen minutes. We truly and desperately wanted these patients to survive, no matter what it took.

The next issue we needed to focus on was the efficiency of ambulances and the way CPR was performed by paramedics. This included resuscitation at the scene of an incident as well as inside the ambulance en route to the hospital. This was essential training for medical professionals in Syria in preparation for the disaster that was coming, and it was a great encouragement to see both the capability and the confidence of all of these different teams grow during this time.

★

I completed my training and did the exams for both emergency care and cardiac surgery, and I finished my residency with two specialisms. My specialisation in ICU came a little later when I moved back to my home city. I took an ICU job in an established hospital in my city and fought as hard for my patients' lives as I would for my own. I began to gain a reputation as a hard worker who was efficient and reliable, setting new standards and ways of working.

Soon, some doctors from another hospital told me they were building a new, dedicated ICU in an old hospital. They wanted my experience and were aiming to revamp their image through establishing this ICU. The concept for how it was to be delivered was new and revolutionary for this area, and I attended a meeting with the doctors who were partners in the hospital. Each of them was investing in their own specialist area, but when I met with them it was clear that none of them had engaged properly with the concept of a specialist ICU and none of them had any passion for it. It is an expensive specialism which is not viewed as profitable.

They were keen for me to run this department (given my experience in cardiac ICU) but advised against me investing financially in this department, claiming that it was not worthwhile. When I saw their complacency, I was all the more keen to invest and take overall responsibility for the ICU, so I committed there and then.

When I returned and spoke with my father-in-law, he asked whether they had managed to persuade me to buy into it. I replied that, on the contrary, they had advised me not to, but I was willing to invest because I saw the potential. It felt like giving a gift to my city, a gift that was desperately needed and long overdue. Over the years I gained so much more from that hospital than the comparatively small amount I initially invested, and we raised the standards of ICU care across the city.

Over the coming years, I began to work further afield, providing ICU services not only to all the other hospitals in my home city but also to many other hospitals beyond. My reputation and profile soon grew, along with my patient list. One by one, each hospital asked me to implement new protocols and ways of working in its ICU department, and I invested in partnerships in a number of hospitals across the city. I chose carefully how I spent my time, focusing on my patients, my career and my hospitals at times when others would instead be socialising or sleeping. Even on the day my brother got married I carried out an operation before and after his wedding.

Soon I was approached by another group of doctors building a new hospital in the city. They had allowed for a larger, more advanced critical care service[6] than any of the other hospitals in the governorate, and they asked me to be responsible for all four of its specialist ICUs. I was really happy to have the opportunity to further expand and develop the ICU services in our city. When I went to see the building, it was almost finished, but they had not yet started equipping it. I could see the vision and knew it would be a fantastic hospital. I was keen to get involved, and this was even better than the hospital I had been planning and dreaming about since medical school.

I committed a significant amount of money to equipping and establishing the four ICUs in this hospital. It was my new baby. As I chose and bought the equipment and began setting up the critical care services, my dream was beginning to come to life, and I could see it growing and developing. I put all my energy and hope into making these the best intensive care services in the city. It was unique in this city, and I spent a lot of time recruiting and training the best ICU team, implementing protocols and procedures and creating an exceptional service. This hospital felt like my child; I truly loved it and was so proud of it.

One day, in a different hospital I had a partnership in, a patient died. The staff were terrified as the family of this patient were notorious for being very violent, dangerous and armed. When we talk about families here in Syria, sometimes they are *big* families. Not just father and brothers, but all their extended branches can be huge – hundreds or even thousands of people. Historically, if a member of this family came to the hospital for treatment, some members of staff refused to even go to work as the family were so formidable. They were unmanageable, and people were very scared of them – there was no reasoning with them.

After this woman died in our hospital, the staff became anxious that the family would destroy the hospital and maybe even kill some of the staff. The surgeon turned off his mobile phone and ran away, and the majority of hospital staff followed close behind. Around a hundred members of the deceased's family gathered outside the hospital, mostly men, threatening to beat and kill all of our staff. Eventually, the only people who remained in the hospital were me and two female colleagues! But God put it in my heart to simply go and face them.

The leader of this Muslim family was standing outside, so I called him in but asked him to come alone. He was so angry that it was hard to get through to him. I recited a number of passages from the Quran that related to the situation at hand, and also referenced some about accepting death, as I hoped this would be something he could relate to. I took him to the ICU and showed him all the equipment and described what we had done and how we had cared for his relative. I showed him how we had treated her with great respect and dignity and had done everything in our power to save her. I explained that we now needed him to help us control the people outside.

It took a long time, but in the end he agreed with me and even thanked me. To everyone's amazement, the extended family all turned around and went home! No one was hurt and no damage was done. It really was a miracle. The next day the manager of the hospital thanked me for not running away.

Standing my ground and looking the family in the eye had been the only way to reassure them.

Another morning I was leaving the ICU at the same hospital having worked a very long night. It had been extremely busy and we had carried out a number of cardiac operations. While I was changing my clothes and preparing to leave, a surgeon rushed up to me saying, 'You can't leave. We have an emergency!' They had a patient who had needed cardiac surgery, but when they had opened his chest, they discovered he had other serious complications and could potentially die at any moment. Because he had been intubated and was on a mechanical ventilator, his predicament was exacerbated, and there was nothing they felt they could do to treat his condition or change the outcome. The surgeon didn't know what I could do, but asked me to stay nonetheless.

The patient's family refused to accept his situation. They were very rich, and at times like these some unscrupulous doctors try to increase the prices and squeeze as much as they can from a tragic situation. In a matter of minutes many doctors appeared in the ICU. They asked me to stop working on him and made a plan that was unethical, but profitable. Having seen that the family was wealthy, the surgeon brought his own team to work on the patient so that they could share between them the money they would receive.

I was tired from a long night and I wanted to go home to sleep. The doctors had said there was no hope for this man, and he would die. I felt so sorry for him. He had a lovely family and beautiful children, but I continued towards the door because I was so fatigued and simply outnumbered by this group.

As I walked out of the door of ICU, an older man stopped me. When he asked where I was going, I told him I was going home. When he asked what would happen to his brother, I realised that no one had explained his brother's prognosis, so I told him. At this, he dropped to his knees, begging at my feet for help and pleading with me not to leave his brother to die. 'I'm a very wealthy man and I have many companies in the Arabic Gulf,' he said to me. 'I will pay you whatever you want and send you anywhere you want in the world. Please, don't let my brother die.' This man had been like a father to our patient after their father had died.

I replied to him that all the doctors working on his brother were after his money. 'But,' I said, 'I don't want your money. I will treat him for nothing. I won't accept any money from you. But if I'm going to work on him, I don't want a single one of those doctors in there to continue working on him. He will be under my care alone.'

The man accepted.

I looked him in the eye and said to him, 'Tomorrow morning, I will return your brother to your hands.'

I can't explain what motivated me to make that statement. It's not the sort of thing any doctor would normally say to the relatives of such a sick patient, especially when every doctor treating him had confirmed that he was dying and had no hope of survival. But at that moment I didn't feel it was me talking. There was a heat, or some kind of electricity, that passed through my body, hands, chest and shoulders. I felt I had said what God put in my heart.

I walked back into the ICU and, if I'm honest, I was afraid. I prayed, saying, 'God, I really hope you're going to help this man because there's nothing I can do for him.' Standing next to the patient, I looked into the eyes of each member of staff around him. They looked at me with questioning eyes, as if this was some kind of joke, wondering what I intended to do. None of them was a Christian, so I said to them, 'My God will heal him.' Usually in environments that utilise a lot of technology, people feel embarrassed to speak of 'God' – even in Syria. People working in these places tend to believe only what they can explain through medicine, science and technology, so for them it was illogical.

The nurses working there at the time had a good relationship with me, as I had trained them and we spent a lot of time working together. They trusted me, so they worked with me on this patient even though they struggled to believe that he would recover or that God would intervene. The patient was still intubated and his breathing was being performed by a mechanical ventilator. The team were waiting because at any moment he could die. The ventilator put more pressure on his vulnerable lungs, but the other doctors believed he would die if they removed the breathing tube. The patient was still sedated and unconscious and it was an impossible situation for us to deal with – but for God, it was easy.

I felt exhausted, but there was nothing I could do except stay and pray. It was like a dream, but finally the day passed, then the night, and I found myself sleeping on the chair beside the patient.

Suddenly, I heard the team rushing to him. I thought perhaps now the worst had happened. As I looked at him, I could see he had pulled the airway out of his own trachea. The team wanted to re-intubate him quickly.

In a loud voice I told everyone to stop. Protesting, they said his oxygen saturation was too low and he wouldn't survive, and they pressed me to intubate him again. I said, 'God removed this airway. Leave him.' We started to work on him without inserting another airway. Slowly his oxygen saturation began to improve. Over time he started to become more alert, and all his vital signs were better.

As the patient's situation improved, morning rays of golden sunlight began to shine through the windows on to him. Suddenly remembering my promise, I called for his brother to be brought to his bedside. When he arrived, I called the patient's name loudly, asking if he was awake. He responded, asking who I was. His brother began to weep, saying, 'Doctor, you kept your promise to me. The sun is rising now, and my brother is alive and okay.'

I smiled softly and replied that it was God who had kept *his* promise.

Some of the doctors asked what all the fuss was about – the man had extubated himself, where was the miracle in that? But I replied that they had been afraid to extubate him after surgery and were sure he would die, no matter what anyone did for him. The funny thing was that I didn't actually do anything at all for this man; I simply stepped back and allowed God to heal him. I trusted God with what he had put in my heart, and he demonstrated once again that he is always trustworthy.

About a month later, the patient came to thank me. He said he had no memory of his experience, except for being in a very light, bright place, then hearing my voice calling him. When he opened his eyes, he saw me. He said he felt I had brought him back from another world to this one.

I replied that it could have been the morning light coming through the windows that he had seen.

'Maybe,' he said thoughtfully, with a distant look in his eyes, 'but it was really, truly the most beautiful moment. I will never forget it for the rest of my life. I was dead, and I have another chance now. Thank you, God.'

This man kept in touch with me for years afterwards, even after the war began. I believed I could see in his eyes that Jesus had touched his heart. He always had a big smile on his face and looked so contented and satisfied whenever I saw him.

6

Fleeing Back to Syria, Early in the Conflict
(continued from Chapter One)

There was a stark contrast between Joseph's friendly, childlike face and Dr Khalifa's piercing eyes and death threats a couple of days before. Joseph was a dear old friend who was quick-thinking and had a great sense of humour; he was always making jokes. He had been through tough times growing up: his wealthy father had lost his business and his family had suddenly become destitute. Joseph had worked hard since then to make his own business profitable, having started from the most menial manual labour, and he now owned a beautiful home and a Jaguar car, and was raising a lovely family. His sunny personality diffused situations that others might feel burdened by. It was hard to know whether he felt any pressure from the situation at hand, but, if he did, his warmth and humour provided a very good front.

'Of course, you need to get back to Syria and to your family.' His friendly smile was reassuring. 'We will take care of it. Now, you have been sitting here alone in your hotel room for so long. Why don't we go down to the pool? I can't believe that after all these weeks here you still haven't used the spa!'

I had said so little, yet he understood my predicament. True friends don't need to ask questions, know all the details or even consider the consequences. Discussing the threat from Dr Khalifa and his armed, extremist group could have caused more problems in the long term for either Joseph or me. He was like my brother; I trusted him, he trusted me and we both trusted God.

A discreet return to Syria was needed, and quickly. My life depended on it, and Joseph knew what to do. Every couple of days since my arrival in his country he had come to see me.

On previous visits there I had always stayed with him and his family. But now, with the war and the increased security situation, the stakes had changed. I had felt my employer should take responsibility for my safety as they had extensive safety procedures and resources. Yet now that I had received a direct death threat from Dr Khalifa's group, I could see that my employer would not even understand what we were dealing with, let alone be able to provide a safe evacuation.

Joseph was an especially welcome sight now, and we had kissed hello with warm affection in the traditional Syrian style. He was the only person here I could trust. I hadn't said anything over the phone or acted any differently from the way we usually interacted. Since Dr Khalifa's visit, I was on high alert. If my calls were being monitored, it might have aroused suspicion if I had asked Joseph to meet me. Instead I waited for his spontaneous arrival, which came two days after my meeting with Dr Khalifa. Joseph was the only person I knew there with the connections and discretion to get me out of the country safely, now that this armed radical group were watching me. They had made it clear they would kill me if I tried to return to Syria. I had no enemies on either side, but my presence in Syria with my expertise in disaster management and running medical evacuations and my ability to work effectively in the desert was unhelpful to their agenda.

The next morning, as dawn broke, the city began to stir. The car engine hummed as it waited for me outside the hotel. I slipped discreetly through the polished lobby while the weary night staff were changing shift and got into the car.

There were belongings I had to abandon at the company offices. The most valuable was my training dummy and the equipment I used for the life support training courses I ran. It pained me to leave that more than anything else, as importing many items into Syria had become increasingly difficult in the war. Yet I couldn't risk arousing anyone's attention. I was concerned that someone from Dr Khalifa's group was working inside the company. Having seen what had happened around my home over the last eighteen months – the planning that he and his group were involved in and the mechanisms they had set up to support this conflict, months and even years in advance – my capacity for trusting others had almost vanished.

As the car navigated the undulating streets of this foreign city, I tried to swallow the overwhelming sense of dread that was washing over me in waves with each rise and fall of the vehicle. Despite the movements in the streets and people bustling on the pavements, everyday noises seemed strangely slow and suppressed. An emptiness encompassed me. The journey seemed somehow surreal, as if travelling through a film set. There was a disquiet in my heart that felt like the stillness on a battlefield before the fighting begins: the calm before the storm.

I had made a life-changing decision. Until this point in my life, I had lived a relatively normal existence. But that day, choosing to return to Syria determined a totally different course for me and my family. It was like boarding an aeroplane with the knowledge that it would probably crash, and that you couldn't get out if you changed your mind. In fact, all the odds were stacked against me. At that moment, I didn't feel like a doctor or a man. I felt weightless, as if I had no gravity, and I was simply falling, waiting for the impact of the crash.

My mind was flooded with questions. Would they let me leave this country? What was I going back to? Would we be in more danger from their people in Syria now? Should we move home, as they knew where we lived? Had I made the right decision for Miriam and the children, their safety and future?

Despite having visited many times before, it had been a deeply humiliating experience to enter this country this time to fulfil my training contract. The doors were closed to ordinary Syrians now that the war was raging. At the airport I had been led by the arm like a criminal, past staring faces, to an overcrowded room filled with other Syrians. Some had been kept there for days, some even for a week. In the absence of chairs, thirty or so men sat on dirty, stained mattresses that covered the floor. The smell of unwashed bodies filled the hot, stale air. Their tired eyes and captive souls tried to portray confidence, but their broken spirits stared back at me. They laughed cynically at me when I said I would soon be in the country.

The authorities detained me for hours, interrogated me, then informed me that they would send me straight back to Syria.

The attitude of the officials changed to shock when they received an order from the king to grant my entrance. My contacts at the company had managed to resolve the issue, but in the hours in between I had felt so vulnerable. One by one, many of my contacts in the country had stopped answering my calls. In my fragile moments, people I considered friends had closed their ears, unable or unwilling to help. This became the Syrian experience. The social rejection confounded the humiliation created by our political situation. We were treated as though we were somehow dirty, like convicts. Yet I had been invited to this country for a professional purpose. I struggled to shake off the feelings of shame I was left with. My only crime was being Syrian.

As I got into the shiny black Mercedes Benz that had been waiting while I was detained, the driver, a simple man, expressed his sympathy. He told me how he had tried to help by calling relatives who worked for the government. He treated me with respect, but his eyes revealed a different attitude. He was looking at a second-class citizen: a Syrian. Over the coming years, we began to feel like the untouchables, the cursed, the undesirables. We became the globally unwanted: a burden to all and rejected by every country around the world.

Yet for the rest of my visit I was treated like royalty. As he drove me to the extravagant hotel, I tried to process the stark, unfathomable contrast of the events of that day. It had been a bewildering and disillusioning experience I would never forget.

But now, on my escape journey, there was a loud voice in my head that nagged continuously, undermining my decision to leave. The closer I got to the border, the more insistent it became and the louder it shouted: 'Why are you going back to Syria when there are *millions* scrambling to get out? You saw how hard it was for any Syrian just to enter another country: this is your only chance to leave and keep your family safe. It

was a miracle that you got out of Syria at all! Are you about
to throw that away? You have the chance for a brilliant new
start outside Syria with a highly paid job. What kind of life are
you sentencing your children to?' My head swam with questions
and accusations. Had I really made the right decision?

The voice was exhausting and persistent. The weeks I had
been away had marked an intense deterioration in Syria. As I
watched the situation from the outside, my anxiety increased as
the area rapidly became more dangerous. But I knew in my heart
that this anxious voice did not come from God. God does not
speak to us through accusations or fear. But now, as I sat in the
car, I knew without any shadow of a doubt that I was leaving
the easy, comfortable way behind and was choosing instead the
hard and painful way. I should not expect a peaceful journey.

I turned my attention instead to the other sound in my heart
– the gentle, calm, small sound: 'You were born in Syria and
trained there as a doctor, for free, and you are a specialist in
disaster management. You have this training and experience to
serve your people through this difficult time. You were created,
trained and equipped for this very hour.'

Despite this assurance, my heart felt so heavy. I kept thinking
of how Jesus might have felt in the Garden of Gethsemane,
before his crucifixion, when his soul was overwhelmed with
sorrow and he prayed that the cup of suffering he was about to
drink would pass. But even with the knowledge that pain and
suffering were in front of him, he submitted to God's will,
saying, 'Not my will, but yours be done'.[1] He accepted the
hideous and excruciating events that were about to lead him to
the most barbaric beating, torture and death.

As I travelled closer to Syria, my hand unconsciously drifted
to the inner breast pocket of my suit jacket. The feel of the
paper was reassuring as my fingers slid in, carefully removed it
and unfolded it to read once again. I had been alone in the hall,
finishing some paperwork, when a Christian man I had been
training came in. 'God be with you,' he said softly, handing me
this piece of paper. My eyes met his gentle yet deep gaze as I
took it, thanking him. I smiled when I saw his handwriting on

the page. A warm sensation spread through my body as I began
to read the words of Psalm 91:

Whoever dwells in the shelter of the Most High
will rest in the shadow of the Almighty.
I will say of the LORD, 'He is my refuge and my fortress,
my God, in whom I trust.'

Surely he will save you
from the fowler's snare
and from the deadly pestilence.
He will cover you with his feathers,
and under his wings you will find refuge;
his faithfulness will be your shield and rampart.
You will not fear the terror of night,
nor the arrow that flies by day,
nor the pestilence that stalks in the darkness,
nor the plague that destroys at midday.
A thousand may fall at your side,
ten thousand at your right hand,
but it will not come near you.
You will only observe with your eyes
and see the punishment of the wicked.

If you say, 'The LORD is my refuge,'
and you make the Most High your dwelling,
no harm will overtake you,
no disaster will come near your tent.
For he will command his angels concerning you
to guard you in all your ways;
they will lift you up in their hands,
so that you will not strike your foot against a stone.
You will tread on the lion and the cobra;
you will trample the great lion and the serpent.

'Because he loves me,' says the LORD, 'I will rescue him;
I will protect him, for he acknowledges my name.

He will call on me, and I will answer him;
I will be with him in trouble,
I will deliver him and honour him.
With long life I will satisfy him
and show him my salvation.'

My heart swelled as I considered his care and compassion in taking the time to write these precious words by hand on paper for me. The psalm would carry such a special meaning over the coming days, weeks and years. I took them everywhere I went in my inner pocket, as close as I could keep them to my heart, as over the years to come I passed through terrifying, life-threatening situations. I had already lost friends and colleagues and would lose many more over the coming years. These words felt like a prophecy over my life. They were my weapon and my protection. I kept them with me until the ragged, dog-eared paper disintegrated. But even when the paper was gone, the words remained, written on my heart.

That man probably never knew how much his handwritten psalm would mean to me over the years. But this assurance stayed with me, encouraging me through the ugliest and most terrifying scenes and events: experiences no one could ever imagine which unfolded as the war progressed.

*

So, as millions of desperate Syrians flocked to cross the borders into other countries, I travelled against the current, back into Syria. I didn't know what to expect as I re-entered my country. Perhaps a naive part of me hoped for an improvement. But I was shocked by what I saw and felt. I had only been away for six weeks, yet the first scenes I saw of newly destroyed areas in the cities were frightening. It was as if a strange blanket of silence had been laid over previously bustling areas. The stillness was perforated at intervals by the roar of cannons. The contrast of the eerie quiet created by the absence of people and life being broken by the insistent sound of distant gunfire and occasional sniper bullets bursting through the silence reminded me of a bad dream where nothing felt right or real. It seemed as though life itself had been muted and we were waiting, just waiting, for all the killing to end.

As we approached my city the car started to feel as if it were moving more slowly. It was travelling reluctantly, like a stone that had been hurtling quickly through the air and upon entering the water was slowed by the density of the liquid. It seemed that the closer we got to the city, the resistance to enter was all the more palpable.

Reaching the road I always used to enter the city, we could not pass. The street was empty, with neither cars nor people to be seen. Ahead stood a checkpoint that had been established since I had left, with the red, white and black of the Syrian flag painted on oil drums on either side. As we slowed to a stop, a young soldier with a rifle slung over his shoulder stooped to answer my questions. A neighbourhood between here and my home had been taken by jihadists and the whole area was now under siege. We couldn't pass, and we shouldn't get too close.

We turned, searching for an alternative route. My heart started to beat harder and faster as I craned my head, looking from side to side, wondering what was going on. We were completely alone.

Suddenly, the loud crack of a sniper's gun punctured the stillness. The harsh sound echoed through the empty street, as if it had emanated straight from hell. A cold sweat of adrenaline broke out on my back and shoulders as a nauseous feeling rose from my stomach. Where had the shot come from and where was it aimed?

Another crack. Somehow, the single sniper shots seemed even more ominous than the bursts of machine gun fire that would stop and start, as these shots were so targeted. Standing on the roof tops and in doorways, snipers hid from view, aiming carefully and intentionally killing us one by one.

With each crack that perforated the atmosphere, I glanced down to check myself. I had treated many sniper victims since the war had started. Many of them described how, at first, they had not realised they had been shot. Initially they felt nothing. After a little while they started to see blood everywhere, before realising it was coming from their own body.

Although my instinct was to shut myself away in the car, I remembered the advice of a friend some months earlier. If I was in an area with snipers and feeling afraid, it was safer to open the car windows to protect myself. If the sniper bullet missed me, the imploding glass could injure me. As I opened the windows, I was changing my behaviour to that of someone in a war zone. It made a very harsh contrast to the atmosphere at the luxury hotel I had left that morning. I had travelled from a peaceful country where people were living ordinary lives, bustling in the streets, and suddenly found myself surrounded by snipers, worrying about shattered car windows and being shot.

Crack. The memories started to fill my mind of the many people I had already seen at my hospital who had been killed by snipers. My body shuddered as a I started to imagine myself in their situation.

We continued driving and I saw from a distance an area where I had been at Christmas, with my friends, shopping for gifts and having parties. Back then it had been decorated nicely with trees and lights, but it was now under siege. I could see the damage from a distance: many houses and other buildings had been reduced to rubble. Making out the homes of my friends, I could see some had been destroyed.

Some of these friends had already left the country. One was an architect who had left Syria. His house was now obliterated. From this distance I could also see what was left of another house belonging to a friend from school – it was in ruins too. Suddenly all my friends and acquaintances from this area swamped my mind as I wondered who was still alive. Had they been killed when their homes were hit by one of the rockets? Did they manage to escape in time, or were they still trapped and imprisoned there? Had they been killed immediately by the jihadists when they took the area?

When I had left Syria just weeks before, my city was the part of the country where there had been extensive damage. But when

I returned, the damage was more pronounced in other areas I travelled through. With this understanding came the realisation that this fighting was not going to be over any time soon. Even after eighteen months of inconceivable violence, the war was only just beginning. I could sense that something big had happened in my absence. All this escalation, in just six weeks!

Stopping in front of a building, I was suddenly breathless as I digested what I saw in front of me. In disbelief, I got out of the car, registering that this was the building where Miriam had wanted me to buy an office for her. The walls were now destroyed, and just three of the four structural columns were still standing while the fourth had been demolished. The floors and roof of the building had all collapsed in layers, like dominos, on one corner and were hanging down, while still connected by metal strings. It appeared so precarious.

It had been a prestigious building, like the jewel in the crown in a sought-after location. Yet something at that time had not sat right in my heart and I didn't feel comfortable buying it. It hadn't been obvious why. I couldn't shake the feeling in my heart that it wasn't the right place, and I didn't buy anything in that area in the end.

When I saw the roof hanging there, it looked as though it could collapse completely at any moment. I felt as if I was like that too, that my whole life could collapse at any moment. I stood in the street, looking. Waiting. Wondering whether it would crumble now, or after a few hours or weeks. In the same way that the floors of this building lay hanging, attached by just some small metal threads, I felt it resembled how our existence in Syria would continue over the coming years. All it needed was one gust of wind and everything would come crashing down.

The deformed building stood like an elegant lady with a deep scar running across her face and body. Spoilt by this intense structural damage, the building was crippled, never to walk, talk or smile again. There was a pain in my heart, and I found myself asking whether I was lucky not to have bought this building or whether I was unlucky to have returned to Syria. I could not decide. Had I made a good decision or a bad one? This building was meant to be the most distinguished in this area. I kept my eyes on it as we got back into the car and drove on, in case it chose this moment to disintegrate, taking us with it.

'Is this what we are now?' I sighed from the bottom of my stomach, no longer knowing what to think or feel. It was emotionally exhausting to see all this destruction. The building next to it had been destroyed too. The next building had been spared by some miracle, but the next building was damaged. I could not hide from the chaotic nature of this place. There were no rules any more.

Driving a little further, I saw walls with gaping, jagged holes of varying sizes. I could hardly process my shock as I remembered standing on the corner next to the building in front of me with my friends, chatting while we drank our coffees. It was one of the places we would stop and talk over our paper cups. My mind raced as I wondered, where were the friends I used to stand and chat with on this corner? Were they standing here when the rockets hit? Were they killed too, or had they been somewhere else? There was a ragged, round blast hole in the wall right there, perhaps made by a cannon.

I could hardly believe I had been walking in those same streets just weeks before. There were no civilians left in these public areas. It was as if I had entered another world. Surveying the landscape, looking around and seeing what had become of these places, I wondered what had happened to humanity. To life. I felt as though the devil was laughing at me, saying, 'Welcome to hell. You were stupid to return!' My heart felt as if it was being pummelled as the sights of my country overwhelmed me. This was my home!

My home was now a war zone. It could have been any war zone. Except these destroyed and damaged buildings weren't anonymous buildings in a picture or video. I recognised each one. I knew the buildings that should have been standing but were now just piles of stones, rubble and dust. It was a sinister perspective from which to see a war zone – my home.

★

Over the following weeks and months, I defiantly threw myself into my work, determined to fight back against Dr Khalifa and his group and the threats made against me and the way they were destroying our country, in the only way I could. I could not *fight* the people who had threatened my life, humiliated me and created this conflict. That was not my fight. But I could fight for the lives of the innocent people they were torturing and killing in my community. My heart was wrung out when I saw their injuries and suffering, and when I saw how many mothers' hearts were shattered by the deaths and murders of their sons and daughters. That was my fight.

As an emergency and ICU doctor, my skills were needed now. I began to set up medical points and small life-saving field hospitals.[2] They were a world apart from the quality of the hospitals I had been striving to establish in Syria in the preceding years. But over the years that followed, people ran out of money, hospitals were destroyed and the remaining hospitals ran out of resources. I learnt, brutally, how this was the only way to provide care for the multitudes in a developing war zone of this intensity.

7

Losing It All

'How much would you pay as ransom if we kidnapped you, Dr A?'

I sat in silence for a moment, unsure whether I had heard him correctly. Dr Zuhaer's green-and-brown flecked eyes burned into mine. He was deadly serious now, yet his voice sounded normal. He could just as easily have been asking what I wanted from the supermarket. I shivered inwardly as the realisation began to dawn on me; suddenly, in my colleague's dark eyes I saw all my friends and acquaintances who had disappeared unexpectedly over the previous few months.

Their relatives had received calls demanding huge sums for their release. Terrified, and desperate to see their loved ones freed, they had handed over enormous amounts of money. But only a very small handful of those for whom ransoms had been paid were ever seen again.

Rage bubbled in my chest as he laughed at me.

One of the male nurses with him nodded in solidarity, and echoed, 'Yes. How much *would* you pay?'

I fought back the scream that was urging to break through the stifling heaviness in the airless office.

The door opened and Dr Zuhaer's secretary walked in, carrying a tray of tea. She put the tray down for a moment and pulled out two small wooden tables before placing a glass of tea in front of each of us. Was she one of *them*? Silently, she backed out of the room. Dr Zuhaer's conduct remained calm and professional. Sitting in his ostentatious office, he had the manner of discussing a patient's treatment.

As I looked from Dr Zuhaer to the two colleagues beside him, it was apparent that I was now a stranger among them. The ice-cold winter had somehow seeped in from outside and permeated the atmosphere in the hospital. I had worked here for years, managing the high-dependency work. I thought I might be feeling something similar to what Jesus experienced at the moment he was betrayed by one of his closest friends. These three men had been my friends and colleagues for years, and I had always been Dr Zuhaer's first choice as ICU doctor for his patients. I had taken on, treated and saved many of his hopeless cases. Just a month before, I had run a training course for the staff in this hospital. He had been one of the best surgeons I had worked with there and he had always behaved like a polite and respectful gentleman. Yet at that moment the scales fell from my eyes and I saw a totally different person, one who had been hiding behind a facade the whole time. I realised I had never really known Dr Zuhaer at all.

No words came to my mouth as the threats of my colleagues echoed in my head. Would they try to stop me from leaving? What were they going to do to me?

I did not touch the tea – it might have been spiked. Just as I was calculating how I could get out of his office, the door opened again and a young man entered to ask questions about a patient. As Dr Zuhaer became occupied with giving answers, I seized the opportunity to escape, jumping up and swiftly leaving his office without another word. I almost ran towards the hospital exit, not stopping to speak with anyone or take anything, expecting that at any moment someone would try to stop me. All the way home, my neck bristled with fear that someone might suddenly try to abduct me, as had happened to many of my friends already. This group had people everywhere.

Perhaps this was actually a bizarre nightmare. This kind of thing didn't happen in real life. But over the last few months, we had been acclimatising to a new reality in my city. Surely, I would wake up to find normal life restored to how it had been some months before, with friends and colleagues who could be depended upon, trusted and respected, and a community that made sense.

I suddenly felt a deep and aching longing for that world I had taken for granted before. It felt like a distant memory, a beautiful dream that was fading quickly on waking. But rather than waking from a nightmare, relieved to find that everything was okay and as it should be, we instead were waking from a wonderful dream to a *real* nightmare. We had woken up to find that the individuals we had dreamed were beautiful were instead filled with ugliness and hate. Something had taken hold of our friends, colleagues and neighbours, and I no longer knew who or what they were.

As the simmering climate of jihad began to rise to a boil in this city, Dr Zuhaer, Dr Khalifa and their ever-growing group had begun to steer some of the hospitals. It soon became obvious that these hospitals were under the control of radicals, and they served only those who supported them. They had begun to talk candidly about their schemes, and over time my co-workers stopped making any effort to hide their ideology and growing hostilities towards outsiders who didn't support them. In fact, they now seemed proud of their conduct and efforts to humiliate and break the rest of us down, and even appeared to enjoy the feeling that our lives could be manipulated or expended as they saw fit. We became like putty in their hands.

Never had I made a distinction between Shia, Sunni or Christian areas, and I had lived in a Shia area. Later I had moved to a Sunni area where I had been very happy. I had good relationships with my neighbours, and many of my very close friends were Muslims, both Sunni and Shia. No one had ever given me the feeling I didn't belong or had ever made me feel unwelcome there as a Christian. Until now.

I had worked with all the hospitals in the city and had always liked working with Sunni Muslims. They were disciplined and respectful and would pay your salary straight away without any problems. I found great fulfilment in serving my city through my different medical specialities. As mentioned earlier, it was my dream of making the best hospital in the city that had motivated me through my studies in medical school. Over the years I had worked hard and had finally achieved this dream. When a group of us built and established that hospital, it was brilliant: clean, inviting and beautiful. It had the most comprehensive ICU in the city, even in all of Syria. It also had the most efficient emergency department (ED) and the best tumour centre. It was the perfect hospital in my eyes – my pride and joy.

The problem was that my dream hospital was located in an area that had begun to be controlled by an armed Islamist group. When the conflict started to heat up, we could feel the climate around us shifting. I was aware of a growing hostility towards my Christian community, and many bizarre comments were being made to us that we didn't understand. There was no way for us to comprehend these signs as indicators of the events to come. We were simply baffled by the strange and surreal events and behaviour. We knew something was very wrong, but we didn't know where it was leading. It was only when we looked back in retrospect that we saw, with absolute clarity, that it should have been glaringly obvious what was coming. But by the time we could see it and understand it, it was far too late.

★

One evening, after I returned home from one of the other hospitals I worked at, my phone rang. It was the manager of my dream hospital. Bewildered, I listened in silence as he told me not to return. They knew I had paid for a share in the hospital, he explained, and that the ICU and ED were mine. They knew I owned part of the hospital, but I was simply not welcome there any more.

'We don't want you here. There are big changes happening in Syria now, and because you are Christian, we don't need you. There will be problems if you return, and we can't guarantee your safety if you do.'

I was dumbfounded. What could anyone say in response to a statement like that? The equipment had been paid for from my own pocket; I had spent time selecting it all, choosing the design, training the staff and working night and day to set the highest standards possible. I had put all my energy into making the very best ICU and ED I possibly could. It had taken me years to get the hospital working to the level I wanted. People trusted our service, and I had put all my hope into that hospital.

These people seemed now to be above the law. There was no one I could go to for help. The strange thing was that the hospital manager who had just delivered this shocking news had felt he was being very generous in letting me go so easily. Others were simply killed or kidnapped. He felt he had treated me in a more honourable way. The same thing happened to all the Christian and Shia doctors working in my hospital.

The manager had been right in what he said: big changes were happening in Syria. But we could never have conceived at that time just how far-reaching those changes would be. They were not just life-changing for us. The whole fabric of our nation, our community and our humanity changed.

The area around the hospital quickly became tense, and kidnappings started. The victims didn't have political motives, they were just wealthy people who could afford to pay the ransoms. This was one of many ways in which jihadist groups raised funds. So many people I knew were kidnapped, a lot of them doctors, as they were well off. Yet when the ransoms were paid, most of them were killed. Only a very small number were ever released.

The radical converts soon stopped anyone except those sympathetic to their cause from setting foot in my dream hospital and the area around it. Only the people working with them were allowed to enter.

We had been living normal lives, going to work each day, doing ordinary things. But, over time, the strange talk between those radicalised doctors and nurses and many others outside the hospital had become commonplace. My friends began telling me the shocking things that had been said to them. Suddenly, I too found myself on the receiving end of similar, inexplicable threats. They talked about taking our homes for free, laughing and joking about it in front of us. Another Christian doctor who was a friend of mine told me that one of the radicalised doctors had demanded that he sell his house to him for just $100, when it was worth tens of thousands. He was warned that this was his last and only chance, otherwise he wouldn't receive even one dollar for it when it was taken. Shortly after, a different doctor from their group told me that if I didn't sell him my home for $100, I would lose everything.

We found out afterwards that they had been dividing up Christian villages, allocating our homes to different people in their group. History was repeating itself: the same thing had happened to my great-grandfather when people with anti-Christian ideology simply came and seized land from our families, just a few generations before us. Areas that had been populated entirely by Christians for generations suddenly became devoid of them altogether. Most were murdered.

Even though it was clear to us that an enormous tension had been rising for a long time before the war had officially started, none of us truly understood at that time what it meant or what was coming. Before the documented start of the conflict in March 2011, I remember treating a patient in the hospital when I suddenly saw a man running in the street with a huge gun. It was an extremely unsettling sight, as it was so at odds with our way of life. Soon there were large numbers of people, armed and coordinated, everywhere in the area. So many people came carrying weapons – previously ordinary people, now radicalised.

After this warning from the manager of the hospital, I didn't dare return. The situation quickly deteriorated even further. New satellite TV channels sprang up, broadcasting radical religious programmes, brainwashing the masses and aiming to create an army of extremists. These programmes started giving instructions; they spoke to their followers and told them what to do, encouraging them to fight for *Khelafi*.[1] They were told they should follow Mohammed and God. They stirred people up, giving them reasons to go down the street and ask for a new Islamic government. They started asking the president to leave; they beat policemen in the streets and destroyed shops. They destroyed everything that belonged to the government, even the electricity.

We lived very close to a mosque, which was unfinished and

had windows missing, and we watched as the men went upstairs and the women downstairs every Friday. After their prayers, they moved out into the streets, shouting and protesting and being disruptive.

One night, while Miriam and I were lying in bed, we suddenly heard voices shouting, '*Allahu Akbar.*' At first, we thought someone had lost their mind, but it continued all night, then our neighbours joined in. The demographic of the area we lived in at that time meant a lot of people around us were shouting it all night. We couldn't understand what was going on around us. *Allahu Akbar* translates as 'God is the greatest', and was a war cry used during the early establishment of Islam when they were fighting against non-Muslims. A sheikh broadcasting on one of the religious satellite TV channels told them if they fasted for three days and shouted '*Allahu Akbar*' every night, then the government would crumble by itself. Soon they started fighting.

It became a declaration during this war: people connected to these groups shouted '*Allahu Akbar*' before firing rockets or detonating suicide vests, among many other acts of jihad. I remember the next day going to the hospital and noticing that Dr Khalifa had a really hoarse voice. I asked him whether he was feeling sick. He whispered no, he had spent all night shouting '*Allahu Akbar*' and had lost his voice.

Perplexed, I asked him how he could be involved in that. I reminded him that he was a doctor who had been to medical school and studied science. He did not say anything, and even seemed ashamed. But the next night he did it again. There were so many voices shouting, and many people were banging pots and pans as they did so. It was rising hysteria.

★

It wasn't long before I began to worry that the same thing would happen to my home as had happened with my hospital. The people in our neighbourhood started looking at me with hatred in their eyes, giving me the feeling that I didn't belong in the area. The way they spoke to me was very disrespectful, but what made it so much harder was that I knew most of the people treating me like this. They had been my friends and patients. I had helped many of them and treated them in my hospital. Yet suddenly their attitude towards me and towards the rest of the Christian community changed. I could barely recognise these people I had once known. Then they started making comments to me about being kidnapped. By this time, many people I knew had been kidnapped, so I understood they were not empty threats. It was a deeply distressing, painful and traumatic experience. I had become a successful doctor, so could easily be targeted. I knew these threats were serious, and that my life was in danger.

When the situation had begun to boil over like this, I already had a young family. It disturbed me to see that even our children started to be affected by the hostilities. How could I explain this aggressive behaviour to such young children when it didn't even make sense to us? We used to walk to a nearby park on Fridays, but we had to stop because one Friday we suddenly found ourselves surrounded by a large group of people with long beards and hijabs. They started saying obnoxious things about us – especially Miriam, as she didn't cover herself – then shouted insults at us simply because we were not one of them. I don't know how we got away without being harmed, but after that we didn't feel comfortable leaving the house even in daylight. We felt unsafe in our street and even in our home.

The radicals became dangerously aggressive, so we decided to take some time out in a different area. We stayed elsewhere and I was fortunate to have a lot of work in that place. Then one day I got a call from a man saying I couldn't return to my house. When I asked why, and how, he replied that their group had put another family in my home. They had broken the door in – it was simple. When I asked how he knew who I was, he replied that they had been looking at the pictures in our photo albums. He commented on the pictures, on our wedding, and even on what people were wearing! They had not just moved into our home; they had also violated all our deeply personal possessions. When I protested, saying the house was full of my furniture and belongings, they told me to come and take them. My father, family and friends warned me not to go, as I would inevitably be kidnapped.

Not long before this, one of our relatives had been killed because he had stayed in his home when his area was taken. He had wanted to see a change of government and supported the idea of a revolution, so had stayed when the radicals took his neighbourhood and continued to run his business there. He had hoped that they would bring the changes that people were being stirred up to fight for: freedom, democracy and a different life. He even supported the group who took over. But one day they came to his house while he was eating his dinner and took him. Terrified, his wife and children just managed to escape. They were told that this group had stolen all his money before murdering him and moving into his home and into the homes of the others they had killed and forced out. They killed hordes of ordinary civilians and did not bring freedom or democracy. Instead, they beheaded and murdered civilians, raped girls and women, imprisoned ordinary people and established terrifying Islamic caliphates in every area they occupied.

These events had begun to feel inevitable. I had wanted to remove our belongings from our house when we left. My father said it was unnecessary. Instead, he offered to put some big iron bars on the doors. They were expensive to fit, yet they didn't stop the jihadists from getting into our home. Strangely, it was the money I had spent on the iron bars that I felt most sad about, because I had known in my heart as I bought them that I should have simply taken our possessions as we would not be able to return. Maybe this is one of the reasons my father returned with some of Miriam's relatives to my house after it was taken, to reclaim some of our personal items, as he felt responsible for that loss. He took just a few of our personal effects, like our wedding photos and pictures of the children, and some special and private things, like our underwear. It would have felt strange if these had been used by the people who had taken our home.

When our relatives returned to our house, they found another

family living there, in my home. The jihadist leader responsible
for the area was armed and told my father that if I had been
there, they would not have let me leave as they needed me.

Our possessions and our home were simply stolen from us in
broad daylight, and the same happened to multitudes of others.
I am just relieved that we escaped with our lives. I am thankful
that neither Miriam nor any of our children was taken – it
would have been too awful to bear. I can accept losing material
things, but I can't accept losing one of my children, my wife
or anyone else I care for.

When the nature of the fighting became more obvious, every
Friday was marked by the radicals going to the mosques and
then into the streets, where they started shouting and killing
people. Suddenly it became evident that they wanted to fight
heavily. They attacked the free general hospital of the city, which
had been provided by the government. Armed fighters went
inside and killed the doctors and nurses working there that day,
many of whom I knew, after which the extremists treated
that hospital as their military base. They then took the whole
surrounding area and started killing the army, the police, the
Christians and the Shia people. Next, they took all the surrounding areas near my dream hospital, and more areas still. And then
they took my hospital.

Because of the tumour treatment centre, there were floors
underground where we dealt with nuclear medicine and radi-
ation. The jihadist group used the hospital as a military centre
for organising their attacks, because of the perceived protection
underground. From there, they attacked people and buildings
outside the area they had taken, killing many civilians. It wasn't
long before the army counter-attacked this area and hit my
hospital with a rocket designed to destroy all the floors, including
those underground.

My relationship with that hospital was akin to that of a father
and son. When the manager told me not to return, I was devastated. Yet I knew it was still there, providing services for people.
But one day, a colleague elsewhere told me that my dream
hospital had been reduced to rubble. I could not answer him.

I could not do or say anything. My shock was immense. I felt as if I had just been told that one of my children had been killed. To me, it had been more than a hospital and a workplace. It was like my home.

My beautiful hospital had been destroyed completely. A pile of stones and rubbish was all that was left of the precious hospital I had invested so much time, money and passion into, and which had saved so many lives. This was one of the worst moments in my life. It took me a long, long time to even begin to get over that loss.

Another free government hospital was also taken over by the jihadists and used as a base, then was destroyed in the same way as my hospital had been. I had worked there from time to time as an ICU doctor, as I had for all the hospitals in the city. Some of the doctors and nurses I worked with were executed by the armed group that took over.

At the time I was working outside the area in a paediatric hospital, but soon that hospital was attacked too. My friends were targeted in both hospitals. One of them, a Christian anaes-thetist, was shot in the leg by a sniper. They tried to kidnap these doctors, but they escaped. Many other doctors I knew were killed. I was told afterwards that this paediatric hospital had also been made into a military base for the jihadist group, but we didn't go to that area in the same way our people had gone back into the area where my hospital had been, to see for ourselves.

They took this area, then the next and the next. They seemed unstoppable. Every day and every week they were invading and taking over new parts of Syria. All the Sunni areas were taken, and the only remaining areas were Shia and Christian. Soon these groups became known as the Free Syrian Army, Jabhat Al Nusra, ISIS and many others.

After experiencing these awful things, I visited a friend in another city, who said to me, 'What madness. I can't believe what is happening in your city.' Soon the radicalised people in our area started calling on their friends and relatives in other cities to stand against the government too. In one city, the people

connected with the radicals were hesitant to protest. I heard the
extremists in my city saying they were cowards for not joining
in this fight. They called them betrayers of Islam. It wasn't long
before other large cities began to descend into the same chaos,
death and destruction that we were contending with daily, and
the fighting spread across the whole country.

Many of the Sunni Muslims lost their homes when the fighting
began, and ended up in the streets of other mixed areas, angry
about their losses. The residents of these areas then felt uncomfortable surrounded by angry people, so they stayed in other
areas. The homeless people then moved into their homes, the
homes of the Christian and Shia people, and so perpetuated the
cycle of displacement.

No one should look at what has happened here in Syria as
an isolated event. Look at what happened across the Middle
East in Tunisia, then Libya, Egypt and Iraq. All of the 'colour
revolutions' are connected. They are packaged differently on the
outside, but underneath they are the same. There is a larger
global agenda, which is not related to my desire as a citizen of
Syria. I have never liked politics and have always kept myself
away from issues of a political nature. Even when there were
general elections in Syria, I didn't vote, but none of the entities
trying to take over ever asked us what our ideas or vision were
for our government.

But one thing I can say with absolute certainty is that before
the war, our situation in Syria had started to become better than
it had ever been before. The standard of living had been
improving, and people had a greater ability to buy everything
they needed. They were living better lives. Before the war, I
had bought two brand new cars and had started buying and
building houses. Many others were doing the same. People were
beginning to live with more affluence than had previously been
possible for many.

Although our system was very different from the situation in
the West, we were also beginning to feel a greater sense of
freedom of speech than we had ever had before. There were
still problems and limitations to that, but we could talk freely.

Practices that have spanned generations don't change overnight. It takes time. But they were beginning to change, even if it was a slow change. We also had ambulances for emergencies in all the cities, good healthcare and, compared with what we currently have at the time of writing, there was much greater law and order on the streets.

We had a good system of education, and I studied for free at school and at medical school. The people who gained the highest scores at school could study whatever they wanted, at any college, free of charge on a scholarship. Whatever my thoughts and feelings about our government, it would be ungrateful and dishonourable for me to speak against it because it educated me and put me through university. It was because I studied medicine for free that I was able to work hard and establish a good career.

I, like other Syrians, just wanted to build my life. I wasn't interested in being a politician, being the president or having a position of power or authority. I just wanted to be an ordinary person living a normal life, to have a house and a car, to raise my children and maybe sometimes have a trip away. Those simple things were my dreams, but I lost all of them. I lost my home, my hospital and my workplace. My children lost their city and we moved from house to house to house. We have been forced to move more than seven times during these years of conflict, just to protect ourselves and stay safe.

When we had to run from our homes for safety, some people whom we thought were very close to us made us feel unwelcome. Some people said that we didn't deserve to be there as we should have stayed to fight for our city. The bitter irony is that most of those people who judged us for fleeing from our homes have now left Syria altogether. They did not stay to 'fight' for their country in any way.

When you lose your home, you lose your dignity. You become vulnerable as you have nowhere to be safe or to belong. But I was in a much better position than most because I am a doctor and continued to work in many places. I was able to support my family and to survive. But many people who didn't have a career like mine, or the persistence I have, couldn't do what I did, and they really did lose everything. Many found themselves literally swimming in the sea, trying to find a rock to stand on.

It wasn't easy for me to lose everything I had worked so hard for, but I am thankful that my family and I are alive and well. I am thankful that most of my children don't remember these events, and I don't want to remind them or make them relive any of what we have suffered. We survived.

But for me, and for every Christian in Syria, life was better before. The same can be said for *everyone* in Syria, regardless of their political views. Not one person in Syria can say that the situation is better now than it was before the war, whether they wanted a change of government or not. Our nation, our culture and our humanity have been destroyed. What is left in the wake of this dirty war? Not one thing in this country is better than it was before the war. Everything is broken, damaged or destroyed. Most of all, the people. Our society lies in ruins.

If what we have lived through and what we have now, compared with what we had before, is what anyone calls freedom, then I will say no thanks. I would rather go back to the restricted freedom I had before because, after many years of war, our freedom is far more restricted now than it ever was before the war, and we have lost everything. I don't want this kind of 'freedom' that the war has supposedly brought us. Look at Egypt – they are not happy. Look at Libya – they lost their country. What about Iraq? Yemen? The people there are far from happy with the situations they now have. If these 'revolutions' – which is just a word to make war sound more acceptable and even desirable – are a good thing, then why has the experience failed in every country it has touched? We haven't seen any country in the Middle East end up better after these supposed revolutions. They are all far worse than they were before.

I can give one hundred reasons why I am still here. My sister left the country and is a refugee in the West. When we speak, I don't feel she is in a better situation than me. When you lose not only your home but also your country, you lose a big part of yourself. You lose self-respect. You lose your family. Most Syrians who have left the country don't feel they can return even just to visit, and as most Syrian people are not granted visas to visit other countries, it is possible that the families who have been separated in this way will never see each other again. At best, it will be many, many years until they are reunited.

Millions of families have been destroyed by the refugee crisis produced by this war, not just by the killings here in Syria. Many couples I know who have left Syria are divorced or separated now, as the meaning of their marriages, and the culture and community that supports our way of marriage and of investing in our future generations, have lost their meaning in the foreign environment. In other cultures, divorce is common and the focus of what is important in life is so different.

If I were to run away, and everyone else were to run away, who would run and inhabit this land? The people who have committed these atrocities against us ordinary people would be the leaders of our country. It is better for me to live and die here than to live somewhere else and spend my life pining for my homeland, Jesus' homeland, watching as Christianity and humanity are stamped out altogether in Syria.

8

A Cup of Tea and a Baptism of Fire, During the War

A cool summer breath swept over me, the breeze gently ruffling the hairs on my arms as I stole out of the emergency room. Blinking in the sunlight, I clutched a cup of sweet red tea.[1] The hot vapours rose, leaving a film of moisture on my chin. We had been on our feet since the day before and I had lost track of the operations we had performed during the night for the victims of the attacks of the previous day.

I needed some fresh air and to remind myself of the world outside the hospital for just a moment. The street was silent. Unoccupied. Empty of people and lacking life. Inhaling as I walked, I tried to fill my lungs with something fresh, wanting to somehow breathe in new life. As I took a sip of the sugary liquid from my cup, my eyes drifted to the public park across the road. I stopped to survey the old playground in front of me. Faded toys lay deserted on the ground, surrendered mid-game. Eroded by rust, their ragged edges and surfaces were now covered with a thick layer of dust. How long had this park stood abandoned?

Memories came flooding back of how it used to be. Noisy children laughing, jumping and fighting. Where did they go? Were they ever really there, or had I imagined them and the life before? It had been a long time since anyone had allowed their children to play outside. It was as if childhood itself had been left behind and abandoned with those toys. I too had stopped letting my children play or run outside. Instead, we kept them locked safely indoors. But was it really any safer inside? I took another sip of my hot, sweet tea to warm the cold that had settled over my heart.

As I began to walk, my shoe scuffed over something on the ground: an unspent bullet which my foot had been resting on. How many kilometres had it travelled? Perhaps, if I had taken my tea twenty minutes earlier, it might have hit my head as I stood here. In an instant, the summer breeze felt a little colder. A shiver ran down my spine as I considered how easily death attacks. Faces flashed through my mind of the people I had seen in the hospital who had been shot in the head. Some were dead on arrival, while others were left with permanent neurological injuries from bullets just like this one. A mother just trying to earn a living on a normal working day at the market. A little boy, simply playing in front of his house. There were too many to remember.

I raised my cup to my lips again, steadying it with both hands. As I peered into my red, very sweet tea, my mother's words echoed in my mind. She always told me not to put so much sugar in my tea. We have a family history of diabetes. 'You will die before your time if you keep taking that much sugar,' she would warn. She struggled even when I was a young boy to get me to do things her way. I always had my own ideas, and unless I could see the benefit myself, or wanted to, I had no will to compromise. But I also knew how much she loved me, even if I was the most awkward of all her children. I smiled at the image of her, and my heart warmed a little.

Suddenly, a deafening explosion tore through the peace. With my ears ringing, for a moment I lost my sense of direction. I couldn't tell where it had come from. Was it nearby or far away? Was I okay? In that split second, my heart began to pump adrenaline and a cold sweat broke out over my body. The roar continued to reverberate. Everything seemed to vanish into a vacuum of silence as the rumble of the detonation diminished. The world seemed to cease. Even the birds had stopped singing. Waiting, perhaps, to see whether they too had exploded with that bomb, or whether they were still alive. A few seconds passed.

There was no smoke in front of my eyes and no obvious damage in front of me. The explosion hadn't occurred in this street. It must have been somewhere else nearby. Relieved, I could be sure that I was still alive and unharmed. My brain began to spring into action and a torrent of questions flooded my mind. How far away was it? Will there be another? Would I be safer inside? Maybe outside would be safer if they were targeting this hospital building. Should I leave the hospital? Or maybe it would be better to leave Syria completely. Suddenly, my relief gave way to concern. I was okay, but what about others? Someone would have been harmed.

I stared down again into my tea. Suddenly the cup became heavy in my hands and I felt tired of carrying it. I longed to put it down somewhere. The tea now seemed a darker shade of red, thicker and opaque. I took another mouthful, but it had lost its sweetness. Now, the liquid in my mouth tasted bitter and claggy.

I thought again of Jesus in the Garden of Gethsemane, praying that the cup of suffering he was about to drink from would pass from him. But he said, 'Not my will, but yours be done.'

It was just another day here. Just another bomb. I began to rebalance myself. My mobile began to ring.

'Hi, Mum. Yes, I'm okay . . . No, it's further away . . . Don't worry, God will save us . . . Yes, I will . . . I need those prayers.'

As I returned my phone to my pocket, I stepped on the unspent bullet again, twisting it into the ground as if trying to crush it, to crush death. I thought of the passage in Luke: 'I have given you authority to trample on snakes and scorpions and to overcome all the power of the enemy; nothing will harm you.'[2]

My name was being called. The nurses wanted me in ICU. As I retreated back into my medical world, my phone rang again. Miriam. She was afraid too. The boys were with her and had heard the earth-shattering boom. They had all frozen on the spot. The older ones knew the consequences of these war sounds, but they couldn't understand. Even I was struggling to understand what was happening in my country. And in my heart.

The sirens wailed, announcing in advance the arrival of

ambulances. One by one they started to appear, alongside cars carrying victims.

'I need to go. I don't think I will be home tonight, either. Kiss the boys for me.' I breathed my goodbye, unsure whether it would be our last.

Pushing open the door to the emergency department, I knew in my heart just how much I needed my mother's prayers. A soul-full of my own went up too. I prayed that the defibrillator would work if someone had a cardiac arrest. We hadn't been able to get a new battery and the current one was not charging properly. It was unreliable. We had power cuts every day, and when the electricity came back on, power surges damaged the equipment. Once damaged, it was impossible to repair much of it, as gaining spare parts was so difficult. The siege of sanctions Syria was under by many countries in the world meant that many medical devices were now out of service. We tried to keep going with the few items we had left, but it was an impossible job.

It was a great mercy of God that this hospital was even still running. So many others were not. The lift had been broken for weeks, but when we called the company that supplied and serviced it, we couldn't get an answer. Later we were told the owners had left the country, like everyone else who could. It was the same story time and time again. Doctors, nurses and people from every profession.

That questioning, undermining voice in my head became louder. 'Why did you return, Doctor? You could have a better life elsewhere. What are you waiting for? You could just leave now, like everyone else. Don't be stupid. Run now while you still have the chance.'

After searching, we found someone who was able to botch a repair for the lift, but it didn't last long. We needed parts that weren't available in Syria, and we couldn't import them easily because of the trade restrictions.

Looking at the old, partially broken patient trolleys and ancient ventilators, I realised that, lately, I wasn't sure whether I was praying for the devices to work or for the patients to get better. I missed having newer technology. I kept dreaming of working in a developed medical environment with everything I needed. ICU and emergency medicine are so much more advanced in the West. I dreamt of working in one of those ICUs where everything is nice, new and organised and, most importantly, has all the correct equipment for each procedure, all the medication needed to treat each patient and all the trained staff. I wished I could experience all of these things together, on the same day. From my position at that moment, it looked like an impossible dream from another galaxy.

Making my way through the dim corridor towards the ICU, I reminisced that those hallways used to be so bright. We had got used to doing so much in the dark, or from the light on our phones. Corridors like that one were now lit by borrowed light from the windows in the rooms or, if there were none, by a small strip of LED bulbs hung anywhere that could be found to prop it up. In winter, fuel was too precious to use for heating the hospital. Instead we wore our coats as we worked, and our patients were fully dressed in their beds in many layers, with the few blankets we could spare.

Before I reached the department, a wrinkled, grey-haired woman with a shawl loosely covering her head came rushing towards me. 'How is he, Doctor?' I recognised her from the day before; another car bomb had grievously injured her son. He was a plumber and a father to three young children.

He had been in very bad shape when they had brought him in, caked with blood and dust. His injuries were extensive and covered his body. He had internal injuries too. Her pleading eyes and the intonation of her voice conveyed her desperation. All she wanted was for me to tell her that her precious boy would be okay. I wished I could tell her that, but I couldn't give her false hope.

The lines on her face moved, expressing a multitude of emotions: anger, pain, frustration and fear. No one could imagine the feelings saturating her broken heart, except the ocean of other mothers here who, like her, had lost a son or daughter in a senseless terrorist attack. The previous day we had had an influx of victims to our ICU from that car bomb.

Another man had not been so lucky. Or perhaps he *was* the lucky one; his injuries were too severe and death had embraced him quickly. He had left this hell. The faces of his mother and brother flashed before me after I broke the devastating news to them. The look in their eyes is something I will never forget. The mother of the plumber, on the other hand, felt blessed that her son was still alive. In spite of his mangled, bloody, unconscious body, there was some hope she could cling to.

She had pressed for answers, asking how he was and what she and her family could do for him.

I had replied, 'He needs you to pray for him. That is the most important thing we can do.' It was the best advice and treatment I could offer.

She had fallen silent, understanding. The younger woman standing in the corner of the corridor had been quiet all along. She looked disoriented. What was going through her mind? What would happen to her beloved husband? What would the future hold for her children, or for her? She was trying to understand something that was beyond her ability to grasp. Why was this happening? He was a good man and didn't deserve this. He was just trying to feed his family. She didn't say a single word, yet I felt I could hear the voice in her heart.

An image of my mother and Miriam faced with the same situation passed quickly through my mind. How would they cope? What would they feel?

I opened the door to the ICU and escaped the questioning, pleading eyes and souls that searched me, desperate to hear a promise that I couldn't make.

The man was still unconscious, but stable. 'Doctor, we don't have the medications he needs. I can't give them to him.' The nurse's brow creased. 'Can we ask his family to find them somewhere else?'

My heart sank. Every day I dreaded hearing those words. I knew these families. They were so poor. They couldn't afford this hospital in the first place. They struggled even to eat. Where would they get the money to buy these expensive drugs? But we didn't have another option. The nurse handed the paper to the man's wife. She stared at it for a moment before covering her eyes with her hands. Her shoulders began to shake. I asked God to help her, as patients from the morning's bomb attack started to arrive in the emergency room.

My focus had to be on them now, to stabilise the critical patients, to rush the injured into the operating room and to X-ray. Our team was so small. We had lost too many doctors and nurses. Those who remained were willing but simply weren't enough. Some had been killed or kidnapped; many had left the country. Others had been conscripted to the army and some had simply stopped working because they couldn't face the safety risks in coming into the hospital. We were trying to train new staff, but the colleges were damaged too, so training programmes had been disrupted.

Here in the early morning, things were calmer than they had been the previous day. This attack had been smaller, and the injuries were not as complicated. However, all the patients still needed a full assessment and examination to ensure we didn't miss anything important. They still needed treatment for their wounds. It was always harder to manage when the patients arrived all at once.

While I was examining one of the new patients, the plumber suddenly woke up. He was terrified, confused and yelling. He didn't know what had happened to him. We needed his family to calm and reassure him. I rushed out to fetch his mother and tell her he was awake, but she wasn't there. I couldn't find anyone outside. Maybe they would come back soon. Alone, I walked back into the department to continue examining my new patients. Maybe everyone else would come back soon too.

★

Later that night, I returned home for the first time in two days. I had just fallen asleep when my phone rang. A friend from medical school was asking for help; immediately I knew something was very wrong. It was a mutual friend of ours who had studied at the same university as us. He had recently married and moved to another city. I had spent time with all his family: they were like my own relations.

His father was having a heart attack. I rushed to the ICU, but he was already dead. I tried desperately to resuscitate him. As we worked on him, I prayed with all my heart and soul that God would raise him from the dead, like Lazarus. But he didn't. There was nothing I could do for this man I cared so deeply about. It is an extraordinary experience to feel that the life of a loved one is in your hands, yet you are powerless to change anything for them or their family.

As I sat beside his wife and told her of her husband's death, we were both shell-shocked. She and her husband had been watching the news that day when he saw that the area his son, my friend, had moved to had just been taken by jihadists. Perhaps it was the shock, or perhaps the desire to leave this miserable world had been too much, and my friend's father had had a heart attack.

'Please, tell me this is not true,' this new widow begged me through her tears. 'They just called me now. They told me now, they have killed my son! I don't believe them. I could hear him screaming in pain. This can't be real. It can't be happening.' The jihadists they had seen on the news had tortured then murdered my dear friend. They had called his mother so his family could hear the sound of his suffering as they abused, then killed him. This agonising barbarity had taken place while we were trying to revive her husband.

I could barely look this bereaved, confused woman in the eye. She had lost her only son and her husband in the same hour. I felt ashamed that I had been unable to save her husband at the very least. I wished with all my heart that I'd been there earlier. Maybe then I could have done *something* to save him. There was nothing I could do or say to bring even a tiny glimmer of hope to this woman in her grief.

I couldn't blame my friend's father for not wanting to return to this world. Who would want to return to the news that their only son had been savagely tortured and murdered? How does a mother or father go on living with such knowledge? Perhaps, as we worked on his body, his soul had passed to heaven, and perhaps he had already met his son there. What motivation would there be for either of them to return to this fractured and sick world? They were the lucky ones, to have escaped this painful mess.

I was too choked up and ashamed to go to my friend's funeral. I couldn't face his mother; I felt guilty that I was still alive when her son was dead and that I hadn't been able to save her husband either.

She couldn't accept that her son was dead, because they never found his body. She lived in denial for a long time, unable to believe that both her husband and her beloved son had been snatched from her at the same time in such an appalling way. Her son's death was deliberate, intentional and calculated. He was not in the military and did not have any political links. He was just an ordinary man, a civilian and a professional, who had studied hard and had a very good job. He should have had his whole life ahead of him. They killed him, just like they killed so many other ordinary people, for no reason, just because he was not one of them.

I wish I could say that this story is unusual or a one-off event. It isn't. Every area in Syria that came under siege – and there have been far too many – started and continued in the same way. The jihadists came, killed, raped, tortured, kidnapped and took hostages. So many of my friends and acquaintances across Syria told me about their own experiences. The goal of these armed groups was to bring a reign of terror, devastation and fear, which they achieved everywhere they went. They created jihadist-controlled areas across Syria, wanting their own Islamic government to rule these places and take over the country. Yet many people who had supported their ideology and goals to begin with became disillusioned when they saw what these radicals were really doing, how they behaved and how they did not bring the freedom they had promised. These events became the daily, weekly and monthly items perpetuating the news around us. Our lives became a living nightmare.

9

The Degenerating Climate of War

My family and I found ourselves living in the middle of the most brutal, advanced and deceptive war zone of this generation. The nature of the war and the politics surrounding it were so complex. What happened to us, our friends, our neighbours and our relatives, what we saw with our own eyes and what we lived and survived through, was so different from what was being presented to the rest of the world. The attacks went so much further than what most people associate with war: bombs, shootings, missiles, knife attacks and, of course, the poverty caused by a collapsed economy. In addition to those obvious things, deception and propaganda have been some of the most damaging weapons in this war.

Owing to my role as an emergency and ICU doctor, plus my experience in disaster management, in the height of the crisis I was dealing daily with the dead, injured and maimed. I saw every disgusting crime against humanity that could be imagined. My connections to every hospital in the city and to many others beyond the region meant that I and my teams were the first to know about every death and almost every attack that took place, and their consequences.

But there were other kinds of attacks against humanity that I could never have dreamed would become the day-to-day experiences of my community. I lost count of the number of times I asked myself whether I had truly made the right decision to keep my family in such a terrifying and violent place. Watching my people suffer in front of my eyes and between my hands almost felt worse than undergoing the same afflictions myself. I had to remind myself every day why I was still in such a horrendous place.

During these years I guarded my family very closely, trying

to protect them as much as I could from what was going on around us. There were some things I couldn't hide, of course. The explosions, the guns and the soldiers became part of our landscape, plus the numerous times we had to move home. But I refused to have television channels in our home so that at least they wouldn't be subjected to all the hideous media messages that drove fear even into adults.

My great dilemma was that I needed to be close to the hospitals, yet since the very start of the war I had seen too many targeted, attacked and destroyed. We lived in close proximity to some of the most brutal battlefields, so I saw everything that happened. I had established the emergency response system for the entire governorate, which I coordinated and managed throughout the war. I was not employed by the government but worked as an adviser to serve the hospitals and people in my area as a specialist doctor and disaster management consultant. I was acting simply as a human being responding to the extreme suffering around me.

One by one, my friends, colleagues and acquaintances were killed or kidnapped or they left the country. No one could blame them for leaving. But while I continued to deal with the torment and anguish that shaped our day-to-day existence, living in hell on earth, I was periodically reminded by phone calls and photos on social media of a totally different world that continued to turn outside the abyss we were drowning in. While I dealt daily with bloody, mutilated bodies, rape victims and the abused, and the monstrous chaos we were overwhelmed with, I would see friends, now living in other countries, posting on social media pictures of what appeared to be normal life.

I looked at those pictures and wondered if they could be real: the latest fashions, expensive restaurants, exotic holidays, parties, new cars, stylish homes. Could this kind of existence really occur in the same world I was living in? Were people genuinely focused on such things, while I was daily covered in blood, breaking the devastating news to broken mothers that their child had been beheaded, but we couldn't find the right head for their body because there were too many? A volunteer sutured the heads onto the bodies so families could take their loved ones and bury them. One day he told me that they had sutured a thousand heads.

The disparity between these two worlds felt like a strange and complex mathematical challenge that couldn't be solved: the figures simply didn't add up. How could these two opposing realities coexist on the same planet? Yet I soon realised that the marvel is not that they coexist; the marvel is that each exists as it is *because of* the other. As I processed this bizarre contrast of lifestyles, I realised that the people I could see from a distance were not living in the real world. They had been deceived into believing, as I had been before the war, that the small details in their lives (which gradually became major priorities) were important. They were living a lifestyle built on things that don't matter and which have no true meaning. Materialistic pursuits have no significance when it comes to the bigger picture of what is important in life, or our place in eternity. Love, sacrifice, honour, forgiveness and surviving in this world without losing your faith or humanity – these are the things that matter.

Walking in the street and seeing the orphans of the patients I had dealt with only increased my frustration. I found myself wondering whether the activities their parents had been carrying out as they were killed had been worth sacrificing their lives for. It amplified my intense feeling that people all over the world were living a futile existence, not focused on activities with long-term value, while sedating themselves with unimportant things. When those parents had been killed, they were simply doing what most people around the world hope to spend their time on: buying a new car, getting a cake for their child's birthday, having a party, shopping for clothes. Were these concerns and day-to-day preoccupations worth losing their lives for? They did not die pursuing something significant in life, serving God or serving humanity. Those activities they had been spending their lives on suddenly seemed empty and pointless when they were gone.

Each of those people who had died was fighting their own battle in life, just as every one of us is fighting our own battle.

Maybe someone is fighting on behalf of a bank, another for a technology company, or something else. The question is, when each of us returns from our battle, will it have been worth it? Will it have been worth the time, energy and focus that each of us dedicated to fighting for it? How did we each choose to spend the precious gift of time God has given us on this earth?

My eyes have seen too much: people who had been savagely tortured and killed, those who had had body parts cut off, groups of fighters in Syria cutting out the heart of their enemy and then eating it. After seeing these atrocities, the meaning of most things that people focus their lives on was lost to me. I found myself asking, what is worthy of spending your life on? The conclusion I came to is that only God and his values are worthy.

From where I stood, even being able to walk freely in the street with your little child running in front of you was something I could only dream of. We could hardly imagine that, after a few years of war, we would be forced to avoid as much walking in the street as possible. Instead, when we had to walk in public, we avoided any parked cars in case one turned out to be a bomb. Car bombs were more numerous than anyone could count. It got to the stage that people would erect barriers in front of their homes to stop anyone from parking there. No one would allow you to park near them unless they knew you well.

We also tried to keep out of sight as much as possible in the street, as the tops of buildings were regularly used by snipers who intentionally killed ordinary civilians. We tried not to go out after dark except in emergencies, as kidnappings took place more often after dark, especially in certain places. I remembered a time before the conflict when we had slept with our doors wide open, but now we dared not even leave the house at night. I learnt to take a different journey to and from work each day and never told anyone where I was going, not even Miriam. This was the time when I was most vulnerable to being kidnapped, as doctors were specifically being targeted. I never allowed my mobile to connect with my car GPS, sound system, location service or anything else that could be used to track my whereabouts. I changed my mobile number every few months and used closed communication systems with my team. I lived in an extraordinarily paradoxical state of both intense fear and complete trust. The world around me was terrifying and I had to take many measures to keep myself safe, yet I also had a quiet confidence in my heart that God had put me here for a specific purpose. Serving my people through this nightmare was my destiny and my life's mission for him, yet existing here was so tough. I needed to keep reminding myself that I was here because God wanted me here.

In my busy life as a doctor before the war, I used to travel from city to city in the middle of the night if someone needed treatment. I would drive along empty roads and across the desert without seeing another soul. That became impossible during the war because of the frequency of kidnappings. Before the war, if a doctor refused to go out at night to see a patient, they would find themselves in court, having to explain why they had let someone down in their hour of need. But as the war progressed, many of my friends and colleagues were lured to their kidnapping, torture or death by someone pretending to be a patient in need in the dark hours of the night. We started advising all doctors to remain in the building they were in when it got dark. Likewise, if I was treating a patient in the hospital after sunset, I would spend the night there rather than risk a journey home in the dark, even if it was less than a kilometre.

The people who were kidnapped were usually the ones who didn't believe it could happen to them and didn't adapt their behaviour to the changing climate. If I was at home after dark and received a phone call saying someone was dying, or a member of staff in a hospital I was working in needed help, I could not go to their aid. Many times my heart was torn in two, as I imagined it was my own mother or father in need. But we doctors had to protect our families who needed us, and to think of the bigger picture – of all the people we would help over the course of the coming years if we were to remain alive.

This was part of our disaster management training: to protect the leaders at the centre of a project.

With each rocket, car bomb or suicide attack, we lost our ambulances. This began very early in the war and we soon found ourselves using any van or vehicle we could find to evacuate the injured from the mangled scenes of carnage and death. Usually they were nothing more than empty tin cans on wheels, with no equipment. Sometimes there would be a mattress on the floor of the vehicle, but often they didn't even have that. They were just a means to extract people, move them through hell and get them to hospital. Sometimes the hospitals were many miles away and were usually ill-equipped when the patients arrived. On the worst days, we had no choice but to pile as many bodies as we could fit at one time into these makeshift ambulances, the living on top of the dead. On those days, the vehicles would hang low on their suspension as the engines groaned, objecting to the heavy weights they were forced to carry.

The snipers knew these vehicles usually carried people, so they would shoot at all the vans that passed on the roads, but the vans had to continue their journey, regardless, through the valley of death to arrive at the next medical point or hospital. We prayed there would be another qualified team to take over their care. There were times when armed groups would threaten our teams, trying to take our ambulances at gunpoint. Driving our tin cans on wheels through snipers and fields of landmines, narrowly escaping bombs, kidnappings and killings, was only possible because of Jesus. He protected me.

Sometimes I felt as though my position was no better than that of the people being killed, whose bodies were left abandoned on the side of the road. I was ready to die too. Life had lost its value, and death became more prominent than life. The monotony and inevitability of the rising death toll made us feel that there was nothing unusual about being killed and that surviving is the stranger of the two things. Some of us blamed ourselves, feeling guilty that we were still alive when so many others had died around us. Friends, family, colleagues, strangers:

everyone. When I looked into the eyes of my old schoolfriend's mother after he was killed, I wondered what was going through her mind. Why should it be her precious son whose life was taken, and not mine?

The funerals were too numerous to count, but I avoided them as much as possible. I couldn't bear to inflict more pain on my battered heart than it already bore every day. I didn't have enough time or emotional energy. People in business say, 'Time is money,' but for me, time is life, and my time and energy had to be spent serving those who could be saved.

There were a few, however, that had a special meaning for me.

One day, I entered the funeral hall for my brother's best friend. He had been an engineer and a true gentleman. I cared very much for him. He had been a good-looking man with a shy smile and had not yet had the chance to marry. I can never erase from my memory the moment my eyes met his mother's. In our culture, women and men are separated at funerals. She ran over to me in the middle of the men's hall, breaking the custom. She hugged me, tears streaming down her face. As she held me so tightly, I felt as though she was searching for the scent of her son on me.

'He is gone,' she said. 'They didn't even give us a body.' Her shoulders shook. He had been kidnapped. His family never saw him again, but they saw the video of his cruel and gratuitous murder posted by his killers on social media. It showed them gloating over his torture, execution and dead body. 'They didn't even let me hug his dead body just one last time. I can't even have a grave to put a rose on. My beloved son is gone, A!' She could barely utter the words through her sobs.

My brother wasn't able to attend this funeral of his best friend because he had been conscripted to military service. They had sent him to the front line and, at this unpredictable time, he couldn't be excused even for a funeral. So I went in his place to represent him and our family. My heart felt heavy thinking about my brother, his family and little daughter too. It could just as easily have been his funeral that day. This encounter spelled out the inescapable reality of where he was and the danger he was in.

At that moment, I couldn't convince myself that my brother's situation was any better than his dead friend's. I clung to our friend's mother, fighting back the tears that were threatening to overflow from my heart. In that moment I wondered whether it was me now trying to catch the scent of my brother on her. I prayed that Jesus would bring him back safely.

In later years, when my brother was finally discharged from the army, he would visit this woman and her husband and ask them to consider him as their son now, and he tried to take care of them. Often, his late friend's mother would go to my brother's workplace. He would invite her in, but on days when she saw he was busy, she wouldn't enter; instead, she would stand at his doorway, just watching him as he worked.

This mother had reminded me so much of my own mother over the years. She was so strong, and she even looked like her. But after the death of her son, she withered away. It aged her, and she lost the sparkle she had always had before. My mother told me so many times how she had seen what had happened to her friends whose children had been killed. She begged me not to leave her.

On another occasion I went to a different funeral. I heard one bereaved mother talking to the mother of the person being buried. Both women had lost their child, but one said to the other that they were lucky to at least have a body to bury. So many grieving mothers didn't even have a body, a funeral or a grave. Their precious child simply disappeared. I heard those mothers saying, 'You can bury your child. At least you have a grave to cry at. We don't have anything, not even a body. We don't even know whether our child is dead or alive.'

What troubled me more was that people who had lost their humanity learnt how to manipulate the emotions of the bereaved and vulnerable for their own depraved gain. They knew what those mourning mothers were going through, and they preyed on the grief, vulnerability and desperation of these heartbroken women. Without seeing their deceased children, these mothers would cling to any speck of hope that perhaps, just perhaps, their child could still be alive.

No mother anywhere in the world would call the bluff of someone who claimed to have kidnapped their missing child and was offering their release for a ransom. Even women who knew in their heart that the self-proclaimed captor of their child was lying were unwilling to risk potentially losing their precious child. They would do anything for a splinter of a chance to see their beloved again. Having already suffered immeasurably because of the disappearance of their child, to then be told they were alive and they could see them again was torturous. They would pay the ransom, even if they had to borrow it, rather than take the chance that if they didn't, perhaps their treasured child would suffer more, or their fate would be sealed forever. So many of those desperate mothers paid, but their children were never seen again.

*

During these years of conflict, I have also seen how sex has been used as a weapon of war. In the conservative culture that we have preserved through the millennia in Syria, this has been heartbreaking and disillusioning to see. Girls and women have been forced into prostitution, in addition to many others who have been groomed and then used to deceive and blackmail men in positions of influence. Others have been 'married' off to armed radicals, and many of those girls did not enter into a consensual marriage. Others simply became the girl who was passed from jihadist fighter to fighter, each one of whom would 'marry' her for a couple of hours, then divorce her simply by saying, 'I divorce you.' She would then be 'remarried' to the next jihadist, with this monstrous act being perpetuated under the perverted pretence of marriage until she was no longer useful to them. But huge numbers of others were simply taken and repeatedly raped, abused and degraded.

One teenage girl from our community was taken by the extremists. She, unlike most others, was released after some time.

She was part of a deal made between the Syrian government and the jihadist group who had abducted her – if the jihadists would release some of the women and children they held, the government would release some imprisoned jihadists in return.

This girl had psychologically crumbled under the abuses she had suffered. They returned her, having repeatedly raped and traumatised her. By that time she had detached herself from reality and could no longer speak or function. Once in the safety of her parents' home, she withdrew to her room with the door closed. Each time the door opened she ran to the wall, pressing herself against it, legs apart, presenting herself for the next assault that she had learnt would result from someone opening the door. She had given up trying to make any sense of the degenerate world she had encountered in her short life. A young girl like this, molested and violated in such a debased manner. There are no words left.

It was not only the women who suffered. Sometimes even men were targeted. A personal friend of mine, a true and faithful Christian man whom I had known for many years, was one such target. He was an honourable teacher who was respectful and honest. When he spoke against the atrocities and violations against humanity that were being committed by the armed radicals, they taught him a lesson. Some of his students, who had connections with these groups, kidnapped him. He was tied up, tortured and raped, over and over again. They starved him, bound his hands, then humiliated and degraded him, day in, day out. When he was released, the marks on his wrists remained from where his hands had been tightly tied, and he needed treatment in intensive care for his internal injuries. They abused him and then let him go, as a lesson and a warning to anyone else who might dare to speak out against these groups who had descended into evil and depravity.

After his release, he was a completely broken man. They had robbed him not only of his self-worth but also of his will to live. He could no longer work or interact with his community. Word travels quickly in Syria. He had been humiliated and shamed on every possible level. He no longer felt like a man.

His pride and dignity had been mercilessly torn from him. Even if he were to be able to recover enough to leave his house and engage with people, how could this man ever stand in front of a class of students again? Every time he would look into their eyes, he would be wondering whether they would be the next to betray him.

This is how evil silences truth and integrity and leaves in its place a web of dirt, lies and deception. We have lived under a cloak of falsehood here in Syria for many years now, where truth has been replaced with the fabric of disinformation. This faithful Christian's life has been martyred, for daring to speak out for justice for our Christian community.

10

Fighting for Our Inheritance

One summer day while the war raged around me, I was sitting at my desk, thinking. We were losing city after city, village after village, and people were starting to feel that ISIS were totally surrounding us, eclipsing everything in Syria. It is a terrifying experience to see your country falling to the control of jihadist groups who just want to kill, rape and take everything you own, and turn everything that was good in your country into darkness. No one could have anticipated that the war would escalate to the level it did, or that it would span so many years. Everyone hoped it would finish quickly and that life would return to normal, but after a few years I had started to feel anxious. Remembering what life had been like for all of us before the war felt like a dream. I could hardly believe that, once, all the things we had lost had been available to us. We could have anything we wanted at any time of the day or night. What were we living in now?

I asked God for guidance: 'You have been here with me from the beginning, step by step. You created me here in this country for a reason. What do you want me to do?'

I was in a good position financially as I had done well before the war. During the war, my services had been especially in demand as my specialist skills in emergency care and ICU had been needed more than ever. The situation for so many others (financial and otherwise) was far worse.

I had set up numerous medical points and field hospitals in addition to my work in various city hospitals and I was serving a lot of different people. Many companies asked me to provide medical services for them. But I was not happy about the advantage that the war had given to my work, and I felt that what lay ahead in the future would be even worse. I kept thinking and praying, as we seemed so helpless. I felt that nothing would stop the things that were happening to us. This attack on Syria had come like a flood, killing people, burning homes, consuming all – taking everything and everyone.

There was another reason I stayed in Syria. This land is my inheritance, passed down from our ancestors, and it should also be the inheritance of our grandchildren and their descendants. Yet so few would choose to stay here if they had another option.

Day by day, it was easy to lose the ability to see clearly. I needed to keep listening to the sound of God in my heart, giving me directions, telling me to go right or left, to stop or to start. I felt that he was saying, 'A, you are here because I gave you this inheritance. I gave this land through a promise to your ancestor Abraham and then to his children. You are living here because your ancestors were obedient. When Jesus came, your ancestors believed in him when he died to create the New Covenant. Your ancestors before Jesus were given this land as a gift from God.'

When Jesus came, he said he hadn't come to change even a single letter of the law, but rather to fulfil it.[1] Through his sacrifice on the cross for the forgiveness of sins, Jesus gave us another inheritance: eternal life, or 'land', in heaven.

In my heart I felt that if I were to leave this land, I would not only lose my physical inheritance here on earth, but I would also sacrifice gaining my full inheritance and helping my people here to gain their full inheritance both here and in heaven. God wanted me to stay and complete my mission of serving my people here, fighting for this land not with physical weapons but with love, compassion and kindness. Jesus told us not to store up treasure here on earth, but to store up treasure in heaven. Wherever our treasure is, our heart will also be there.[2] I wanted my heart to be focused on heaven, not on the comforts of this world. I felt I was staying here to 'fight' for humanity, to keep the promise of the land my ancestors had gained directly from God, as we were fighting now for Jesus. Those of us who have stayed here have been fighting to keep his words, teaching and presence here because we believe in him. We have the right to this land both on earth and in heaven: on earth because we are descended from Abraham and Jacob, and in heaven because we believe in Jesus.

Imagine this land, the place where Jesus lived and where Christianity was born, losing its knowledge of him, becoming a place where Christianity was stamped out and eradicated. It would be a travesty. Yet these years of war and the related attacks on Christianity and on Jesus have made that prospect a much greater possibility. So many Christians have been killed or driven out of our land since the start of the conflict. Hundreds of thousands. If I were to leave, I would set a precedent for others to follow, and the people who respect and trust me might feel that they too should leave: our actions influence the behaviour of others. But when they see me standing with them, living with them and suffering with them, they see that it is still possible to live here, even though it is more difficult than anyone outside Syria could believe.

Miriam gained a visa to live and work in a western country during the war. We could have gone with our children and enjoyed a very nice, comfortable life there. I could easily have found work as a doctor to support my family anywhere in the world. We had many disagreements over emigrating, especially in the toughest times when we lived in the middle of all the fighting. Despite the doubts that surfaced regularly, I knew in my heart we must stay. It was hard for Miriam to accept, but after a number of years, when we were living in a calmer place, she began to see things from my perspective. One day, when her grandmother became sick and needed us, we were there for her. Six of her children had emigrated to the United States, leaving their mother behind. Her seventh child, Miriam's mother, had stayed, meaning we are her only remaining family in Syria. What would have happened if we had left her too?

In our culture it is the sons who inherit property and land, and the name of the family is passed on through the generations by the sons, not the daughters. From this perspective, that family has vanished from this country, as if they have simply been erased from the map. They are living a very comfortable life now in the US, but they left their mother behind. She cannot go to live in the US. Even if she could get a visa it would be impossible for her as she can't speak the language, she can't work and, being elderly, she can barely even walk. When all her other children left, it was as if she became a woman who brought no children into the world. Where are all her family, her children and grandchildren? What does she have to show for all those years and all the love, energy and time that she poured into raising those children? When she is sick, she needs someone to take her to the doctor and bring her medication. We don't have old-age pensions or social security in Syria. It is the family who provide for their elderly relatives. When she's lonely, she needs someone to sit with her, talk with her and tell her about their life and daily events.

I believe this beautiful old lady is a true manifestation of Jesus living here among us. Why do we have trouble seeing that? Could I really leave Jesus behind, and my father and mother? I could not. It would be better to die here than to leave them and go and live somewhere else.

This experience with her grandmother opened Miriam's eyes, and she told me she couldn't imagine not being here for her family. As an only child, her parents will depend on her and on us as they grow old. If we had left, I felt that it would be like betraying and denying Jesus, making a statement that we aren't his disciples, in the same way that Peter denied Jesus when asked if he was one of his followers. It would be a shame if all these things God did for us here in this land were lost, just because I wanted an easy life for myself.

I want my children to grow up here to claim their inheritance, both the physical land here and their eternal inheritance, through serving God in this challenging place of need, bringing his light to our damaged communities. It would be almost impossible for them if they were to start their lives outside Syria and then try to return later. Once they tasted life elsewhere it would be so hard to return to this tough place to live, especially as young people, as it needs enormous perseverance, resilience and persistence to achieve anything here. Those qualities have to be fostered in this environment, and my children will only truly understand our culture and needs if they live here and struggle here with us for the name of Jesus, working for his kingdom by the sweat of their brows.

To work for his kingdom here is my mission in this life, and, if I were to leave Syria, I would have failed my mission. I need to stay here and set an example to my children of how we should stay and fight with love and compassion. An easy life is not the solution. Elsewhere I could have an expensive car, an attractive house and numerous holidays, but these would be temporary delights on earth. I want to stay here in the promised land, and from here build my more beautiful home in heaven.

Compromising in this life can be a big issue. Often it is talked about as a positive thing, but I don't remember Jesus compromising on anything at all. People often feel it is okay to compromise on little things, providing we stand firm on the big issues, but Jesus showed us this is not the case. The real problems between him and the religious leaders began the day he challenged them in the temple. He refused to compromise on the issue of the market traders inside the temple who were profiting from the people who came to worship there. He said they had turned his father's house into a den of thieves.[3]

It must have been obvious to Jesus what the consequences would be of challenging the Pharisees. Surely it was clear that those religious leaders would not accept that kind of confrontation, especially from someone with a low social status like Jesus had in their culture. Such opposition to their power would result in death. If Jesus had compromised and turned a blind eye to the hypocrisy of the religious leaders, perhaps he would not have been crucified. When he was asked about paying taxes to the Roman government, he again didn't compromise. His responses and challenges to the leaders of his time were always unyielding. He did not change his opinions to suit those around him. He stood his ground to the very end.

True faith, which stands firm to the very end, is the faith that Jesus calls for. If you are happy to die even for the smallest belief, never mind the big things, then this is what complete faith looks like. If you look back through church history over the years, prominent church leaders, such as the Pope or archbishops, don't usually compromise on the big issues in faith. They are non-negotiable. Yet if you look around the world you will find widespread corruption and compromise in the established Church. How can it be that all the important issues and ideas are complied with, yet these problems remain? I believe the reason is that some leaders have compromised on what may have seemed like small things. However, once we compromise on the small things it leaves a door open for the devil and gives him the opportunity to change us from the inside. Over time, we will begin to feel that we've lost sight of even the larger issues, and in doing this we can give up our spiritual inheritance. Where faith is concerned, compromise is not an option.

I decided to stay in Syria and trusted that God would send people to help and support me. There was a certainty in my heart that he would protect me and provide for our family. He brought our people to this land thousands of years ago through the miracle of the parting of the Red Sea and many other miracles our ancestors saw while they were living in the desert. We have been living in our own desert and have seen many miracles from God here as we wait to be able to enter his eternal rest. Why should I be afraid now? God brought me here and will fight for me here. We should not accept seeing the name of Jesus banished from his land. On the contrary, we should do everything we can to see it glorified here.

When we do a coronary artery bypass graft, we have to first put in a lifeline. We put in a central venous catheter[4] and an arterial line.[5] These allow us to give blood and fluids quickly. Then we put the patient under general anaesthetic. After we open the patient's chest, we redirect all the blood to an artificial heart that pumps blood to all the organs of the body. Then we stop the unhealthy heart, take veins from the patient's leg and graft them on to his heart. Once this is secure, we then activate the real heart, close the chest and wake the patient.

If you think about everything that has to be done to carry out this surgery, it really is a bloody operation! It is complex and requires a lot of concentration. If we want to perform 'heart surgery' for the Syrian people, we should expect it to be messy and complicated. Despite the challenges involved, we can't stop midway through, because without the operation the patient will die. The same would be true of abandoning Syria. Perhaps God was preparing me through my involvement in complex cardiac surgery for my work in my community, building resilience, tenacity and focus so I have the strength to continue no matter how challenging it becomes.

That summer's day in my office, I started to write. I wasn't sure what I was writing, but I wrote and wrote for hours. I felt the sound of God in my heart, saying to me, 'You need to build an ark.' As I was writing, I could hear the sound of guns firing outside. I could smell death out there. The city was literally burning, and I could smell the smoke from a distance. I sat in my office, surrounded by fear and horror, and kept writing.

It was so hot that day in the middle of summer and I didn't know if the heat I was feeling was from the weather or from the hell we were living in. We had no electricity and no resemblance of a real life. We were struggling to keep any kind of balance.

What I wrote was not like anything I could think up, or any kind of plan I had ever wanted to make. I had spent my life as a doctor and I loved being a doctor. I struggled to think about anything else outside my medical realm and ambitions for hospitals. But I saw how the concept of an ark, or 'vessel', could save and preserve elements of our community, protect our people and help them to survive this enormous attack. It was not a physical building, but rather a combination of services and community to aid us in surviving this war.

We needed a humanitarian arm – we couldn't survive without it – to support people by sowing seeds of compassion, to foster positive feelings of love and sympathy in their souls, which had also been broken, just like their bodies and homes. I wanted to open people's hearts, as over time their arteries had become blocked by their brokenness. I wrote in depth about how we should carry out this humanitarian work. More was required, because whatever you give someone to eat will be gone the next day, leaving them hungry again.

The second area to focus on was business and employment, because everyone needs to earn a living to support themselves and their families. They need independence. We can't simply give aid handouts to an entire country forever, as that would just create a nation of beggars with no self-worth.

The third arm was for a true church that would give our hungry people the real Jesus: fresh bread and living water. So many had lost their faith and needed a genuine church that would feed their hearts and souls, encouraging them in their relationship with God.

I wrote this plan in great detail, spending two full days just sitting and writing solidly about this 'ark'. When I finished writing, I gave it to lots of people to read. Some were people with influence, but they asked me why I was spending my time writing about this if I was not going to do it myself. They told me I couldn't do it. I replied that they were right, I couldn't do it – but God could.

It *was* impossible for me to do all the things we have achieved since then: to start a charity, to distribute clothes and food to hundreds of thousands of people, to establish the additional hospitals, to provide medical care to many additional tens of thousands of people, to support many of the orphans and widows we have helped and to work for a vision of building a large hospital.

But one day someone appeared, as if from nowhere, sent by God to help me, with an 'army' of others behind them. Slowly we started to work towards and achieve some of those things, but it was a long-term vision that would take time. It was as if they were working from the same document as me, from the vision of the ark, which I had written about in such detail. When I did something different from what I had written, somehow they prompted me back to the way it had originally been written, yet without ever having read it. It started slowly, little by little, and the 'ark' began to be 'built'. It grew not by might nor by power, but by God's Holy Spirit.[6]

II

A Broken Cry for Help

At the beginning of the war I was fully charged and strong. Over time, trauma, pain and encountering the most evil acts imaginable began to take their toll. The day-to-day battle of trying to serve people in their most vulnerable moments, in a war zone, with fewer and fewer resources, wore me down. I became exhausted. I couldn't recharge myself properly any more. I found myself wishing I could have the same difficulty two days in a row. But every day brought a different challenge and I never dealt with the same problem twice.

One day, as I was walking along the street, a rocket hit the ground right next to me. By God's grace it didn't explode, or I would not be here to tell this story. The person who was with me looked at me in fear, as if I was some kind of freak, and asked what kind of luck I had. God had made his promise to me early in the war through Psalm 91, that he would protect me from harm, and this was one of many examples of times when I was delivered from dangerous situations that could have taken my life.

The months and years of injustices I suffered personally, the daily fear I lived with and the ocean of atrocities I dealt with were significantly affecting me, both mentally and emotionally. Nothing could be achieved easily, and organising any work took a huge amount of time and commitment. Dealing with people who had lost their moral compass was a wearying and soul-destroying process as daily I was faced with injustice. I was burnt out, yet there was simply no opportunity to rest. But I kept going because the only other option was to give up.

The strong personality I have had since childhood has always put me in a position of leadership. I have always been the capable person others have looked to for reassurance, encouragement and solutions to problems. As the war continued to develop, the needs increased. It was not just individuals depending on me but also companies and organisations. I was being asked to set up new medical centres and field hospitals and to provide more ambulances and equipment. But it was problematic to find the equipment and resources to make it possible. We couldn't even find the basic essentials. Patients' injuries were severe, and the maimed would scream with pain, yet during the worst times we often lacked the anaesthetic drugs or painkillers needed to relieve their suffering. At one stage I was even searching for paracetamol and the simplest of medications. Many people lost such significant parts of their bodies that they were left permanently disabled, and many didn't survive at all. My heart was crushed again and again. I didn't know how to explain to grieving relatives what had happened to their loved ones: there was no explanation.

One day, in a medical centre, I was dealing with significant injuries and was so desperate that I asked a friend to bring me all the medication from his clinic. There were times when I spent hours ringing round just to source enough anaesthetic drugs to carry out a couple of life-saving operations. The alternative was to let the patients bleed to death. I went to every length to provide these things, but in the end we simply had to pray and trust that God would bring them to us. So often, the only treatment we were able to prescribe was 'stay and pray'. I felt Jesus with me, and while I was trying to heal our patients' bodies, he was wanting to heal our souls.

So many of the incidents and situations I witnessed would lead to post-traumatic stress disorder for many people. Yet these were daily, sometimes hourly, experiences for me. As the days of abominations stretched into years, I began to feel more and more isolated and alone. It felt as if I was carrying the weight of the entire war on my shoulders, and I couldn't share the heavy burden with anyone. Although there were many people around me who cared for me, there was no one who thought to encourage me during those toughest of years. Everyone around me was suffering immensely too. We were all fighting simply to keep our heads above water, and not to drown in the torrent of savagery and pain we were immersed in.

We were struggling in the hospitals and medical facilities with missing or faulty equipment, and with insufficiently trained staff or lack of specialist staff. Hospitals had been destroyed, damaged or closed when the owners left when the areas were under attack. The hospitals that remained were increasingly unreliable, and many had lost confidence in them. Importing new medical equipment became a dire struggle because most companies outside Syria refused to deal with companies or people inside Syria. Most hospitals were trying to keep resuscitating old equipment that was well past its use-by date. When machines were really beyond any hope, we just had to make do without.

I was introduced to some non-government organisations (NGOs) who were bringing medical aid into Syria, but I quickly became disillusioned with them. They did not care about the poor and suffering Syrian people, and pocketed or sold most of the money and items they received from outside Syria. Those NGOs capitalised on our crisis – it was just business for them. I felt such anger and despair when I saw what they were doing.

In some of the most basic facilities set up for emergency response, it became an expectation that patients would share equipment intended to serve one person at a time. Single-use supplies were cleaned after use, sterilised, then used for the next patient and the one after. We were so tired of seeing patients die who could have been treated easily if we just had what we needed. We had to choose between the second- or third-best treatment options or no treatment at all, which in many cases would mean death. These were not choices any professional would choose to make for their patients, or that any person would make for themselves or their relatives.

One of the hardest things to endure for me as a doctor was knowing what needed to be done but having no means to provide an adequate level of care for these poor people, who had no one and nothing else to depend on. The conditions were already trying enough – conditions that were an insult to the training I had gone through as a doctor, and to the infrastructure I had worked so hard to build up – then more bombs would explode, resulting in scores of new patients being brought to us in just one hour.

To add insult to injury, the medical services were targeted by bombs as well as by fighters. They weren't only targeted by jihadists. Sometimes fighters belonging to militias would turn up and attack the staff if we refused to drop everything we were doing for other patients in great need in order to prioritise the person they had brought in. On one occasion, while I was suturing a patient, I was physically attacked and beaten by some armed men who had arrived at the hospital. They had brought someone needing treatment. It was not life-threatening, yet they wanted me to stop in the middle of suturing my patient and deal with them immediately.

Our medical teams couldn't cope physically, mentally or emotionally. There were days when I was covered in so much blood that I didn't know which of the stains on my clothes were from which patients. At times, the corridors and floors were awash with the remnants of life that had been poured out of the Syrian people. Their blood and their lives had been spent. But for what? No goal in the world could justify this.

Tirelessly, I worked to improve the conditions we were trying to function in, but it was like attempting to drain an ocean with a single cup. It was impossible. We were in such great need and I kept searching for other solutions for our people. Every day, feeling bone-weary and angry, I prayed from the deepest part of my heart. I was totally overwhelmed. All I could say to God was, 'Help me!' and trust that he would understand my heart. I simply didn't have the words to pray. These prayers were like the prayers I prayed as a little boy in pain, not knowing what else to say. I was just a child calling out to my father, because who else could I call out to? I felt like Peter, sinking while trying to walk on water, who simply shouted to Jesus, 'Lord, save me!'[1] In the last few years I have had to walk on water, doing the impossible daily just to survive and to keep going for the multitude who have needed my help. Every day we survived in that hell was a miracle, yet we saw many other miracles and answers to prayer. But it had become too much, and I was drowning. I called out to God for help. I felt by this point as though my head had sunk below the water and all that was left of me was one hand, reaching above the water, while I prayed desperately that God would grab hold of it and pull me back up so I could breathe again.

One day, I began to speak, and I was sure that the words I spoke came from God, through me: 'I am your protector and helper. No one dares to stand against me. With love and mercy, you will feed my people and lead the blind to light. You will receive everything you ask for, will see all that is hidden, and will hear everything that is silent. I will rebuild you when you break and refresh you when you are tired. Neither food nor sleep you will need, only God. Your army will be brave. I will send you a star from the desert to guide your journey and help you.'

★

As I was drowning, someone did take hold of my hand and pull my face out of the water. But when I surfaced for air and looked up, it wasn't the face I was expecting to see. Someone connected me with an English woman running a charity called Samara's Aid Appeal. I was deeply suspicious of her and was reluctant to have contact with someone outside Syria. Who was she and what did she want with us, or with me? For a start, her surname was Levy. At that time, it was a name that evoked much fear in Syria. We place a lot of emphasis on names in our country and make a lot of inferences about people from their names, even before meeting them. In our culture, someone's name tells us about the family a person comes from.

Levy is a name that Syrians, and many others, associate with the instigation of the 'colour revolutions' in the Middle East. Her name set ringing every alarm bell I had. My fear was that this woman, Samara Levy, might have a connection with a network that was linked in some way to the fighting in Syria, as these groups were notorious for using a cover like humanitarian aid to establish connections and relationships in Syria which could then be exploited to steer the political situation, to sabotage or to influence the fighting in our country. Some of them were also known to use religious groups and charities to serve their political agendas. Something that has especially disturbed me is how entities serving worldly governments have politicised and manipulated the Bible to support the political agendas of secular governments. They have used God's holy words in unholy ways, to justify their military and political actions of gaining power, influence and resources in the Middle East. Suffering and instability has been caused here on an enormous scale over the last century by entities politicising the Bible, and they have a lot of blood on their hands.

Furthermore, she was English! Almost everyone in Syria was painfully aware that the UK was one of the countries fighting against Syria in the war. I struggled to believe at first that she was not linked with an intelligence agency outside Syria. I didn't see how it could be any other way. It felt very risky even to talk with her. We were in the middle of a war, and if she was connected with the enemies of our country, then having any link with her could prove devastating. I could be arrested or, if she had a hidden agenda, there could be more severe consequences for me and our people.

But there was a sound in my heart. When we talked on the phone and exchanged messages, I felt that her heart was genuine. She was openly moved, and even suffering herself when she saw our situation. I sensed as I talked with her that she was human. She felt my pain, our pain. She was authentic, and she dealt with me as a real person. I wasn't used to people like that any more.

In the build-up to this I had lost faith in people, as well as in religious leaders. I had faced significant problems working with a group of people here in Syria who had claimed to be Christians. When I saw what they were really doing, as opposed to what they told others they were doing, I felt that they were sabotaging and dirtying all the words of the Bible and Jesus. They used them freely, but their lives reflected the opposite of

God's way. By the fruits of their lives I saw that they had no true interest in serving Jesus, only themselves and their gods of power, money and status. Seeing their hypocrisy, I was angry and heartbroken. They talked so much about faith, but it was cheap, empty talk which they used in a way I hated.

I couldn't face trusting Samara and then having another experience like that. Those people had said many things that had implied they were Christians: 'God bless you . . .', 'God will help us . . .', 'Let us pray . . .', 'God will be faithful . . .' But in the end, they were just corrupt people taking whatever they could of the money and help intended for the suffering of poor Syrians. They became richer while the poor here became poorer. Sadly, I had seen too many churches and Christian groups profiting from the humanitarian crisis here, who didn't pass on most of what was donated from outside Syria to the people who were really in need. I felt disgusted by their pretence and didn't want to start a new relationship with someone talking about God in a similar way. There was a battle between my mind and my heart. My heart wanted to believe that Samara was true, but my mind was saying, 'You are stupid. You are going to have the same problem with her. How can she be different?'

When Samara saw my struggle, she said we need fellow disciples of Jesus around us, to build us up and encourage us. For me, the most important thing about fellow disciples was to be able to trust them. This issue must have broken Jesus' heart, as he knew before it happened that Peter would deny him, and he felt a heaviness in his heart as the hour approached. We don't know what he felt about Judas, except that he knew he would betray him. It hurts so much when you really give your trust and your heart to someone who then betrays it, especially if it is intentional. I couldn't bear to go through this painful experience again, so I tried to protect myself.

With these thoughts in mind, I did not respond to any of Samara's initial comments about faith. I tried to keep things as simple as possible, so much so that she struggled to even see my faith. I was exhausted by people in public positions here wearing the titles of Christian leaders and then betraying the trust of people in need. To me, they were like the Pharisees, wearing religious clothes or titles but using their positions of influence to whitewash dirty purposes, achieving immoral and unethical goals. They didn't show anything like the love of Jesus in their hearts. It was hard to separate these things in my mind after witnessing the large-scale hypocrisy that took place. It got to the stage where I felt repulsed just seeing people wearing religious robes or who had religious titles. In my mind, they were the wolves dressed in sheep's clothing that Jesus warned us about.[2]

But the sound in my heart overrode these fears and suspicions and, slowly, God began to melt the ice as we talked more. He helped me forget the people I had been burned by before as we shared about our lives, families and childhoods. I began to see who Samara was and to feel her true motivations. Over time, God's Holy Spirit helped me to re-establish some faith, not only in Samara but also in other people.

I began by telling her only the basic information. I kept a lot back to protect myself and my people. Yet, over time, I began to feel there was something different about her. I tested her many times, then waited for the signs of intelligence interference. Instead, I saw only a genuine, faithful woman and mother who really cared about us. She didn't ask for anything, only what I was happy for her to share with her people, to encourage them to help us. When we were suffering, I saw she was really moved. She was *with* us. She rallied her people together to pray, and even to fast for us in the most awful times. Her prayer group sent personal messages which she forwarded with Bible verses to encourage me, to inspire me and build me up. I asked myself whether people like this could be real.

After everything I had seen and lived through, I had lost confidence in humanity. I hadn't known anyone like this before, even though I came from a Christian community. It took time for me to begin to trust Samara, and even when I felt sure she was true, I was still so careful what I said. She might be a genuine, true follower of Jesus, but how could I be sure there weren't people beside her using her for another purpose, trying to steer the situation or gain something? That is the nature of war.

For the first time, I felt there were people who really wanted to encourage and support me. I was able to just be real and vulnerable and to feel understood. Whenever I felt concerned, I remembered the words of Jesus: 'Thus, by their fruit you will recognise them.'[3]

When Samara appeared, suddenly there was someone helping me to achieve more, although it didn't make my life more comfortable. Beforehand I had just been dealing with hospitals, but with her I started to deal with containers full of aid and humanitarian work too.

As well as talking about faith, we began to pray together. I had never prayed like that with anyone else before. We simply talked with God in a conversational way. There was no formality or prescribed words. We simply shared our hearts with him. This helped me to draw closer to Jesus, and I saw different faces of him that I had not known before. Being surrounded by true, faithful people developed my faith.

I was surrounded by a physical war, but I was also caught up in a huge spiritual battle. There is a lot of noise and stress involved in both. There was so much spiritual noise in the physical war that many things were drowned out. As it dragged on, it prevented me from even being able to hear God. But through deeper prayer and fellowship, I became closer to Jesus. That connection increased the intensity of the battle we were facing, though; when we are doing the work of Jesus, we face a much greater level of opposition. This can be uncomfortable at times, yet this relationship also enabled me to achieve so much more than I had been able to by working alone.

A significant challenge Samara and I faced was our different understanding of what was really happening in Syria. What she understood was largely based on heavily biased reporting she had seen in the media in the UK. Likewise, it was a struggle for me to believe how entire nations and continents could be steered and conditioned to have such a different perspective ingrained into their minds of the events I had seen with my own eyes and was experiencing each day. It was impossible for her to comprehend what we were experiencing from the information made available to most westerners. It took significant time and trust for the two of us to digest that the real events that were taking place could be so wildly different from what was being reported. In the beginning, neither of us realised the enormous discrepancies between how we each saw the situation. We had many misunderstandings over issues resulting from this, until we both gained a more balanced grasp of the other's position.

One example was early on. It had taken time for us to build a reasonable level of trust in each other, and Samara had been asking me to send some videos showing our medical situation here. In trying to give me an idea of the kind of videos that would be helpful, she sent me an example from one of the largest, most respected media sources in the UK. When I saw it, I couldn't believe what she had sent me. I was shocked and angry with her for sending something so insensitive and abhorrent, when I had shared such personal stories of my losses with her. Samara was also upset, as she had no idea why I was so appalled. It took a lot of time for us to unravel this issue fully, to analyse the details and discuss what was so obvious to Syrians looking at the same video. It could easily have driven a big wedge between us, but we both had to be willing to understand what vastly different perspectives we had of what was happening in Syria, from our distinctly placed vantage points.

The video had clearly been filmed by one of the jihadist groups responsible for kidnapping, torturing, murdering and raping my friends, relatives, work colleagues and neighbours. That was obvious to me because of the area it was filmed in, the date and many other details. And she had asked me to film something similar! The jihadist group were being presented as innocent victims being attacked for no reason, when in fact they were the ones who had taken the area they were occupying, with brutal violence, by murdering the original occupants and forcing others out. I knew exactly what they had done, because many of those who escaped became my patients, and many of those who didn't managed to call us to say goodbye minutes or days before they were murdered. Likewise, I had lived in one of those areas before being forced out in the same manner.

I couldn't believe that anyone in the world could be so blind to what was so glaringly, painfully obvious to me, or to anyone else in Syria. But disinformation has been one of the most evil, divisive and sophisticated weapons in this war. I'm sure we Syrians have seen plenty of propaganda here over these years too, but no amount of deception, no matter how sophisticated, could colour my understanding of what I have directly experienced at the hand of these jihadist groups, events I have seen with my own eyes, or my injured patients and the stories they have told.

Samara accepted my opinions, but I could see she struggled to fully appreciate the extent to which this kind of deceit was possible. The money pumped into creating networks to feed the propaganda machine was immense. It wasn't until she came and saw our situation for herself, meeting multitudes of displaced families from different areas that had been under siege, hearing their stories directly and weeping with them over their tragic suffering, that she was finally able to comprehend the sophisticated indoctrination she had undergone. It took years and multiple visits to Syria for her to truly understand the extent of disinformation that has warped the perception of our reality and prolonged our agony here.

Our environments and cultures were so different, it was fascinating for us both to get to know more about the other's way of life. We are the same age and have children the same age, so had plenty to share. But she had never been to the Middle East, and I had never been to the West, so it was an interesting time as we learnt which of our customs and expectations were similar and which were very different. These differences provoked many interesting discussions. One day I was talking about a girl I employed. Samara seemed surprised and asked her age. I said she was about thirty, to which Samara replied that in her culture it would be considered disrespectful not to call her a woman. For us, on the other hand, it would be offensive to call an unmarried female a woman, as that implies she is not a virgin. From a Syrian perspective, especially in the Christian community, every unmarried female is a virgin. If not, she will struggle to find a husband and might never marry.

Samara was helping the Syrian people, yet it took a lot of groundwork to enable this. However, I was able to speak with people outside Syria with honesty, which helped to restore some of the trust I had lost in those outside our living hell. The world were not all monsters, as we had begun to believe. There were a few people trying to help and protect us, happy to even sacrifice their own belongings for the poorest of us. They were genuine. Until this point, we had seen too many using our suffering to take something for themselves or to serve a political agenda rather than help us. This had been our increasing experience of humanitarian organisations and foreigners during the war. Samara and her fellow believers helped to restore my faith in people and humanity.

12

Renewed Faith and a New Vision for a Church

I believed that we, as Syrian Christians, knew Jesus better than anyone else in the world, especially Christians in the West. Many other people here feel this way too. I had an arrogance in my heart, although I didn't come to this realisation until I got to know Samara better. When I was first introduced to her, I would never have accepted that she had an understanding of Jesus that I didn't. After all, we are living in the land of Jesus here in Syria. When I read the Bible, the place names are the areas where we live. My relatives come from some of the villages named in both the Old and the New Testaments. These areas around us are the same places where Jesus walked, slept and ate. This is where Christianity was born. He was *our* Jesus, and *we* were the ones who had carried his message to the rest of the world.

Maybe Mary or Joseph still have relatives living here; perhaps they are my ancestors. I would never have accepted that anyone from the West could help me in my relationship with Jesus. It would have been like accepting that a nurse with less training could help me to read an ECG,[1] when I am a specialist ICU doctor and cardiac surgeon. We have a general attitude here in Syria that people in the western world don't know Jesus. Their understanding of him is second-hand, while ours is first-hand.

In some ways we are wrong for thinking this way, while in other ways perhaps we are right. It was our perception that it was impossible to live the kind of life people live in the western world as well as living the life God asks us to live, as the Bible is very specific. We have lived here in the same manner in which people lived in Jesus' day, and in which people before him lived.

So much of our culture remains unchanged, preserved since then, so we tick many of the boxes in terms of the practices and behaviour that the Bible prescribes.

For example, the Ten Commandments. We see how many in the West have relationships before marriage, and many have additional ones after. Christians don't live like that here. Physical relationships are for marriage, and anyone who ignores this pays the price. Then there is the issue of divorce. People don't get divorced in my Christian community here in Syria. In worst-case scenarios, people might separate, but they wouldn't normally get divorced or remarried. If someone were to go to one of our priests to ask for a divorce, it would be as if he were asking for the moon. There are a few exceptions, and the war has changed some perceptions towards this, but generally speaking this is our way of life. Yet when we look at the West, it seems to be the normal way there, even among some Christians, to have physical relationships outside the sanctity of marriage.

Families in Syria are committed to each other, even through our differences, yet in the West many families seem to live very separate lives. We take care of our families, honouring our mother and father, financially supporting them in their old age as well as living close to them. This has always been our duty and culture. No one here would spend money on a holiday or buy a car instead of giving money to their elderly parents or taking care of them. Instead, people would sell their house here to pay for an operation for their elderly mother. But in the UK, people put their parents into care homes instead of bringing them into their own. No elderly person here would ever worry about being a burden to their children, as caring for our parents in their old age is our responsibility, not someone else's.

Whatever someone's religion in Syria, most people believe in God, yet in the West there are so many who have turned their backs on God completely. We can't understand how there can be so many atheists in the West. Changing religion is something that no one here can imagine, or even changing your name. Names are so important here; they say everything about who you are and where you are from. When a woman gets married, she keeps her father's surname, but her children will take their father's name.

These are just a few of the many reasons Syrian Christians feel that people in the West, even western Christians, don't *really* know Jesus.

What I realised, however, is that we have been living here according to the Old Testament and the old covenant. Samara was led to me by Jesus, carrying a fresh perspective of the same faith. It was a new way of understanding Jesus, with more compassion and without judgement. She showed me what they were doing at her church each week, sending me videos and talks from their services. I saw the way they sang and worshipped Jesus from their hearts, and she told me about their leaders and what their faith looked like. It touched my heart, as I had never seen a church like that before. I had seen evangelical groups and churches here, but I didn't gain a good impression of them. In Samara's Christian community I felt as though Jesus was dancing with them, in the same spirit of his miracle at the wedding in Cana.[2] I could picture him collecting clothes and filling containers with them, then crying with them as he did when his friend Lazarus died, when I told them about my friends who died here. I felt we were joined as one family by sharing such intense emotions. I loved them and felt safe with them. Every Sunday it was as if I was being taken to church in England, and I felt as if we prayed together as one church. In spite of the distance, our different worlds touched.

I was interested in understanding more and began to embrace this vision of Jesus, woven with ours. We shared our different perspectives with each other, and she too learnt more about our understanding of Jesus. I was absorbing everything we talked about, digesting it, adding my own insight from what I have experienced here, and our faith evolved together.

Knowing Jesus more intimately and feeling his presence in me changed the balance in my heart. He changed the way I measure right and wrong, which is exactly what he did when he came to our Jewish ancestors, as recorded in the Gospels. Jesus still taught the Ten Commandments, but he brought them to life in a new way. He taught people about using mercy and grace in understanding right and wrong, instead of judgement. He taught people how to adopt and follow the Ten Commandments with a deeper understanding of their meaning. To the people who were about to kill a woman caught in the act of adultery, he gave an instruction that whoever was perfect could throw the first stone.[3] Naturally, not one of us has the right to throw a single stone. Yet we are still living in a culture here in Syria where people who are guilty of adultery might be punished by family members by death, not just in radical Muslim communities but even in Christian ones. Our culture and mentality here remain almost unchanged.

The way Samara's church had been living felt very different from the way we were living in Syria as Christians. We had been living the Old Testament, almost as if Jesus had never come. Yet we are Christians, and Christianity only came through Jesus, his teachings and his beautiful grace. Somehow, we had forgotten about grace.

Interestingly, Peter and Paul are not thought to have been buried here in our land, but rather in Europe. Jesus told Peter that he was the rock on which he would build his church,[4] which demonstrates the significance of what has been happening, according to God's plan, outside our land. Likewise, in Jesus' home city and governorate, Nazareth and Galilee, Jesus performed fewer miracles than he did anywhere else.[5] The people in the very community Jesus came from didn't accept him.

Many Syrian Christians have acted in the same way as the people from Jesus' community who struggled to accept his teaching. Even though we have heard his teachings first-hand and identify as his followers, on many levels we have continued to live according to the Old Testament, as if our Bibles didn't contain a New Testament. Too many Syrian Christians have been living like the Jewish people and have missed out on so much because of this.

I sensed that in Samara's Christian community, this merciful, compassionate understanding of Jesus was very strong. When we talked and then prayed together, I felt the Holy Spirit start to move in my heart. It wasn't that I didn't have him before, because I have always loved Jesus, but there were chains around his living Spirit in my heart. Those chains were my perception that I would be saved and gain eternal life by following the old Law of Moses. The truth is that humans have proved that we cannot earn our salvation by following the Ten Commandments. It comes only through recognising that we *fail* to live by these commandments and that our place in heaven comes through accepting the undeserved gift Jesus bought for all of us with his blood. Simply, he died to take the punishment we deserve, because we are so far from perfect and can never fully live up to those Ten Commandments, no matter how hard we try and no matter how righteous or good we believe we are.

Perhaps our greatest sin is believing that we have managed to get closer to God, have been doing the right things or have been living by the Ten Commandments, while simultaneously looking at others around us and feeling we have done a better job than they have. We are so quick to look at the speck of sawdust in our brother's eye while our vision is distorted by the plank in our own.[6] Anyone who feels they have a good, strong faith, or who wants to help or teach anyone else in their faith, should walk very carefully, as this is a precarious place to stand. Humility and understanding our own shortcomings and our need for God's grace are the only safe ground from which to view anyone else's life or faith. Our place in heaven only comes through his grace, because he paid the ransom for our sins and our lives, which cost him *his* life. We didn't deserve what he did for us, but that is the real meaning of grace.

Through this new understanding, the Holy Spirit was set free in me, and he fed and nurtured my heart. Through the Holy Spirit I received fresh bread that is the real Jesus, warm and straight from the oven. I was released when I surrendered my arrogance, superiority and feeling that we Syrian Christians were better than Christians elsewhere in the world. My mistake in feeling more pure and good, and the spiritual pride I had carried, had prevented me from truly understanding and being intimate with Jesus and therefore being able to become more like him.

Jesus began to stir my heart to start supporting the poorest people through non-medical aid too. At first, I resisted Samara's desire to involve me in helping to coordinate containers of aid: I was a doctor focused on medical work, not a humanitarian. But I started to see the way she was helping the poorest people. My way of helping them had been different, but when I accepted and started to work her way, I felt I connected with Jesus even more deeply. My way had been based on serving people as a doctor, which is important too, but in the medical sector we would help patients in a more formal, restricted manner with appropriate boundaries in place. When I participated in her humanitarian work, she wanted to go and sit with the poor and bereaved in their destroyed and dirty homes, walking the muddy streets to reach them. We hugged them, wept with them and felt the passion of Jesus in our hearts as we sat with them, as equals.

I was moved by and grateful for everyone who helped us by collecting and sending aid from the UK. The clothes warmed the bodies of our poor and displaced. When we saw the smiling faces of each child and person who received something, it warmed our hearts too. They are humans – brothers and sisters, not statistics. We wanted to establish personal connections with them based on unconditional love. It was a relational approach, more in touch with the human beings themselves rather than their conditions or circumstances. Medical work doesn't facilitate this kind of relationship in the same way, as it needs to be professional.

In the same way that our resuscitation team had fought for the physical lives and bodies of our patients in hospital, I felt Jesus was now calling us to fight for the spiritual lives of our people. Before, I only concerned myself with the survival of their physical bodies, but now, after all these years of war, I began to understand spiritual death as their greatest danger, as this has eternal consequences.

We moved to a different level when we started using this one-to-one, individualistic approach. I felt as if Jesus was smiling at me in a new way, and I was grateful for the faithful army of believers in the UK who were praying for and encouraging us every day. This was the greatest blessing.

There were times when Samara and I felt so weighed down that we were tempted to stop doing this work. We encountered many problems and challenges along the way. On these occasions I was encouraged to know that Jesus identifies with that feeling too. When he arrived in Jerusalem, he asked God to remove his cup of suffering and let it pass from him.[7] He showed us our own human nature in that moment. His purpose was about to be realised and he was doing what he had come to do, yet in his humanness he wanted God to stop the painful process that was unfolding. Regardless, he put his human desires aside to show us what God's love looks like and that, no matter how hard, we can do it too.

We will find ourselves facing similar battles, and we will want to run away from our cup of suffering. It is painful when we truly follow Jesus and his example. It is like giving birth, which is painful, but in this distressing process we give life to something new and precious. We will all experience pain when we commit to following Jesus *his* way, as he didn't call us to an easy life but one that is full of challenges. Yet it has eternal consequences more beautiful and rewarding than we could ever imagine.

Every Christian journey follows a different pattern, even if we have many similar experiences and lessons to learn. I am keen not to make the mistake of feeling that everyone has to follow a set pattern, or the same steps to faith that I did. People start in different places. This is especially true of my Christian community in Syria. Our story as Syrians doesn't follow a structured model. We are complicated and unholy; we are a suffering people. We need to be real and authentic, because we are all imperfect. I dream of a church here unlike churches in the UK, US, Africa or anywhere else in the world. An authentic church that understands us as Syrians and the atrocities we have lived through and survived here. No one else can understand what we have suffered here, only the people who have lived it. Our body of believers must meet the genuine needs of the

Syrian people, relating to our understanding and experiences of life and faith, which are so different from western experiences.

The only way to God is through Jesus, who we meet in our hearts when we seek him. We all have different experiences of him, as he is sensitive and responds to each of us as a unique individual. Jesus said, 'Anyone who loves me will obey my teaching. My Father will love them, and we will come to them and make our home with them.'[8] He continued, a few verses later, 'But the Advocate, the Holy Spirit, whom the Father will send in my name, will teach you all things and will remind you of everything I have said to you.'[9] When we love Jesus and are willing to accept him into our hearts without reservation, the Holy Spirit will come and live in our hearts, guiding us in everything we do.

We have the opportunity to grow and be purified in our faith through our suffering. I have been growing here in the oven of the Syrian war. No one can understand the intensity of this heat unless they have been cooking here in the same oven. You can sense the temperature if you put your hand into the oven for a moment, but you can take your hand out again, so it will never be the same experience. It is different altogether to be shut in the oven with the door closed, with no way out.

Samara has experienced much of the heat over the years we have been working together, as she has passed through many tough experiences with me over these years in this work. One experience was the night she spent in Damascus under rocket attack. It's real heat, and the people here have been sitting in the oven for many years, feeling all of it, with no escape. So many people here have lost their souls, and many have lost their faith in the heat.

The saddest thing is that so many have spent these harsh years in this oven but haven't reached the understanding of how they can have an intimate relationship with Jesus based on grace. In spite of their suffering, they have not reached this level of faith. Many have been pushed in the opposite direction and have lost their faith completely; they have no one to lead them, because few spiritual leaders here have this kind of faith themselves. I have been blessed to have found this in Jesus, and to have been filled and moved by his Holy Spirit. The noise of the battle here has drowned out the voice of the Holy Spirit for so many. Countless numbers have turned against God because they have been so damaged and hurt. Some people have managed to stay as they were before the war, with their faith still intact. But few of those people can provide fresh bread to others who are hungry. We need people here, living among us, with God's Holy Spirit living inside them, who will walk through the oven, letting the fire purify them, enabling them to emerge at the end with faith like refined gold.

At the beginning of the war, we Syrians started to read the Bible more often than we had before. I dipped into the Bible, reading passages when I was desperate and needed to refresh myself. Lots of things pointed me back there, perhaps going to a funeral and hearing certain passages which I would then revisit afterwards. Psalm 91, which was written on a piece of paper and given to me at the beginning of the war, took on a whole new meaning for me as I began to live this psalm and *depend* on God's promise to me in it. I kept reading it over and over again. What changed was that I began living the Bible and feeling involved in these passages. Living them for real is different from simply reading or hearing them with a limited life context.

It is essential that each of us focuses on helping others, even while we are still in need of help ourselves. It doesn't matter that we aren't yet perfect or don't feel prepared. God wants us, just as we are, to accept Jesus into our lives and to start serving him with all our heart and soul right now. We all still have so much to learn, and we need to ask the Holy Spirit to work in our own hearts as we serve. But we make a mistake if we feel that we aren't yet ready to do something for him. No matter where we are on our journey of faith, Jesus wants us to start serving him, his kingdom and our brothers and sisters. If we keep asking him, he will teach us *while* we walk and *while* we serve. We should be able to help people find their way to Jesus even while we ourselves are far from perfect. That is something God put on my heart and has been reminding me of. I am not better than anyone else because I chose to stay in Syria, but I do have a mission here.

Jesus helped me to do this, to help people on their journey of faith even though I still have so much to work on in myself, and he will help every one of us, both in Syria and around the world. I'm glad to have been able to know Jesus better. At the moment there are few who will survive this oven in Syria and end up as pure gold. What Jesus did in my heart has enabled me to survive this heat. I desperately needed this new relationship with Jesus, which I received because it was brought to me by a faithful follower of his. Now we here in Syria need to do this for each other, because is it hard for Syrians to trust foreigners. This freeing of the soul and spirit, by spending time talking, learning and teaching, has kept me human. It has stopped me from turning into a damaged monster, by drawing me close to Jesus, who has healed my heart. I am grateful for the servants of Jesus willing to walk alongside me, sharing my faith, praying with and for me. My heart is now to rebuild my Syrian community here, in this intimate relationship with Jesus.

13

A Narrow Escape and a New Trust

I could be discovered at any of the checkpoints and taken into the army if I were to go with her. It was an enormous risk.

A week earlier, Samara and I had met in person for the first time. My mind had been full of questions and 'what ifs'. It had been a surreal moment to meet face to face, in spite of having worked together daily for nearly two years. This was the closest working connection I had had with someone from another country and culture in my life. As well as developing a strong working partnership, Samara and I had become good friends, and Miriam and I welcomed her into our home to stay with us, as a member of our family. We had already passed through many extraordinarily difficult situations and events, but in doing so we had achieved a huge amount by way of support for the Syrian people and seen some wonderful work being accomplished. But it didn't come without significant challenges.

The previous evening we had begun an important and complicated conversation. It was awkward and had been left unfinished. We were struggling, as we often did, with the clash of our vastly different cultures. Each of us had such contrasting understandings of the two opposing worlds we lived in, which had a huge bearing on the issues about which we needed to make decisions. We were both influenced by the conditioning we had received in our respective lives and countries. I respected Samara's pure and honest heart, and I knew that she cared deeply for all of us. She was having to accommodate a totally different way of understanding our world compared with what she had learnt in her country. Our worlds were like two different galaxies.

With the previous evening's conversation unresolved, the issues replayed in my mind. Instead of sleeping, I had spent the night pacing the house, trying to shake off the uneasy feeling I had.

I don't sleep as much as most people, but with this on my mind I didn't feel relaxed enough to go to bed. Instead, I sat on the balcony and watched the sunrise, breathing the fresh air and trying to dissipate the frustration from the previous day and my fears about that day's trip. I lifted the cup of milky Nescafé to my lips and took another sip. The stillness of the crisp morning air was broken only by the chirping of the sparrows.

Even after all the years of bloodshed, problem-solving and burnout, the most demanding time in my life was now unfolding. Somehow, in the midst of the awful cacophony of explosions, pain and death, I had kept going because so many lives depended on me, but my situation changed the day I was advised by a reliable source that I could no longer delay being conscripted to do military service. I would soon be taken into the army.

I had been hoping and praying that this time would never come. However, over the years I had learnt that God doesn't give us what we want, and instead gives us what we need. Often, we don't realise the difference between the two until we reflect back after passing through difficult times and events in our lives. After all I had been through, I desperately needed a rest, and some intense spiritual nourishment. But nothing on earth would have induced me to step back from my career unless I was forced to, as I also felt an enormous burden to serve my community, especially when there were so few reliable doctors and medical services available while the needs were so overwhelming.

Suddenly I was faced with a decision of such magnitude, the outcome would change the entire shape and direction of my life. There were only two choices for me if I planned to stay in Syria: either I accept the fate of being conscripted and becoming part of this war, and sacrifice all the humanitarian work God was doing through us to help the Syrian people with Samara's Aid Appeal, or I would have to go into a self-imposed captivity, or 'lockdown', and sacrifice my freedom to travel and even to work as a doctor. I would need to retreat to a place where I wouldn't be found. Although it crossed my mind as a fleeting thought during the problematic years to come, leaving the country illegally, as so many others in my position had done, was not an option I was willing to entertain.

Over the years I had managed to avoid military service. Training courses, additional studies and the work I was involved with gave me many legitimate reasons to avoid it in the early days. But when I was advised that I could no longer escape serving my country in this way, I had no rights to exercise as a conscientious objector. I had seen it happen so many times to men around me that I knew what to expect.

Men would be taken at one of the many checkpoints when their documents were checked as they drove, or the military police would go to their workplace and simply take them. I had watched this happen to many of my colleagues. The officials would simply come to the hospital and walk away with our doctors and male workers. At some of the worst times men were even rounded up in the street, then taken to be processed. If they were eligible, they were conscripted; if not, they would hopefully be released. But no one could escape unless they met the exemption criteria: being a religious cleric, an only son, in full-time education or significantly disabled.

People in the army had told me I would have a high-status position if I was enlisted. Doctors were in demand, especially with my background in emergency care, ICU and the additional niche of disaster management. Many said it would be a boost to my career and, unlike most other professionals who were taken as officers, I would be able to continue earning money. Many men's careers would be damaged or even destroyed after years in the military, but I was told it would help mine. In Syria, soldiers and officers are viewed as heroes and are treated with great respect and honour. People's lives would depend on me as a doctor and, in the middle of this relentless war, my skills would be like gold dust. Yet I felt God was asking me to make a life-changing decision, by choosing what I wanted to be and who I wanted to serve. It was either Jesus or something very different.

If I were to be in the army, I would have to stop any kind of connection and communication with Samara and her charity, and therefore stop all the humanitarian work we had been doing to help my people. The medical facilities we were running were saving many lives, and the aid we had been distributing to hundreds of thousands of people was not something to simply walk away from. There was no one at that time who would be suitable to hand the work over to who had the ability, desire and mentality to run it effectively. It is messy and complicated, involving daily battles. It takes a huge level of trust, ability and a specific kind of personality to get this work done, as well as the need to speak English fluently. I didn't have faith in anyone else to do it. The poor people around me were in such great need and I felt a deep compassion for them. If we didn't help them, I didn't know who else would.

Once in the army, I would not be able to have any connection with any foreign party outside Syria, especially someone in the UK. The UK government was an enemy of the Syrian government, and if I had a position of authority in the military, I would be accused of spying if I had contact with an English person. It would have been considered treason to talk with any foreign person in an enemy state while in the military.

Even if such communication were accepted in Syria, it would have significant repercussions for Samara. She, representing a British charity, would not be able to justify that her work was humanitarian if she were connected to or dealing with someone in the military, and she would quickly find herself in breach of the sanctions imposed against Syria. The best outcome if I were to be conscripted would be for us to stop all our work serving the poor people, but the repercussions would be severe.

One of our faithful prayer team in the UK helped confirm my decision when, knowing nothing about my predicament, she was given a prophetic picture for me at the end of a day of fasting. She had a picture of returning to an old place that had not been visited for some time, with the words, 'Go back.' I believed it meant I should leave the area I had been in and retreat to another place, where I wouldn't easily be found.

That day, Miriam had been caught up in a shooting at a petrol station. We had been suffering from a fuel crisis for months in Syria, caused by the sanctions and the number of oil fields that had been taken over by other armed groups. But it was an excruciatingly cold winter. It was almost impossible to buy fuel, and whenever we found some there were huge queues.

On this particular day, someone had started shooting people and vehicles at the fuel station. Thank God Miriam was unharmed, but she was in shock and I began to feel guilty. I felt we should move yet again to get my family out of this tense area. We had already moved six times during the years of war, and it was an exhausting process. Having made the decision to stay in Syria, I felt it was now time to find a safer place for my family. If the military were going to come looking for me, I ought to be somewhere they wouldn't think to look. I needed to get out of the place where my pattern could be predicted.

In my new place, I confined myself to the house. Even going to the church at the end of the road was off limits. There was a checkpoint beside it and there were occasions when intelligence officers were there, checking people at the church as they went in. There were also times when they searched the area, taking any men they could find. Usually the officials didn't take men from their homes for conscription, but we heard rumours about this happening when we moved to our new place, so I didn't risk even going to the front door when the bell rang. It was like being under a strange kind of house arrest. I could count on one hand the times I left my house in those first few months. What magnified my intense feelings of frustration was the knowledge that my skills and experience as a doctor were needed so urgently. It was like being tortured.

I couldn't risk people asking questions and finding out where I was, or my status becoming known, so even contact with friends and community became restricted to only the closest and most trusted people. I could not confide in anyone about my situation, even to the very few who did come to my house. The only people in Syria who knew were my parents, my brother, my wife and her parents – not even my children, who lived with me. The fewer people who knew my predicament, the safer I would be. In the hell that our country had descended into, people who used to live respectable lives would resort to any means possible to make money. Having already been directly threatened with kidnapping a couple of times and having lost so many friends and colleagues to these kinds of criminal activities, I had many safety procedures to avoid putting myself at risk of blackmail or extortion. It took serious discipline to live this way.

But today's schedule for Samara had already been arranged. As the sun began to peep over the horizon, spreading a pink, pale golden glow beneath the clouds, I recalculated the risks once again, making an alternative plan for each possible scenario. It was important to show her the reality of our world, our work and how important it was. She needed to see the damage to the city as well as to the people. My wish was for her to feel more connected to everything that was happening here. Our small field hospital was prepared for her visit and I had briefed our team as to where to take her after. But that morning, God gave me a different plan from all those I had been making. There was a sound in my heart: 'Go with her. Don't let her go alone.'

'Really?' I wondered. Did he *really* want me to travel such a distance, between cities, passing all those checkpoints? It felt like suicide to me. How could I pass forty or more checkpoints that day, twice, without being caught and taken to the army? It would destroy all the life-saving humanitarian work we had been doing together. As soon as my ID card was checked on their computer it would all be over. It was as simple as that. They would almost certainly examine my card and data on the computer at the checkpoints between cities. That was how many of my friends had been taken. I had barely set foot outside my house in the last months, even to go to places within one kilometre. Today's journey would entail a few hours' drive, with dozens and dozens of checkpoints. Each one was a massive risk.

But the sound of Jesus' voice became firmer and more serious. 'Go, A. I am with you. You can walk on water. Trust me.'

The sun rose higher and the darkness began to vanish behind the hills and trees. The household began to stir as people woke from their slumber. I told Samara what I felt, and we sat and prayed. The sound of Jesus was louder than the sound of my fears. I told her I was sure. This was what God wanted and I would travel with her. She recounted the promise God had made her before she came to Syria: 'I will protect you and I will protect the team.'

As I broke the news to Miriam, I saw the furrows in her brow and the fear in her eyes. She knew what this meant, and the possible consequences, not just for me, but for her and our children too. 'Are you sure, A?' she asked. I had a churning sensation in my stomach, yet there was no doubt in my mind.

We didn't know what to expect but were prepared to pray through everything. That day, we were to have an encounter that neither of us would ever forget. Knowing that prayer cover that day was essential, Samara set up a message group as we drove, adding faithful people to it and asking them to pray for protection as we travelled.

Miriam and I had known Dr Jon for many years; he was a faithful Christian friend. He worked in a different field of medicine and had been working with our team for a little while. He had specific instructions for Samara's visit: I had asked him to take her to his area which had previously been under siege, then to find somewhere appropriate and safe for her to take photos and videos. If she were seen, the consequences could be severe. It wasn't illegal, but the Syrian people had developed such a heightened sense of suspicion that people didn't dare do anything that might evoke questions, especially in a post-siege, damaged area that was still under close military control. A British citizen taking videos in an area like this would provoke a significant and justified suspicion that she was working for a foreign intelligence agency.

Cars sped along the highway beside mine in the busy morning traffic. I put my foot down as I drove, wanting to be quick so we could return before sunset, as it was more dangerous to travel after dark. A makeshift military vehicle was a few cars ahead of us: a simple pick-up truck with a machine gun erected on a stand at the back. A soldier stood on either side of the gun. The sound of Jesus again told me to hang back and slow down, so I let my car fall back a little. Another car began trying to overtake the military vehicle. Suddenly a burst of piercing cracks was fired into the road. Immediately, a gap appeared between the military vehicle and the cars behind. They had been warned.

As we approached the city, a tall, thick column of black smoke stretched up from the horizon over the cityscape and sky, dispersing to the left with the wind. It was like a banner, announcing and advertising the most recent air strike in the area. It was impossible to play anything down for my foreign guest or protect her from our reality. We were in the middle of a war zone.

As every checkpoint loomed, I braced myself with prayer. It felt as though my heart sank with my foot each time it pressed down on the brake. Every time I handed over my ID card and the soldiers examined my name, I prayed with all my heart that they would be blind and not notice us. I wanted to appear relaxed, both to the soldiers and to Samara. But there was no opportunity to relax that day. We were on edge at every moment on the road.

After we had finished in the field hospital, I had an uneasy feeling and a sense that we should go straight home. Yet visiting this destroyed area and taking some videos and pictures there was one of the main reasons we had come that day. Going against the reservation in my heart, we continued into the city. I felt a sinking dread as we passed an unusually high number of checkpoints, which hadn't been there the previous time I had been in the area. They were everywhere! We stopped again and again and must have prayed our way through at least twenty of these checkpoints over a short distance. Every time I felt we must have passed the last one, another one suddenly loomed ahead. I could hardly believe my eyes. We did not stop praying.

Samara had been briefed on how to behave. No cameras around checkpoints or soldiers, and she knew not to say a word in front of strangers. English people were under great suspicion of having connections to one of the intelligence agencies working against Syria, and one wrong move could induce a whole string of unpleasant events and questioning. There was no knowing where it could lead if someone felt suspicious of her motive for being there. It was imperative to avoid anyone asking questions about her and her reasons for being there, even though she had entered the country legally, with all the correct documents and with a genuine motivation to help us.

It is hard to explain to foreigners who haven't lived through this politically complex and advanced war in Syria. It didn't matter that her reasons for being there were good and legitimate, or that she had entered the country with an official stamp in her passport. There has been such a breakdown of trust in Syria that most people are suspicious of anyone they don't know, and often even of people they do know. We have learnt to avoid having to answer questions at all costs during the war, especially where a foreigner is involved. The most obvious complication was that if the authorities were to ask about Samara, they would *fully* investigate me, checking my ID on the computer, among other things. Being taken to the military would jeopardise not only my safety, but also the whole future of our work. The impact on my entire extended family who depended on me being there for them would also be immense.

This once busy and bustling area was still under heavy military control and now largely deserted. Dr Jon indicated where to park outside his apartment. He and his wife were now the only residents in their abandoned block. He was keen for us to have tea with them, but I had an apprehension in my spirit. As I surveyed the destruction, the remains of Elie's house captured my attention.

Elie had been the best man at my wedding. My memory drifted back to a conversation we had had here, standing in his doorway, opposite the place I stood now. As we approached our end-of-school exams, he was worried that he would fail. These exams would decide what we would each study at university. He asked for my help, and I spent time revising with him. I had put my hand in his and prayed that Jesus would help him to gain a good mark. I felt in my heart that he would. Looking him in the eye, I told him I felt Jesus had showed me that he would achieve the same mark as me. He didn't believe me, as I had always been the top student, while Elie had always struggled and only ever achieved a lower mark. Yet I felt sure.

'Will you go into medicine if you do?' I wanted to encourage him. All the top students in Syria go to medical school.

He smiled shyly. 'No, I don't deserve it,' he answered. 'I promised Jesus that if I do well, I will take a different career in the medical field.'

To his amazement, he achieved the same mark as me. He could have gone to medical school with that grade, and most people would have jumped at the chance. But, faithful to his commitment, he followed the career path he had promised God.

Elie and his family had fled when the armed radicals came and the fighting there became intense. They were some of the lucky ones who got out in time, but many we knew did not. Maybe one day Elie and his family might be brave enough to return and overcome the painful memories that place would bring back for them, of their friends and neighbours who had been mercilessly killed in their homes.

Further down the ruined street, Dr Khalifa's clinic caught my eye. The modern glass front of the building had been shattered into a thousand pieces. Remnants of the broken glass lay scattered among the other evidence of a different existence long ago. The doorway was now a gaping hole with tattered edges. I felt no desire to go and see how far the damage went.

My mind drifted back a few years, to his confident posture with his ankle resting on his knee and his smug smile, sitting in the lobby of that luxury hotel outside Syria. It had been our last meeting. I shuddered, wondering where he was now. Was he still practising his high-level, strategic jihad wherever he was now? It seemed impossible that his radical ideology, which had been so strong and deeply rooted in him for years, could have altered even in a different country. The last I heard of him was that he, like many others, was living in a western country now, where it would be hard for the local communities there to have any understanding of his history here in Syria.

He had repeatedly asked me to visit him here in this clinic.

For a long time I avoided it, as his conversations with me were always the same. He wanted, again and again, to assert his viewpoint that the radical Islam he had become entrenched in gave him a superiority and an entitlement over me. It became so tiresome to listen to him endlessly repeating the same rhetoric and the relentless insults that he felt justified in directing at me. Eventually I could no longer find excuses, so I obliged, but it was a bizarre social visit as, true to his personality, he kept reminding me of his perceived religious supremacy. I soon found a reason to leave his clinic. As I walked away, I knew that his lies were a distortion of everything I had read in the Quran about Christians, and I had read it many times.

It seemed strange now, thinking about how I was still here, in our homeland, and he was not. He had left his home, his family and his country. It would be impossible for him to return now after everything he had done. The remains of his clinic stood obliterated and abandoned. He had been so instrumental in stirring up unrest and injustice here, yet soon after the fighting became really intense, he was one of the first to leave. I wondered if he had achieved any part of his objectives. He was one of the multitudes of hardcore extremists who been trained in Syria but had left to go and live abroad. Significantly high numbers of them had moved to the West by that time, having disguised themselves among the floods of genuine refugees: they were in Europe, the US, Canada, Germany, the UK and many more.

What would the future hold for these countries with such hardened jihadists in their midst? They have made the way harder for the innocent people who have fled, and have increased the animosity towards refugees entering foreign countries. These radicals had played a dynamic part in planning and engineering the infrastructure of strategic jihad; they had already tasted blood and power and had felt the adrenaline of an uprising.

We walked down the dusty, rubble-filled street bordered by empty, damaged buildings. This was the first time I had been here since it had been taken by jihadists and then taken back by the government. Many of my Christian friends had been living here when it was attacked and put under siege. It was a prominent central shopping area, with a lot of businesses and homes. When the jihadists came, they tortured and murdered the Christians living here, then moved into their homes. Some of the Christians had managed to escape.

It had been under siege for years, but the jihadists had been forced out now. Much was ruined in the process. So many buildings were just wreckages now. The damaged and shattered bodies had been cleared away, but the injured buildings couldn't be hidden. Now, the maimed properties and piles of rubble heaped on the sides of the streets told their own story of the atrocities that had taken place there.

Dr Jon led us through the scarred streets. We had walked less than a hundred metres from his home before he stopped and indicated a place for us to take a video. The wreckage and rubble were extensive. Opposite this empty and damaged shell was my godmother's house. It had also been destroyed, but I recognised the location and the unusual stones that had differentiated her house from the others. It had been built in the classical Syrian style around an open-air *baha'* in the centre, with a fountain and trees. Stopping for a moment, I remembered her warm smile to all the children. She had emigrated to the US, and her brother and his family had occupied her Syrian home until the moment the jihadists came. They escaped just in time, but the dark stones of her house lay scattered now on the street. I sat on one, wondering whether the lemon tree in her courtyard had survived, while Samara walked inside the carcass of the building opposite, looking around the ruins and picking a place to film.

She stood next to a large, rusty bomb case that had been discarded and started to film it, describing what was around her. Within seconds we were taken by surprise. Out of the blue, a motorbike sped down this otherwise empty road, but we were too slow to react. It was too late. The soldier on the motorbike stopped beside her. He had seen what she was doing before she managed to put her phone away. Even standing where she was standing, in the skeleton of this building away from the road, would provoke questions.

My heart lurched. This was the end. My life suddenly flashed before my eyes as my mind raced, digesting what was happening. It would be disastrous if he were to speak directly to her and realise that she was English. There had been too many foreigners involved in the war propaganda and they were often connected with foreign intelligence agencies or criminal groups. Our government viewed them as very dangerous. Realising immediately that I had to take control of the situation, I started to speak with the soldier and to answer his questions. One wrong word or gesture could be catastrophic for all of us. I was thankful that he was respectful to her as a woman and therefore didn't address her directly, and instead asked me about her and what she was doing.

'You need to come to the checkpoint,' he informed me after a few moments. Wow! What a disaster. How far would their questions go, and would he check my ID? I looked sideways at Samara. Her eyes were wide. I gave her an intense look as I told her and Dr Jon, in Arabic, to wait there. I started walking towards the checkpoint. My expression must have said a hundred things, but in my silence I prayed. The soldier turned his motorbike around and stopped beside me to let me climb onto the back.

Reminding myself how much I used to love riding on the back of my grandfather's motorbike, I tried to relax as I swung my leg over the vehicle to straddle the bike. In the moments it took us to reach the checkpoint, every possible outcome flashed through my mind: being taken to the army, Samara being arrested and put in prison for as long as it took for her honesty to be proved, the extensive process, for me, of trying to get her released, and all the work serving our people having to stop.

If I wasn't careful, I would be overwhelmed by fear. I couldn't let the devil's whisperings swamp me into an even more vulnerable position. As the motorbike sped along the street, the breeze cooled my face as I quickly calculated the possibilities and how to respond. I needed to keep the focus on her, not me, by being her advocate. I could not show any sign of weakness or fear.

Meanwhile, Samara frantically quizzed Dr Jon. 'What did he

say? Where are they going?' Dr Jon had tried not to look worried, and repeated my instruction to wait there. But, feeling responsible for the situation, Samara wasn't willing to let me out of her sight. She began to follow us down the road, praying and messaging her prayer group with an urgent request. Dr Jon followed quickly to keep up with her.

As the soldier and I reached the end of the road, the motorbike slowed to a stop and I was ushered into a deserted building. We were a couple of metres from the shop where Miriam and I had ordered our wedding invitations. It stood empty now. The soldier fired questions at me, then asked for my ID card. With my heart pounding, I fished it out of my pocket and reluctantly handed it over. He looked at my card and recognised my name as a doctor working in the city. We talked for a few minutes. Praying all the while, I reassured him, confirming that Samara was harmless. As he quizzed me, I had the feeling that Jesus was reassuring him, making him feel relaxed in a situation other soldiers might have taken much further.

After a few minutes, his eyes lost interest and he seemed to switch off. We said a relaxed goodbye and walked out of the door.

As soon as I got out of the makeshift office, I saw Samara and Dr Jon outside waiting for me. I was touched that they hadn't deserted me in this hazardous moment. But I realised I had a new problem: Dr Jon was telling Samara, *in English*, about the souks that had been in this place before! She smiled tightly, not saying a word in response. It hadn't occurred to me to give Dr Jon a safety briefing too. He should have known better, but sometimes in tense situations people do the strangest things.

The soldier's posture immediately changed. He was alert and poised, and his attention was fixed on Samara now. Fear was visible in his narrowed eyes. He stared at her for a few seconds, then his attention turned back to me. Ordering me back into the makeshift office, he had lost the relaxed posture he had had just moments before. I wondered how we could get out of this now.

'Is she English?' He fired at me, the suspicion evident in his expression. I understood his alarm, and I tried to calm and reassure him. 'Why,' he demanded, 'is he speaking to her in English?' His tough, doubt-filled eyes pierced mine.

I smiled at him softly. 'Because,' I said simply, 'he is showing off!' I prayed with all my heart that God would close Dr Jon's mouth. He fell silent outside.

The soldier glared back at Dr Jon, then at each of us, one by one, weighing the situation in his mind. The seconds felt like hours as he stared, looking at us all once again. Suddenly, his gaze dropped and he grunted, waving me off for the second time.

'*Fadal!*' I instructed Dr Jon and Samara, marching quickly away from the building before anything else could go wrong. 'Let's get out of here!' I breathed as soon as we were out of earshot of the checkpoint. I politely declined Dr Jon's invitation for tea with his wife. Their house was almost opposite the spot where this encounter had started, and I couldn't wait to get away. All I could think about was getting back safely and as quickly as possible before it got dark. We prayed intensely as we passed through the twenty or so checkpoints again on the way back out of the city, and then through the rest en route. The release of nervous energy and relief afterwards, as we replayed the situation over and over again in the car, seemed to make the journey home pass quickly. God had been so generous and faithful to us.

As we drove home, I thanked God for instructing me to go with Samara that day. I kept thinking how differently things could have turned out if I hadn't been there to deal with the situation that arose. I dread to think what might have happened. Dr Jon clearly struggled with his discernment and decision-making that day. Samara would likely have ended up being arrested, interrogated and imprisoned, and who knows what would have happened to her, or to me, as I would then have tried to solve these problems for her. I couldn't have resolved that situation without totally exposing myself, then likely would have ended up being conscripted.

It had been such a close call. But in our weakness, God is strong, and his power works best in our weakness.[2] We simply have to trust him and obey his voice, even when his instructions sometimes seem to be the opposite of what we believe we should do or want to do. At times, God's instructions can seem to be illogical or even foolish, but if we are working under his guidance, truly listening to him, we can be sure that he sees things we don't have the ability to see. Somehow that day, putting myself in the most exposed positions while within God's will had been safer than hiding in the perceived safety of my home, against his will. Obeying him in things we can't see is what it means to trust in God.[3]

14

Breaking Down Idols

I had established an extremely successful career as a doctor and was respected for my expertise in each of my specialisms. I had treated many rich and powerful people and built a strong network of connections. In one of the most brutal years of the war, I was given an award by the Doctors Union in Syria for my service to the civilian population. I sent one of my team to collect the award as I wanted them to take the credit.

The Gospels of Matthew, Mark and Luke all tell the parable of a rich young man who asked Jesus what he needed to do to inherit eternal life.[1] Jesus quoted five of the Ten Commandments: "'You shall not murder, you shall not commit adultery, you shall not steal, you shall not give false testimony, honour your father and mother," and "love your neighbour as yourself.'" The young man replied that he had kept all of these since he was a boy, and asked what else he lacked. Jesus looked at him with love and told him that if he really wanted to be perfect, he should sell all his possessions, give to the poor and follow him. The young man left disheartened, as he had a lot of possessions.

As I looked back, I realised that I was like that rich young man, but not in the area of money. I had never had a problem with giving anything to anyone. Although I had made a lot of money, I did not worship it in the way I saw many people doing. I was similar because I felt, like the rich young man, that I had kept all these commandments since I was a boy. All my life I had been happy to help others, giving them money if they needed it, doing operations for free for poor people or giving them treatment without charge if they couldn't afford it. It was my pleasure to do that. If God had asked me to give up everything I possessed, I was willing. Over time, I developed a false impression of myself as being very good, especially because I came from a hard-up background and therefore had earned all the money I gave away. I was not obsessed by earning or accumulating money.

My status and reputation as a doctor, however, had become too important to me.

I felt Jesus had brought me to a crossroads. It was as if he looked at me, smiled and said, 'It's not your money I want; it's you. I am not interested in your money; I want you to give up your reputation as such a reputable doctor. I know you will give me your money, but have your status and position become your idols? It's not money you are worshipping; it's your career, your business, your reputation and your image.'

He was right. These things had become my idols. They were the things that I gave priority to in my heart. Although on many levels I felt I was doing these things *for* God, they were also things that came between me and God. I knew that if I were to go into the army, I would have an extremely good position as a doctor in my specialist areas. Maybe I would become one of the most important doctors in the military, with a very high and well-respected position in the army and therefore in Syria. I couldn't be certain, but I felt it was unlikely, as a doctor, that I would be posted in a dangerous area, and I wouldn't be asked to fight. I could gain experience that would be good for my career, and I would be able to earn money in ways that others can't when they are conscripted to the army.

My father, who had been a high-ranking officer many years before, told me that someone like me would be given a very high position and treated with great respect and status, 'like God'. Everyone is desperate for a medical professional with my skills and experience and would do anything for such a doctor when their life is in their hands. Any injured victim would be in their service, as the doctor is the most important person to them at that time. After helping them, they would feel forever in debt to the medic. I knew this already from my years of working as a doctor.

'Don't hesitate,' said my father. 'Go! I know the importance of being a doctor in the army with experience in emergency and intensive care and disaster management during a war.'

My brother also told me to go. He had been conscripted years before. It was a requirement of every male citizen in Syria. If a family had two sons, only one is required to serve at a time, to ensure their parents aren't left with no one to provide for them in their old age. After a number of years in service, my brother started asking me to voluntarily enlist so he would be discharged. With his first-hand knowledge of the army, he said that if I were to go, I would be much more important than before, and he would be free. He asked why I was hesitating. The officer in charge of him said that if I were to come, I would be the boss: everyone would want my skills and experience, and I could earn a good income.

My heart was torn in two. I felt awful for my brother and his family. But I also had to look at the bigger picture and the number of people who would be affected by the decision. My career so far meant I had been able to financially support my parents and my brother's family while he was unable to earn an income. If the situation was reversed, he would not be able to provide the same level of financial support, as he had lost his high-level civilian career while in military service.

I heard Jesus say to me, 'What do you want? Do you want to stay as you are, or do you want to follow me?'

I still remember how, in the early days, after Samara and I first started working together, she had asked me if I could receive the containers of aid into Syria that she was sending and organise the distributions, because she trusted me and the way I work. But I didn't want to. I kept saying to her, 'Samara, I am a doctor. This is not the work of a doctor! I don't deal with containers.' I considered my status as a doctor to be more important. It was my image. It was who I was, and I couldn't see beyond that. That was all I was thinking: 'I am a doctor!'

This was exacerbated by the fact that the humanitarian aid sector in Syria is filled with corruption and deceit. I didn't want to get involved with this messy world as it meant dealing with people I had previously tried to avoid. If I were to enter this dirty arena, people would probably assume I was just like the other people involved with humanitarian aid who were using it to benefit themselves. I didn't want to be tarred with the same brush.

It was my pride that prevented me from getting involved in this work, reaching out to the poorest of the poor. I'm so grateful that Jesus humbled me and showed me how much he loves the poor. He showed me that serving them and loving them is more than just giving them a physical object that they need, or food; it is about being willing to touch them and spend time with them, or about having our reputation smeared because of our involvement in humanitarian work.

My identity and reputation as a doctor had become my idol, and it had come between me and my ability to make myself available to be used by God. I felt Jesus say to me, 'Is that really what you want to be, A? If you want to put your identity as a doctor first, you can't be a true disciple of mine at the same time.'

That was a defining moment in my life. What was most important to me: the way other people see me or the way God sees me?

I decided to put Jesus first and to follow him, no matter what the cost. Even though it would mean spending *years* excluded from normal life and not being able to work as a doctor at all! I could never have known in advance how these years would feel like centuries. It felt like trapping my heart in an iron cage and dropping it at the bottom of the deepest ocean, then covering it with ice.

Once I withdrew from the life I knew, the devil kept whispering, 'Really? You are going to stay here in prison for three and a half years [until I reached the age enabling me to pay an exemption fee]? Who knows, maybe you will stay here for longer! Can you do it? Is that what you want? Sitting in your house, not daring to leave. You will become a nobody!'

I definitely didn't want to stay in my house, 'imprisoned' for years. I didn't like the idea and I didn't want to do it at all. But

Jesus had been clear with me, and I decided to do not as I wished, but as God wished.

I felt close to Jesus in that moment. He too wanted the cup of suffering to pass from him so he wouldn't have to be tortured and crucified. I was so grateful that Jesus showed us through that moment in his life how vulnerable he felt, and how close he is to us. He is not a distant God; he gave up his royal position in heaven and came here to this broken world, to become human with us, to be humiliated and to suffer with us. He showed us, through his emotions, that he truly understands, from the deepest part of his heart, how hard it is for us to make big sacrifices. He felt it just as we do, and he showed us his vulnerability to encourage us in our weak moments. And just as he accepted his cup of suffering, I accepted mine. Again.

After I made the decision to withdraw from the world, my brother became very resentful and angry towards me. He couldn't hide his hostility, and the next few years were very tense between us. His two years of obligatory service that all men have to undertake had stretched into many years, as it had for so many others in this war, with no sign of discharge. He had lost his income, his home and his career as a lawyer, and his family had had to move to another city as they could not afford to live in their pre-war home. It was not an easy time for any of us. I felt terrible that he and his family were in this position, but I knew that even more people would suffer and lose out if I were to go into the military. Most importantly, God had been clear.

Even if I had gone into the army, there was no guarantee that he would have been released. It would have been a gamble, and too much was at stake.

One day when I called my brother, his youngest daughter answered the phone. When she heard my name, she said, 'Uncle, I don't love you.' I felt how aggrieved they were with me. This war caused huge tensions in families for so many problematic reasons. Yet I felt God had been very clear with me on many occasions that I should not leave my home, for any reason.

Retreating into my house for those years was harder than I could ever have envisaged. No one can imagine the many phases and emotions a person passes through over a number of years. I became increasingly careful and fearful. Initially, I continued to carry out little activities, but as the days morphed into weeks, months and then years, I became willing to take fewer and fewer risks. Before I retreated, I had hoped I could work at a nearby hospital, but I soon recognised I would be too exposed. This reduced to a dream of running a clinic from home, but the more I thought about it, the more I realised it would make me too public and expose my home. Gradually I had fewer and fewer people around me, and eventually only my immediate family.

There were times when I built up my hopes that maybe there was someone with influence who could help me get some kind of exemption from the army. I tried to take control of my circumstances, as that is what I had always done in life. I invested a lot of hope in various people, as I dreamed and fantasised about my freedom. As they failed, one by one, my mood crashed down with each fresh realisation that I still had years left to pass in this agonising place of confinement which my home had become.

It was a real challenge not to sink into a deep depression, as my state of mind hit absolute rock bottom. There were moments when I was close to sinking. The stretch of time ahead seemed to loom for eternity as I sat staring at the same walls. I felt like a wild animal that had run freely in nature all its life, then was suddenly captured and put into a tiny cage.

My absence from the community had other repercussions for me and my family. After some time, rumours began to circulate that I was in prison because of the humanitarian work I had been involved with. This was exactly what I had wanted to avoid! Many people linked with the humanitarian sector did end up in jail because of corruption or worse, but I couldn't challenge these false rumours. Doing so would have exposed me completely, and as my country had changed during the war to a land filled with enemies, I couldn't risk it. I felt for my parents, who were asked whether it was true that I was in jail. I was sorry for putting them in that position, but I couldn't see any alternative. I simply had to hand it all over to God and surrender to his will.

Ultimately, God allowed me to be put in that position for a reason, so my only option was to trust him to get me through it and out at the end. It humbled me. I had to die to myself, my status and my reputation: all the things that had been of such great importance to me before. Only then could I be remodelled according to God's will.

When Jesus was crucified, to all those around him everything seemed lost, finished and hopeless. But God worked a miracle and raised him from the dead three days later, in the most glorious and amazing way. God's way is very different from the way we would choose, and I had to trust that by being faithful to him, he would give me more in the end than I had ever lost through choosing to put him first.

The days turned into weeks, which stretched into months and then years. It was demeaning for someone as fiercely independent as I am to have to rely on others to bring me absolutely everything. There was almost nothing I could do for myself. Even if I wanted to buy my wife a gift, I had to ask someone to go and choose it and bring it to me. We didn't have internet shopping in Syria.

I lost my internal sense of time and space and had moments during those years when I began to wonder whether my entire life before had been real. I started to ask myself whether all the events that had taken place during the war were real, and I even began to wonder whether my entire existence was a dream. Being shut away from the world for such a long time forges a surreal kind of existence. I can hardly describe the strange feelings I had, but it was excruciatingly hard to watch the people around me continuing their lives, seeing my family coming and going from the house, leaving for school and work. That was the thing I most envied – being able to go to work. I would have given anything to be working in my hospital again. I dreamed about it regularly.

One day, my oldest son asked why I couldn't go to watch a music competition he was entering. I couldn't tell him why. It would have been too big a burden for him to carry, to keep this dangerous secret, but my heart was really crushed that day. It was such a simple thing, and I had taken all such freedoms for granted before.

From this 'prison', I was able to keep coordinating all of our work, but even those I trusted enough to work in my house, I didn't tell of my situation, yet I had to ask them to do absolutely everything.

The old Dr A was dismantled, humbled and brought to a very low place. I felt that I had lost my identity. Yet in losing my old identity I found a greater one in Jesus. By this time, I had lost everything that was important to me except my family. I had lost my dream hospital; I had lost my home many times over and I had lost my possessions. I had lost my career and I had lost myself. I started to wonder, 'Who am I now? Who is Dr A?'

This time was a time of breaking down and rebuilding, like a caterpillar becoming confined by the tiny space of its cocoon. In this little chrysalis its body is broken down completely and it loses its original form. It turns into a mush that bears no resemblance to its former self, then a brand new body is born, which takes a totally different form and has a totally different ability. It is rebuilt and metamorphoses into a totally different creation. It was my prayer during that time that I would be able to emerge as a butterfly, with a new set of colours and abilities, and be able to fly for the first time. In my tiny cocoon, I was so desperate to be able to spread my wings and fly.

Disappearing from society altogether is one of the most unreal and bizarre experiences a person can go through. I had to pretend to most of our community and connections that I was no longer there. Even before it got to this point of needing to withdraw, I had removed all evidence of myself from public view. Having seen my friends and colleagues being targeted and kidnapped and having received personal threats, I made some tough decisions. Because I was prosperous in my field of medicine, this made me a target, and I was very concerned about my personal safety. Previously, there had been a lot of information about me online – news articles and videos about my work as a doctor. One by one, early in the war, I fought to get all of those articles and videos removed.

Over time, I simply disappeared from view. It was as though I no longer existed. After a while, many of the people in our team with whom I spoke on the phone were under the impression that I was now living abroad and would be returning to Syria once our projects were established.

This kind of jail felt in many ways worse than I imagined an ordinary jail would. In an ordinary prison, the boundaries are very clear, as are the expectations of prisoners. But in this captivity I was in, my family and some of my contacts could still talk and interact with me. Everyone, even those who knew and understood my situation, still had an expectation that they would deal with the normal Dr A they had always known. They expected me to behave as I always had, that I would deal with the various situations we faced in my characteristic strong and decisive manner. Except I was not the same man and I couldn't deal with things in the same way. The stress of being restricted became an increasingly heavy burden with each day that passed, and the closer I got to the date after which I could pay for military exemption, the more unbalanced and weighed down I felt. It was like fasting for a very long period. After fasting for a few days, you become weaker and hungrier. Your thoughts and words become less coordinated and you are more vulnerable to the attacks that the devil will try to throw at you.

In a normal jail, I perceived that there would be a kind of quiet detachment. Yet to remain with your family, with noisy children running around, just being children, arguing with each other, and then dealing with the day-to-day minutiae of life with a restricted personality, was one of the hardest things I have ever been through.

In addition to all this, my wife was forced to cope with the added pressure my captivity put on her, as she had to do a number of things alone as well as having all the children to look after. It was intense for all of us. She was desperate for me to be free, and there were many times when she too asked why were still living in this hell when we could have gone to live in the West, enjoying good lives and careers there.

At the time of writing, my youngest child had no memories of me at all outside our house. I had never been able to do anything with him except in our home. I had missed all the children's concerts, competitions and sports matches. Even when they were sick, I couldn't go with them to the hospital. For me as a doctor, that really was distressing.

Friends and acquaintances expected me to visit and call them. They felt upset because I didn't, but I couldn't explain to them why. Watching friends who had emigrated living their lives on social media really rubbed salt in my wounds. When one of my children asked me why we didn't go and have a nice life somewhere else, I explained that we had stayed here to serve God and serve our people, but sometimes I asked myself the same question. Staying in Syria was so difficult. The pressure on every one of us was immense. It was like being a bird with its wings tied.

The final year of my captivity was the hardest. I began to feel as if I had been frozen, as if I had stopped functioning properly. From being such a capable person, I found myself battling to have the will to do anything. It felt like I had weights attached to my body and mind. I felt paralysed, as if I was running the last few miles of a marathon I hadn't trained for, yet the end was still so far away. Towards the end of a marathon, your body and legs continue to run but you can barely feel them, and your brain shuts everything out except the thought of getting to the finish line. Reaching the end became my focus and goal, and it was extraordinarily hard to do anything else that needed to get done.

Every one of us has things in our lives that can easily become idols, things on which we lavish our time, attention and energy, which come between us and God. Perhaps sometimes they are even the things we feel we are doing *for* God. Yet these things dilute or even destroy our relationship with Jesus. For me, it was my career, status, reputation and position. For others, maybe its money, possessions or lifestyle. Perhaps it is a relationship with someone or something, whether food or alcohol, fashion or beauty, or even time spent watching TV. It could be pornography. For each of us the temptations are different, but when these things come between us and God because of the time, energy and money we spend on them, we can quickly find ourselves distracted from the things that are important to him. It is essential for each of us to identify the idols in our lives and break them down, so there is nothing to come between us and God.

15

The Milkman, the Carpenter, the Fisherman and the Thief

The roar of the engine reached my ears before I saw the outline of his motorbike speeding up our road. He pulled to a stop and put his foot down to steady his shiny bike before dismounting. He had just traded in his old one for this newer model, and his innocent, slightly rounded face beamed with pride as he untied the ten-litre plastic milk jars from the back of his bike. The pure white *halib* was still warm from the cow. Miriam would boil it later in a huge stainless steel pan, then skim off the rich *ashtar*[1] from the top, which we would eat with honey from my father's beehives. We would sit at the table with the children, tearing pieces off our traditional Arabic flatbread, using them using them to scoop up generous mouthfuls of the creamy, sticky mixture. This was exactly what God meant when he talked of giving our ancestors and their descendants – us – a land flowing with milk and honey.

My milkman was one of the very few people I saw from week to week and month to month while I was in my 'jail'. He visited me every few days and we would chat at the door for fifteen minutes to half an hour each time. He was a simple farmer from the next village, who milked the cows by hand then sold the milk to locals. I could not set foot in the next village or even out of my own front door, yet through his stories and conversations I was able to live their village life through him, enjoying the beautiful day-to-day experiences of an uncluttered and ordinary life. In those uncomplicated conversations, even the way he conveyed pain seemed somehow beautiful.

Sometimes I invited him in, but he always made an excuse about needing to continue with his work, then would chat for another ten minutes before purring off on his bike. I sensed he was uncomfortable about crossing the threshold into my big house, as he was a simple man. Instead, he preferred to sit on his familiar motorbike, ready to flutter off at any moment. Like this, he felt relaxed and unrestricted about sharing his heart. He was like a bird, wanting to fly, not to be put in the cage where I was. Like a bird, his singing was more beautiful as long as he was unrestrained, perching freely on his motorcycle.

Farmers are not used to sitting with people in big houses like mine for long periods, as people in my community are. We had many conversations like this over the handlebars of his bike. His use of language was basic and uneducated, yet his words conveyed a deep understanding of the world, which he had learnt in the hills with the cows and nature, where he worked every day.

He would tell me stories about life on the land, the sea, farming and fishing. Before becoming a milkman, he had worked as a chef on a trading ship. He had visited every continent, and he recounted his experiences of the world from his ship's kitchen to me. He had had the chance at the beginning of the war to leave Syria. He had chosen instead to stay with his mother, saying that Syria was more beautiful than any other country in the world. His stories had many similarities to the parables that Jesus told. They were honest stories about simple, everyday life that people could relate to.

He expressed his frustration over the way people with power would use their positions to benefit themselves. In our culture, the respect people have towards each other isn't based on money or position, but on a person's ability to keep their word and be reliable. This man was important in his community, as milk is something valuable that everyone needs. People could depend on him. He was respected and trustworthy. I felt I could rely on a man like him so much more than I could on many of the seemingly important people I had known in my life, who undoubtedly valued themselves more highly than they would value a milkman. On another day, he shared with me his high hopes for the new cow he had just acquired, optimistic it would produce more milk than the previous one. He had an important, co-dependent relationship with his cows.

Over time, restricted as I was to my house, I felt a connection to this man and I looked forward to his visits.

★

After I had been confined for some time, I felt God put it on my heart to start doing carpentry and woodwork. I had never done anything like that before. I hadn't even used a drill to fix anything in my house, or even put a picture on the wall! In the past my wife and my mother used to complain that I never fixed anything in the house, and would ask why we always had to bring someone else to fix even the simplest things. I had never had any kind of interest in manual work.

Over the course of a year, the urge became increasingly insistent. I started to buy equipment and machines and began to work with different kinds of wood. My heart felt more and more burdened until I bought each item I needed and began to do the work, teaching myself what to do with the wood and how to prepare it, and learning techniques from the internet on how to make things.

It was so much harder than I imagined it would be. But every time I touched the wood, I felt as though I was touching the clothes of Jesus. I felt I could hear his voice speaking to me while I was working with my hands. Each time I handled the wood, I was learning. But I learnt more than just how to shape and join wood.

One day, I was making cupboards for our outreach centre for those who have been orphaned and widowed by this war. It needed to be a large cupboard and the wood was extremely heavy. The planks were thick and long. To carry these heavy planks alone was hard, and then to lift them and hold them on the machine used to straighten them was laborious work. I was hot and could feel the sweat dripping down my forehead and into my eyes. All my muscles were aching while I was trying to balance these cumbersome planks of wood. I was exhausted, but at that moment I felt Jesus at my shoulder saying, "'By the sweat of your brow you will eat your food."[2] This is what it means, A.'

I had read that passage in the Bible many times, but this was the first time I realised, in my heart, how it feels. I felt how tough it is for so many people in this world just to earn the money they need to buy food. I had spent my life working in ICU and in hospitals. These are privileged, controlled environments. As doctors we didn't do physically strenuous work. It wasn't heavy or demanding like this, yet I was paid highly for it.

While I worked with the wood, I heard Jesus saying to me, 'This is what I did. I did everything you are doing now. It's not too heavy for you. You can carry it.' It was a privilege to feel what Jesus had felt.

It was humbling to be able to empathise with the people who normally do this kind of work. I felt ashamed when I thought about all the years I had been so proud of myself as a doctor, the way I didn't feel that *I* should have to do this kind of manual work, as if I was somehow better than those who are uneducated and poor.

As I spent more time working with wood, I saw and felt how much Jesus really loves the poor. He stands beside them, speaks with them and encourages them. He is one of them. Jesus is a carpenter, from a poor but honourable and trustworthy family, not dissimilar to the respectable milkman, who provided a valuable service in our community. Jesus held wood like this before I did, and I'm sure it was much harder for him 2,000 years ago, without the equipment and electrical devices available now. I expect he sweated more than I did and had to work harder than I did.

That day, I felt God was teaching me through this work. He said, 'Hold the plank firmly; don't move your hand. Push it. Keep it straight or the plank will fall. You can't build my temple if your bonds and joints are not straight and strong. You need to focus more, A. Don't listen to your body when it is aching or shaking because of the physical work. Listen to me and keep your eyes focused.' That day, I was a disciple in one of his classes, learning from the Master.

★

During this period, as I stepped back from so many things in the world, the circle of people I was exposed to was very limited. I learnt from the people around me, those whom many in my community might consider too simple and uneducated. Yet I began to feel I could learn more from these people than from many of the sophisticated professors and qualified people I had been surrounded by for many years. It was people like these that Jesus chose to build his church. His disciples included a handful of fishermen, who would have been of a similar social status to my milkman.

One night I wasn't able to sleep well. The next morning, I couldn't concentrate on my work, and felt instead that I should withdraw to pray. While I was praying, I had an encounter with Jesus. I was sitting in front of Jesus, who was standing up. It didn't feel in any way like a dream; it was a real experience, just like talking face to face with another person.

He was teaching and telling me many things, warning me that my road ahead will be very difficult. One of the things he told me is that the life of a Christian is not about accumulating things, but that the only true happiness we can experience is when we are in the presence of God. He showed me that there is no freedom except in God. Wherever you are, if you are disconnected from God, it's impossible to be free. To be with God and experience true freedom, you must give him everything, even your life.

He reminded me of some Bible passages, one of which was, 'I am the way and the truth and the life. No one comes to the Father except through me.'[3] He encouraged me not to be afraid of the suffering I would experience in the future, but rather to be prepared for it and to keep my eyes fixed on the goal of eternal life in heaven. He told me that the pain I experience in this life will release my soul, and that those who give up their lives in this world for him will find true life and their place in eternity. However, those who keep trying to preserve their lives here in this world will lose their lives in eternity.[4]

He explained to me that I am not my body; my body is

simply a vessel that my soul occupies, and death will release my soul. He also reminded me that a grain of wheat must die in order to produce a crop.[5] He said that my 'death' is part of multiplying me.

We talked about marriage and that the true purpose of it is not for pleasure, as many people perceive it to be, but rather to raise more children of God: children who are his children.[6] Everything we do and the purpose of our lives are to serve God and the children of God.

I asked Jesus what he wanted me to do.

He replied, 'What are you ready to do?'

I told him I felt tired of hiding in my home.

He smiled at me, saying that he hid for thirty years before *his* ministry began!

I asked him why all these things happen if has already conquered this world.

He replied, 'My kingdom is not of this world.'[7] He told me to hide from sin and temptation and to run from pride, that if I feel I am powerful, this feeling doesn't come from God, as I am weak but he is strong.[8]

He told me not to spend my time and attention on the things that occupy people: pleasure-seeking or eating for the sake of enjoying food, but to always listen to his voice in my heart. God lives in our hearts, not our mouths or stomachs, so we should focus on feeding and nourishing our hearts more than we do our bodies. He said God doesn't have a problem with us arguing or questioning issues with him, but he wants us to believe in his message at the end. This experience made me feel that I must give Jesus all my time and concentration.

He finished by telling me that I was not forced to accept any of what he said, but rather I was invited to give up things in my life that ultimately weren't good for me or were a distraction from serving him and reaching the eternal goal.

While I was having this meeting with Jesus, I couldn't hear anything going on around me. Afterwards, however, I could see that I had a few missed calls on my phone, but I hadn't heard it ring. I felt as though my soul had left my body for

a little while and gone to another place, to a place where
Jesus was.

After the encounter, I found myself reading Psalm 20:

> May the LORD answer you when you are in distress;
> may the name of the God of Jacob protect you.
> May he send you help from the sanctuary
> and grant you support from Zion.
> May he remember all your sacrifices
> and accept your burnt offerings.
> May he give you the desire of your heart
> and make all your plans succeed.
> May we shout for joy over your victory
> and lift up our banners in the name of our God.
>
> May the Lord grant all your requests.
>
> Now this I know:
> The LORD gives victory to his anointed.
> He answers him from his heavenly sanctuary
> with the victorious power of his right hand.
> Some trust in chariots and some in horses,
> but we trust in the name of the LORD our God.
> They are brought to their knees and fall,
> but we rise up and stand firm.
> LORD, give victory to the king!
> Answer us when we call!

I felt strongly that I needed to start a new phase of life. I needed
to sit with Jesus, pray more and discuss issues with him in greater
depth.

I was left with an overriding feeling of happiness, even though
so much of what Jesus had said was very challenging. Yet it
didn't feel hard when he was saying it. I was left with such a
strong desire to follow him, and my ability to understand him
and his teachings was greater. I felt I had received a fresh
revelation and new understanding of the same Bible passages I

had read many times over; the way Jesus spoke them was somehow different.

During this period of captivity, I genuinely had no other real option but to trust in the name of the Lord. He was my only protection, my only shield and my only deliverer. There were so many situations I faced that were dangerous. Eventually I kept myself hidden from all the team working for me, apart from a couple of trusted people who oversaw the others.

On one occasion I had had to fire a member of our team, and he had been very disgruntled about this. He was someone I had always kept at a distance, and I didn't trust that he wouldn't try to stir up trouble for me. One night, after many weeks had passed and I hadn't heard from him for some time, I had a dream that he went looking for me, and he turned up in a particular city, far from his own and far from where he had been working for us. He was looking for me, trying to track me down and demand extra money.

The next morning, I told my dream to one of our team, Haitham, whom I trusted and was depending on to carry out a lot of the work at the time. A couple of hours later, Haitham received a phone call from the disgruntled former employee. He was in the exact place I had seen in my dream and was demanding extra money. As I had told Haitham about the dream in advance, he knew to be very careful in how he handled the situation.

I felt after the dream that God really was taking care of me to the last detail. When we are doing God's work, we have to depend on him to give us the instructions and guidance we need along the way and recognise when he is warning us of a situation that we should handle carefully.

There have been many times I have visualised the scene of the crucifixion, yet with additional details to those described in the four Gospels: Jesus and the two thieves, bleeding and dying, each on his own cross. Jesus was exhausted, humiliated and in pain. The clouds were beginning to gather, darkening the sky. People were standing at the foot of the cross. From the perspective of the cross, I felt I could see the immense sadness, fear, shock and broken hopes in the eyes of the people gathered there. I visualised Peter – although not mentioned as being present in the biblical accounts – and how he might have felt, as they all struggled to understand and accept what was happening. Was this the same Jesus they had followed? If so, why wasn't he getting down from the cross now, performing another miracle? If he was God, it would be a very small miracle to change the situation now and prove that he was God.

But others were there too: Mary, the soldiers, the religious leaders and many other spectators. They had all arrived at the same place, at the cross, yet each by a different route, through a unique experience and with a different understanding of what was happening. Every one of them, except Jesus, was unworthy.

Although they all came their various ways, with different attitudes and through separate circumstances, the cross was the place where they were all brought together. God put the picture in my mind of Jesus on the cross with Peter looking at him and the two thieves on either side. Jesus looked down at Peter, who had denied him three times, then he looked to the side of Jesus and saw the thief there. In this picture I had in my mind, in spite of their differences, Peter and that thief ended up in the same place, at the cross.

Peter was a good man, a fisherman, and Jesus' disciple from the start of his ministry. He served Jesus, and even stated that he would die for him.[9] Regardless, when the tough times came, he was quick to deny even knowing Jesus, not just once but three times. The thief, on the other hand, was guilty of stealing and breaking the law. He had not followed Jesus at all, but at the cross he truly saw who Jesus was and was quick not only to repent, but also to confess openly before everyone watching that he knew he deserved the death he was dying, while defending Jesus as pure and undeserving. At that moment, the heart of the thief at Jesus' side was pure, honest and surrendered completely. His ability to see who Jesus was, and his statement acknowledging this in his dying moment, is perhaps one of the greatest testimonies to Jesus as the Son of God. He was the first human to cry to Jesus for salvation, and he was the first person on earth to *receive* salvation. Jesus told that thief at his side that he would be with him in heaven.[10]

Both Peter and the thief were unworthy in that moment. Jesus said, 'whoever disowns me before others, I will disown before my Father in heaven'.[11] Yet even though Peter denied him three times, he was still the rock on which Jesus chose to build his church. This picture at the cross perfectly illustrates the beautiful paradox of grace, and the wildly different ways that lead to the same point. And as far as we know, that thief arrived in heaven long before Peter, as Jesus promised him he would be there that same day. Not a single one of them was worthy, including Peter and the thief, but they received the same blessing of Jesus because of his mercy and grace.

Many of us are like that thief at Jesus' side. What a blessing that we too can have hope to be saved by the grace of God, through the sacrifice of Jesus.

As far as we can read, the thief at Jesus' side was the only man on earth who had truly, with all his heart, accepted and believed in Jesus at that moment. Jesus' disciples, although they had said in the past that they believed in him, had all fled the night before. Even though Peter was the bravest of the twelve, he *still* didn't have the courage to publicly acknowledge him when he was asked directly.

As Peter stood there, at the foot of the cross – in this picture I saw – I felt that perhaps his whole world and everything he had believed during his years with Jesus was literally dying in front of his very eyes. But there on the cross, the thief at Jesus' side was convinced of who Jesus was and didn't hesitate to ask for his forgiveness and grace, which Jesus gave to him without hesitation.

For those of us who believe in Jesus, what an encouragement it is that God could still use Peter – in spite of his very signifi-cant shortcomings – to build his church. Not just to *help* build it, but to be the rock, the very foundation on which it would be built. After all, how many of us talk the talk, but when the pressure rises and the tension is turned up, or we wait a long time to see the promises of God fulfilled, we allow that voice of doubt to creep in – the 'what ifs', the 'maybes', the 'surelys' and the 'it can'ts'. How many are truly willing to live and die for their faith, to suffer and give up their lives for Jesus? Or how many say that they will and mean it, but in a group discussion find themselves retreating into silence when someone says something against Jesus?

If you were to ask people across the world who they would choose to be – Peter, the thief who repents or the thief who doesn't, not many would say the latter. Yet many people are just like him, mocking and insulting Jesus, refusing to believe in him in spite of their unworthiness, even while they are dying on their crosses. Not many would choose to be the thief who repents either, although this is the next largest group of people, who scrape in by the skin of their teeth. Most people would probably choose to be Peter. Yet the irony is that not many of the people who would prefer to be Peter are actually willing to choose the narrow and difficult way, and to suffer in the way Peter suffered after the crucifixion and resurrection, to be able to be the rock on which Jesus could build his church. People make many excuses, and even manage to convince themselves that they are following Jesus and are living their lives for him, yet many of their lives bear little or no resemblance to those of Jesus and his disciples. Where is the fire, the passion and the suffering that were evident in the lives of Jesus, Peter and all the other disciples? Are we walking the walk, or just talking the talk?

The interesting point is that Peter's ministry only really began when he was willing to become like the repentant thief, at least in the eyes of the world. He challenged the ways of the world in favour of sharing the grace and radical message of Jesus, and was crucified as a criminal as a result. He was accused of being one of the worst criminals in the eyes of the old religious community. This is still happening today. It is the true and genuine Christians, those who will give everything for Jesus, who are the minority. And the people who perceive themselves to be the most holy are still trying to crucify the true followers of

Jesus. We see that here in Syria, and among other people who identify as Christians around the world now. There are people living under the banner of Christianity who do not have the Holy Spirit living inside them, and they will fight the people who are truly seeking to apply the challenging teachings and passages taught by Jesus to the way they live their lives. The only way to combat this is to keep going back to the words of Jesus and to keep looking for opportunities to apply his teachings to our own lives. When we do this, we are living the true revolution.

*

One Sunday, Samara sent me a photo of her church service. It looked so nice and organised. I saw lots of people worshipping and singing together, raising their hands to God. It was beautiful and I could see one of the leaders standing at the front giving a talk. I thought it looked like heaven.

After a few moments, I saw another picture, this time in my heart, completely different from the one Samara had sent. I saw our destroyed country, my devastated city and our damaged and annihilated houses. I saw poor, broken people sitting in their cold houses because they have no money and there is no fuel or wood to buy. They have no windows and no food. There were poor children sitting beside their widowed mothers, and orphans beside their widowed grandmothers.

I looked deeper into this picture and I saw another person I didn't recognise at first. As I looked closer, I started to recognise him, as his sound and presence was familiar. It was Jesus, but he looked dirtier, thinner and more tired. He looked so much like us, just like the dirty, poor children around him. They were sitting around the *sobia* heater together to warm themselves. He was sitting beside these children, sharing in their suffering. As I watched, I felt I wanted to cry. I couldn't look at his face again because I felt ashamed of myself. I wanted to sit there with him and have something to give to him, as well as giving to these poor children and orphans.

When Jesus walked this earth, he didn't spend his time in palaces or high places. He was on the streets with the poor people, the most vulnerable, the sick and the sinners, with many of the people that no one else wanted to spend time with. It has been a privilege for me to be here in this dirty, unclean place with him in Syria, sitting with the poorest and most vulnerable people. I feel enormously blessed to have been born here in this land. Now, after everything I have seen and experienced here, I have a much greater understanding of the wisdom of God's plan and how he has chosen to do everything. He has given me the realisation that I am no better than the thief at the side of Jesus when he was crucified. I'm sure I have made many mistakes in my life. But I feel blessed to have been able to be crucified at the side of Jesus, to be accepted by him and to be able to join him in heaven.

16

Praying and Worshipping in Spirit and in Truth

While I was in my captivity, our youngest son broke his arm. As it was healing it started to itch. Frustrated, he came to me and asked me what to do. I told him to pray. When he said he didn't know how to pray, I said, 'Just speak to God, that's all.'

Then I watched and listened as he started to pray. He reminded me of the way I had prayed when I was his age. He simply prayed as a young boy, saying, 'Jesus, I want you to stop my arm from itching and you are very beautiful, and I love you.' He spoke from his heart in very simple, childish language.

I asked him afterwards if it had stopped itching. It had. So I then asked if he had said thank you to Jesus. He said, 'Oh yes! Thank you, Jesus!' just like that.

Sometimes he would wake up in the middle of the night and start praying without asking me. Watching how he responded to his discomfort, I saw myself in him, as a little boy, lying in bed and calling for my mother when I was in pain. When she couldn't answer, I called out to God, who did answer me.

When you have fellowship with many people at church, it is easy to pick up their ways, their bad habits as well as the good, without noticing. For me, it is important not to simply follow routines that other people use to pray, or to adopt their customs for anything else, just because that's what everyone seems to be doing. We need to weigh up and test these practices, considering whether we are truly following the teachings of Jesus, as there are so many things that can distract us from his priorities. That was the beauty of the place of confinement I was in, being completely isolated. I couldn't see many people, converse with them or go to church. As I didn't have many people to speak to, it was mostly God I talked with.

It is easy to fall into the trap of trying to be clever in prayer or to think that if you pray in a certain way you will get a better response. Jesus thanked God for revealing his ways to the little children while hiding them from those who considered themselves to be wise.[1] If we can't go back to being a child (most likely a naughty child), then we will struggle. We need to go back to being children, which means we need to be simple, uncomplicated and not dependent on our own wisdom or knowledge. We just go to God our Father and treat him the way children go to good earthly parents – parents that can be trusted and relied upon – not as if we are adults trying to be clever, manipulating situations through our words and actions.

Even when my parents' friends came to me when I was a child, joking and humouring 'Dr A' by saying that they were feeling sick or unwell, I would tell them they should pray. They seemed surprised, but they agreed. I told them I did that when I had tummy ache, but they didn't take it seriously. I told them with the faith of a child that if they would pray, God would heal them.

Praying is not a one-off, daily or hourly event. It is a continuous process. I believe that our whole life and the way we live should be a prayer; every breath should form part of it. We should be continuously speaking with God, just like two people who are living together. Prayer is not separated from the ordinary activities of normal life. Instead, in our daily activities and routines we need to be speaking with him at every step. He is with us. This is what I felt in my childhood, and even more now in this war.

When I was a young child I went to church with my mother. The priest taught us how to pray. He told us not only what to say, but also when and how to say it. I asked him once how he prayed. He explained that he would wear his special clothes and he would prepare himself before standing or kneeling in a certain place. He detailed the things he did before he prayed. It seemed to me as though it was like a performance for him.

Once we start to focus on ourselves and on what we are doing, we lose the meaning of praying. The true meaning of prayer is to simply speak with God, from our heart to his. Why would anyone speak to him differently from the way they speak with anyone else? Jesus showed us that, through him, we are God's children and he is our Father. That's why, when Jesus' disciples asked him how to pray, he made it simple. He is our King, but he is our Father too. Jesus demonstrated that all we need to do is speak to God as we would our earthly father. We need neither prestige nor pretence; just pure simplicity. If I was going to speak to my earthly father, I would just go to him and talk. There is no need to go to a special room or place, sit in a certain way, put my hands in a particular position or use specific words. The same is true with God our heavenly Father – we can simply speak with him exactly as we are, wherever we are, at any time.

The only times I ever felt as if I was unable to pray was when someone told me *how* I should do it. When we went to church, the priest told us how and what to pray, that we should pray this number of prayers for the Holy Father, that number to the Virgin Mary and this number to Jesus. I did it, but felt I was simply repeating words without any true feeling, meaning or any understanding of what I was saying. I tried to pray like this for two or three years, but eventually it felt too robotic. It was like a recording. I was young and wasn't able to tell the priests that I found it unhelpful. When I prayed these kinds of prayers, I felt nothing happened. For me, they were ineffective and lacked power.

I remembered before, when I had talked with God normally and my stomach had got better. The repetitive prayers I had been taught didn't help me to have a true conversation with God, and I couldn't see how anything could be changed by repeating these prayers over and over. After a while, I stopped praying that way. I wanted to speak to God heart to heart, and to say, 'Look, it's me here, God, and I can feel you. You are there, and I'm speaking with you.' If I can't sense the presence of God, then it feels as though I'm just talking to myself, or to thin air. God is real and he is true. If we invite him in and let him fill us, he lives in our heart and we can speak with him directly through our hearts.

Sometimes someone might tell me we should pray, but at that moment I don't feel like it. That doesn't change my relationship with God. When I feel tired and exhausted and that I don't want to pray at a given time, I don't feel it is a big issue between me and God, because he knows my heart and will find countless different ways to talk with me. It's not as though I'm bound by a contract, and if I step outside that contract by not praying at the right time or in the right way I will lose God's favour. No: I'm spontaneous and authentic. When I'm happy, you can see it; when I'm sad, it is obvious; and when I'm angry it's pretty evident too. I wear my heart on my sleeve. I'm not trying to pretend I am something or someone that I am not. I am not a super holy saint. I'm just a normal person.

I believe God wants me to tell my story, which I am doing through this book. Perhaps it is because he wants to encourage other people who, like me, don't see themselves as holy or spiritually perfect. If my story encourages ordinary people to reach out to him and meet with him just as they are, with all their defects and blemishes, I will be happy, because I am no more worthy than anyone else to stand before him. Because of his grace he works with us. Even though we are all sinners, he still loves us.

He came to heal us sick people in this broken world. We are not healthy, which is why we need him; he is the doctor for our souls. If we lose sight of our brokenness, we will just be promoting a fake, hypocritical religion that will mislead others, because most people don't feel they are good or perfect either. Those who do probably need to be humbled.

I don't want anyone to compare themselves to me or to compare their situation to mine. If we don't show others our reality, acknowledging our faults and imperfections, they will feel that they can't do what we're doing because they can't reach the high place that we have elevated ourselves to. Whatever we have achieved in our work here has happened one step at a time, and only because we have trusted and listened to God.

When I pray, I pray as a naughty boy in need of forgiveness from a merciful God, because that's what I am.

God allowed me to experience being in captivity for three and a half years. He squeezed my heart, exposing me daily to the fire. It was as if he was cooking my thoughts and feelings to make me more mature, preparing me to be put on the table of his service. God showed me a picture of a table with bread sitting on top of it. I felt as if God was preparing me, and this book, to be bread for people to feed on. When you make bread, you need to put the dough in a warm place, and then knead, stretch and work it before giving it the time it needs to rise. When you have done this, it still needs to be put into the oven in the stifling heat to make it edible and nutritious.

God has done the same with me. He put me in that place of isolation where I felt as though I was fasting from life itself. But in that time and place he also put me through fire, which was incredibly hot and intense, which is necessary too when making bread. Every day here has been a huge struggle. But it has given me a message to share, which I hope will provide good and nourishing bread for others, on the table of God's service.

*

One sunny day, while I was living in captivity in my home, the boys were playing outside. I noticed that Miriam had been in the bathroom for a while. When I went to see what was happening, she looked very pale. I asked what she thought was wrong, as she is a doctor too. She didn't know, but said she had been vomiting. Suddenly she started vomiting again. After wiping her face with a tissue, she picked up her phone and started to search for something. A few minutes later she looked really worried. She showed me her phone with a look of real fear in her eyes – she had just eaten something poisonous.

There was a tree in our garden with fruit on it which we had never eaten, until that day. Her father had asked someone whether it was edible and had been told that it was. Miriam and her father had been eating the fruit that afternoon.

Poisoning is one of the things I dealt with as an emergency and ICU doctor, so I know exactly how to respond in such a situation, as well as the importance of reacting quickly. I began researching the fruit in a poison reference guide. Miriam had other symptoms, including abdominal pain and a headache. Her father had also started vomiting.

As I read about this plant, the information stated that eating even one piece of the fruit can be fatal, but Miriam and her father had each eaten four or five. We were all filled with panic when we read that there was no antidote for this poison. Even if there had been, I knew we wouldn't have been able to find it in any of the hospitals in Syria, which were totally depleted of resources and many medications. It was a terrifying situation, because my family and I would be at great risk if I were to leave my house. During my captivity, Miriam's father was the one we depended on when someone needed to go to the hospital, because he is also a doctor. But he had been vomiting and was also suffering the effects of poison and thus couldn't do anything either.

We started to really worry for their lives. I felt an enormous sense of frustration about my own situation in the heat of the moment, as I couldn't even leave the house. Miriam was lying in bed, pale, in pain and terrified. Her hands had gone numb and she had become disorientated. We were scared that she was going to leave us. She asked our children to come around her, and was weeping and kissing them, saying goodbye. The boys didn't understand what was going on, but they started to cry too.

We began to pray, because we had no other option available to us. We prayed and we cried, and God heard us. Miriam began to recover immediately and didn't vomit again. Within half an hour she was feeling better. Her father also made the same rapid recovery. It was a miracle. God helped us because we couldn't help ourselves. There wasn't any other option for us that day; we just called out to him in our moment of need, and he took care of us. We were so thankful.

★

During the most violent years of the war, I couldn't specify a certain amount of time each day to pray and read the Bible. I dipped into it here and there when I could and needed to. I was desperate and needed to be able to carry God's Word in my heart, everywhere and anywhere. I didn't have anything else to depend on. With the kind of life I was living, the Word of God in my heart was my only escape, my only survival tool and my Plans A, B and C. I prayed as I passed through challenges that had been written about in the Bible.

I didn't have the luxury of going to sit alone and have a quiet time every day when I was needed at the hospital at all hours of the day and night. But after I connected with Samara and her group of pray-ers in the UK, I started to feel that when I walked those horrible and dangerous streets, I was not alone. There were now people standing beside me, walking the road with me, praying with me and reading the Bible with me. My situation didn't change, but I no longer felt alone in those exhausting and terrifying moments. We used the Bible as a language of communication and kept going back to it to make sense of things that were happening. It was a way of receiving and understanding prophecies. We used it in a very practical way.

Later, when I was in my 'prison', I had so much quiet time on my hands it drove me crazy. My way of having special time with God was to sit and watch the sunset every day, feeling his presence and his closeness. It was a daily ceremony for me to marvel at this beautiful picture he painted for us, and how each one was different from the day before. Clear, cloudy, hazy, different colours – each one was unique and stunning in its own way. Every evening I listened to the birds chirping their evening chorus before they fell silent and the blanket of dusk was rolled out for the night. Just at the moment when the sun vanished below the horizon, a gentle breath would sweep over the land before the darkness settled. Sometimes I would read the Bible at sunset or listen to the Bible in One Year.[2] At other times, I would feel his presence with me and just sit with him, thinking and pondering. At these times I felt he gave me ideas and solutions for handling situations.

I read the Bible when I was a child and while I was at college. But once the war started, I began *living* the Bible. It was totally different from simply reading it as I had done before. In the past I had read various parts and sought to apply them to my life, but not to the same degree as I do now. At the beginning of the war I started to pick up the Bible more than I had in the years before. It was such a shock to go from normal life to this messy and violent existence. Without God's Word it would have been impossible for me to survive what I have experienced over these years and get through to the other side with my humanity intact. I carried the Bible in my heart, trying to digest it every day.

It would surprise me at times when a passage would suddenly come to mind. I would realise later it was the Holy Spirit, the 'Helper', reminding me and putting words of guidance and encouragement in my heart when I needed them.[3]

In my opinion, it's not enough for anyone to simply send physical Bibles to Syria or anywhere else. God's Word should be given to people from your heart, directly to their heart. I don't want to give someone a Bible that will be put on a shelf to gather dust, or even be sold if the person is in great need. If I want to give someone a Bible, I should first walk the road with them as they look for water. I need to walk with them while they go to find bread and when they are searching for fuel to heat their freezing home. If anyone wants to bring us God's Word, they should bring it in their heart. It has little value otherwise. Come and read the Bible with us day by day and live it with us while we are walking these hostile roads, hand in hand.

This was my experience. I received prayers, passages and words of encouragement from our brothers and sisters in the UK and watched them sending support to the Syrian people for years before I received a physical Bible, which I requested from them. I received the spiritual Word of God, carried in the hearts of these people, who tried to meet our physical needs while they also tried to meet our spiritual needs. They lived with me and walked with me every step of the way. They prayed with their prayer groups for us.

These people gave me strength and hope. The combination of physical and spiritual support was essential, as people here really are in such great need after so many years of war. As Jesus said, 'Man shall not live by bread alone.'⁴ We need to show people what God's words mean in practice, and we can only do this through living out God's Word in front of their eyes, holding their hands as they live their lives and we live ours, going through the fire *with them*.

Working in disaster management, I know that effective communication is the crucial factor in determining whether you will succeed or fail. Good communication with your team and with your leader is essential to survive. It is the same in our battle in this life. We need effective communication with our team and, most importantly, to stay in communication with our leader, Jesus. This is the only way we can know the plan for our lives and what is required of us. This is how we can ask for backup when we need it, review the situation if something is not working, decide on a change of plan or find out what the next instruction is.

This life is a full-scale battle, and the aim of this battle is not for our bodies to survive in this world; it is for our souls to survive in order to live in the next, in eternal life with God. As Christians, we are not afraid of physical death. We are willing, even glad, to die for Jesus. I am happy to die to this life for the sake of eternal life with God.

17

Lessons in Forgiveness

While I was still in my 'prison', my oldest son came home from school, upset and crying. One of his best friends had hit him, hurting him badly. As his father, my heart was moved. When I asked whether he had fought back, he told me he didn't have the chance because he was taken by surprise. We spent some time talking and I showed him some self-defence manoeuvres, explaining how to avoid attacks and how to protect himself from being hurt. I even taught him even how to hit back without injuring himself.

After I had finished showing him these things, I explained that Jesus asked us not to get involved with this kind of fighting. When we start to act with violence, however justified it might seem, we give victory to the devil. I gave my son the ability to use his own power, but I also gave him the opportunity to turn the other cheek and practise forgiveness. I told my son about a lesson that I had learnt many years before, when I too was beaten at school.

I was the only Christian student at the school where the beatings happened. I worked hard, and every year I was the top student with the best grades. It made some people jealous. After the grades were announced, a group of students would wait for me at the school entrance. They wanted to beat me up and humiliate me. They attacked me, and I gave as good as I got. We fought for a long time. I can still remember the bitter taste this experience left in my mouth after the fighting had stopped.

They kept taunting me, saying that, as a Christian, I was not allowed to be in first place. They said I had no right, and that they were superior to me. They kept saying, '*Ente Kafr*' which means, 'You are unfaithful to God.' I wanted to fight them because they were so wrong, and I had worked hard to get my grades. Their attitudes and actions towards me were unjust in every way. I argued with them and challenged them, and it took so much of my energy. It took a lot of effort to try to disperse all the negative feelings in my heart. This happened every year at that school when I got the top grades.

Even when I went to secondary school there were problems. When I was fourteen, there was a group who would mess around in the same class every week, and it became very tedious. Some of the children took a dislike to the teacher and thought he was a bad teacher. I didn't think he was a bad teacher, but he was weak and couldn't control the class. With them messing around in class, no one could learn anything.

This went on for weeks. Eventually I got fed up and said in front of everyone in the class, including the teacher, that this behaviour was unacceptable as we needed to learn. I told them either to leave if they didn't want to be there or to be quiet because they were stopping everyone else from learning.

The misbehaving students ended up being excluded from this class and were not happy about it. One of those boys was one of my best friends. He refused to listen to my advice and was excluded. We had been to each other's houses many times and knew each other's brothers and sisters.

At the end of the month we had a final exam and afterwards he asked me to wait for him in a certain place outside the school. It was strange, because after he had been excluded for what had happened with the teacher, he hadn't spoken a word to me. Suddenly, out of the blue, he appeared to be holding out an olive branch. On one hand I felt happy, but on the other, something didn't feel quite right.

I waited for him outside the school, as he had asked. When he came out, he walked straight over to me and kissed me on my cheek, then walked off again without saying a word. As soon as he had done this, a group of other children who weren't students at the school jumped out at me, kicking and punching me and pulling me to the ground. They beat me badly and I had lots of wounds on my face and body.

Immediately I realised he had set me up. He made sure I was alone and away from anyone who might have tried to help me, then identified me to this group. I had been betrayed. I hadn't done anything to hurt this boy; I just wanted to learn so I wouldn't fail my exam. But he was only interested in his damaged pride and taking revenge.

This time, which was years after my first attack, I decided not to fight back. Instead, I changed my attitude and said, 'Thank you, Jesus, because I passed what you also passed.' It was a real privilege to experience the same event and feel something of what Jesus must have felt when Judas betrayed him. Jesus was also betrayed with a kiss, a sign of affection between men in our culture, to show the soldiers who to take, beat and put to death. I did not fight back. Instead I kept saying, 'I forgive them.'

While I was being beaten, my best friend Munzer suddenly appeared, looking both uncertain and angry, like Peter was when Jesus was arrested. He could not understand why I wasn't fighting back. I shot him a look, to let him know that it was okay and not to fight. But I could see the bitterness in his face from having to hold back from fighting against this injustice. When they saw Munzer, the other boys stopped and resorted to firing insults at me instead, before leaving.

I forgave those boys, but it wasn't easy. I suffered great pain over the coming days and nights, both physical and emotional. The betrayal and painful experience kept replaying in my mind and I barely slept. The humiliation of being thrown to the ground and repeatedly kicked in front of everyone else kept occupying my heart and mind. A big part of me wanted to retaliate and take revenge, but Jesus' voice in my heart said, 'No. Don't fight back. Forgive.'

This was a significant event in my life and in our community, and the friend who had betrayed me remained at the school after this assault. He pretended he was not responsible for what had happened and tried to be my friend afterwards. But his involvement in the set-up was as obvious as his involvement in the incidents in class. I did not fight him, accuse him or try to take revenge. I forgave him. Although I had lost my trust in him, I didn't hate him.

The next day, when my son returned from school, I asked him what had happened with his friend and whether he had retaliated. He said he hadn't touched him or tried to repay him for what happened. I was so proud of him. 'But,' he said, 'not hitting him was so much harder than hitting him would have been.' It took more energy to control himself and not fight back than it would to have taken revenge. My young son, who was just a child, had learnt an important lesson in life.

During this war, I have been personally betrayed; I have had my hospital taken and destroyed; my friends, colleagues and relatives have been tortured and murdered. My home was taken; I have faced death threats and threats of kidnapping. I have been beaten while treating patients. I have faced false accusations, and some have tried to blackmail me. One employee of mine tried to take my work contracts under which I had employed him; other employees tried to falsely accuse me to take my position. I have had my freedom taken away from me. The catalogue of verbal abuse I have encountered since my early years is endless, just for being a Christian.

There have been troubles in our country for centuries, but this dirty war has applied pressure to people in a concentrated way. The manners and customs of people have been destroyed, making this a 'dog-eat-dog' environment where survival is against the odds. That's why so many people have left the country, as most ask what kind of future this hostile environment can offer any child growing up.

My earliest experiences taught me to forgive. While I would never want to go through those experiences again, I recognise the value of them in the bigger picture of life, which is greater than the experience we live in these bodies. Forgiving people who have wronged us so deliberately requires double the energy that retribution does. Retaliation feels like the natural option and is very tempting when you feel the sheer weight of injustice, when people have lied about you, have been hostile towards

you or have acted out of jealousy. But by allowing anger or hurt
to grow in our hearts, or by indulging the feelings of injustice
that are boiling away inside us, we will be destroyed along with
the perpetrators of our pain. Responding with forgiveness
requires greater strength of character than responding with anger.
Even defending ourselves takes energy that would be better spent
on something more positive. But forgiveness is a decision that
Jesus helps us with.

Some situations require a defence (if you are taken to court,
for example), but in most other scenarios the energy we spend
in trying to defend ourselves is wasted. We could spend a lot
of time and energy in doing so, and in the end still not have
the result we want.

After years of conflict, of setting up and running medical
points and field hospitals to serve the people injured by the
fighting, one day I received a court summons. The widow of
a doctor who had worked with me had accused me of being
responsible for her husband's death. The place where he was
working when he was killed had nothing to do with me, as
doctors work in multiple locations here. It was the strangest
accusation. It was an enormous shock and I found myself
wondering how on earth someone could make such a huge
accusation about someone totally unconnected to an event.

Even though this accusation was ridiculous in every way, and
I didn't believe I could be found guilty, it was a very uncomfortable time. Being accused of being responsible for anyone's
death is a gruelling experience, especially for a doctor. People
who knew me knew it was nonsense, but what about the people
who didn't?

Weeks later, the court cleared me of all charges as it was so
straightforward. The deceased had chosen to work in one of
the most dangerous places, and he, like any one of us, knew
the risks of simply being there.

There were many times when I wondered about the motive
of this widow. As a doctor, I am aware that bereaved people go
through a number of stages in grief, anger and blame are both
part of the process. When I did some investigating into who

she was and why she would do something like this to me, I discovered that their family was very poor, her mother was sick and they needed money. In spite of what they had done to me, I felt compassion for her. Once the court case was over and my name was cleared, I sent a representative to give her some money. I believed that was what she had wanted from the start, and I tried to think of what would happen to my own wife and children if I were to be killed. Jesus teaches us to show mercy and forgiveness and to love our enemies, and to give more when someone asks the unreasonable of you.[1]

This war has given me countless opportunities to forgive, as I have experienced more injustice than people living in peaceful countries could possibly imagine. But it is the teaching of Jesus, and understanding what he went through, and how, that have helped me to apply this way of living in my own life. Just as I have tried to do with my own son, my father shaped and trained me in how to apply these teachings to my life. He gave me practical models, teaching me by the many examples of forgiveness and mercy he lived out in front of us children as we were growing up. His sacrifices in life formed the most important lessons for us; he demonstrated what being a servant of Jesus really looks like.

My father's second episode in prison when I was eleven came about because another army officer plotted and arranged to assassinate him. Having gone into the military at a young age to gain the education he couldn't have afforded otherwise, my father had worked his way to a high position. He was respected as a man of integrity; there were few Christian men at such a senior level in those days. But exercising fairness in such a place did not come without consequences. There was a man in a lower position with connections to the Muslim Brotherhood who didn't want a Christian above him who could not be manipulated or coerced. He wanted my father's position but found nothing to accuse him of in order to remove him. Instead he plotted and arranged his murder with the aid of some of his own subordinates.

One night, my mother had a dream, warning her that someone

would try to kill my father. My mother was so distraught, she spoke with one of my father's friends in the army and begged him not to leave his side that day, even for a minute. His friend promised my mother and, true to his word, stuck by him. Later that day, two men working with my father's rival came to take him away. My father could see his rival standing at a distance with a gun aimed at him, but his faithful friend stayed beside him. Seeing that my father was not alone, his rival seemed to lose his nerve.

However, my father's friend was overwhelmed with fear as he watched the situation unfold, and he fled. The men who had come for my father took him to a warehouse where they tied him up, planning to set fire to it, hoping to make it look like an accident. It was full of blankets and flammable items. As they were setting this up, they became unsure of themselves, worrying about my father's friend who had seen everything. Concerned about being charged with murder, they ran away. Eventually my father escaped.

As is often the case in such situations in Syria, both my father and his adversary were imprisoned while the investigation took place. My father was put into solitary confinement for six months, in a cell just two metres by one metre, with no natural daylight. It was a life-changing experience for him, but God was good to him and encouraged him during this awful, uncertain time. He had experiences of meeting Jesus while he suffered in captivity.

When the man was eventually brought to trial, my father was confronted by him begging for mercy and talking about his family. My father is a truly faithful Christian, and the words of Jesus about loving our enemies had touched his heart. He made the decision not to testify against the man who had tried to kill him. We all paid a high price for this merciful act, as my father then fell under suspicion of having a deeper connection with this man, who had a darker and more complicated history than just the attempted murder of my father.

These events didn't simply affect my father, they turned our entire family life upside down too. What this man did changed absolutely everything in our lives. Our place and acceptance in the community, as we became outcasts, and our financial situation were two of the most obvious things. My father was discharged from the army after this happened, which was when he opened the supermarket as our livelihood.

Many people would have borne a grudge for life or tried to take revenge if they had had this experience. In doing so they would have become bitter inside. The inability to forgive consumes us from the inside, and when that happens it also manifests on the outside. It is easy to recognise people who cannot forgive because you can feel the heavy burdens they carry when you are in their presence. The only way to keep our hearts soft is to forgive the people who wrong us.

*

When I was around seventeen, another experience had a significant impact on our family and gave us a further opportunity to forgive. My brother and father decided to branch out from the supermarket and started an additional service providing electrical parts for cars, such as lamps and horns. We had a warehouse next to our supermarket and used part of it as a workshop. These premises were inside a building that had other residents. No one in the building had any problem with this, except for one family. They were communists and hated Christians. They hadn't done well in life and their children had failed at school. They seemed to dislike our family, first for being Christian and secondly for working hard to improve ourselves and our situation.

This family complained that this extra service would be noisy, although we were located on a very loud, busy main road. No one else objected. Moreover, we weren't doing extensive work on these cars, just dealing with small electrical parts. The family bribed the police to come and make trouble at our workshop, but as we had all the correct permissions for what we were doing, they were limited in what they could do.

One day, the family stormed into our workshop and started

attacking the employees working there, beating them with wooden objects and vandalising the warehouse. They destroyed a lot, and we needed money to repair the damage they caused. We took them to court to seek compensation.

They paid another poor neighbour to give false evidence against our family, to say we had attacked them in their home rather than the truth that this family had come into our workshop and destroyed it and had physically beaten our workers. As a result of this false testimony, the judge did not award our family any damages to cover our repairs. It was a very tough and unjust experience.

Years later, when I was working in a hospital, I saw one of the women in the family who had been paid to give false evidence against our family. She looked lost, so I was friendly and helped her find the right department; it turned out she needed to have cardiac surgery on her mitral valve. I did everything I could to help her with all the paperwork at the hospital and never mentioned any of the issues that had happened in the past. It was water under the bridge.

Later, I received a call from her son. He and his family were very concerned and were asking for my help. His mother had gone in to have the surgery, but she had been in the operating room for twelve hours and the team were refusing to give them any information about her. The family were terribly worried and didn't know what was happening. They asked me to find out what was going on.

When I entered the operating room, I could see that her operation was very complicated. Her mitral valve had ruptured, and she was inevitably going to die. However, the cost for this surgery was very high, and the surgeons didn't want to lose the large fee that her family would pay them for doing the operation. So they were trying to manipulate the situation to keep her on life support long enough to be discharged into ICU and then would be declared dead there a little later, rather than owning up to their loss in the operating room. Owning up would have been the ethical, honest thing to do. But they wanted the large payment. It was a huge amount of money for a poor family like this.

When I realised what they were doing, I was furious. I challenged them, saying that it was unacceptable practice. I told them I didn't agree with what they were doing, and that this patient should be declared dead there and then in the operating room.

I then went out and told the family the truth. They were understandably distraught, but at least they would not be left with a huge hospital bill they couldn't afford, along with the loss of their wife and mother.

When her funeral came, my father and brother decided to go to show their compassion and hold out an olive branch to this family. They wanted to put the past behind us all and begin a new relationship with them. When they entered the funeral hall, the entire family stood up to welcome them, then confessed loudly, in front of everyone there, that they had done us an injustice. Most of the residents of the street were there, and yet that family stood in front of everyone, loudly admitting that they had made a huge mistake by telling lies about us and falsely accusing us in court in front of the judge. The neighbours in the street were shocked and came to us one by one to express their sympathy towards us, amazed at how graciously our family had dealt with our neighbours. It could have ended up as a much bigger battle, but we let it go instead of trying to take justice into our own hands.

★

Years later, during the war, my family and I went to lunch with my brother and his family. The shish kebabs were delicious, and it was very special to spend time with them. In the lead-up to it, it hadn't been easy to see each other. We lived in different areas and the roads were often closed at that stage of the war. Having been forced to move home a number of times, it was hard to maintain normal visits. We had been laughing and joking during our meal and it had felt as though there was a momentary pause in the fighting. The city had felt calmer.

My brother's daughters were excited about taking us to the

new ice cream shop that had just opened around the corner. It was the best in the city, they had told me. The girls had put on their coats and were ready to leave. I was just about to put on my suit jacket when my phone rang. It was my hospital.

Ten minutes later and still on the phone, I was standing with my hands clasping my jacket, poised and ready to leave. The girls quietly skipped around the room, desperate for the promised ice cream but delayed by my work call. I said goodbye and put on my jacket. Suddenly, BOOM!

With our ears ringing, it took a couple of seconds to register the bomb. My brain immediately went through an assault of emotions: sadness, adrenaline and even for a split second the exhilaration that comes from a sudden rush of hormones. This brief exhilaration was almost instantly replaced by fear and a sinking realisation of what had happened. It would be hours, even days, later that our brains would begin to process all the 'what ifs' and flashbacks, and then the nightmares would come.

Thick with confusion, the moment then began to clear as the sound of the girls crying in terror and chaos broke through the heavy atmosphere. My youngest niece was wailing very loudly. My brother wrapped his arms around his daughters, quickly moving them away from the open window in case of a double bomb. This was a common tactic of the armed extremists who planted car bombs in crowded civilian areas. If the windows were to shatter from another blast, it would send a thousand sharp shards flying into our bodies. He tried to reassure them.

The calls and messages quickly began to come through. It took a little time before the confused fragments of rumours began to form into a solid story of what had happened. A car bomb packed with explosives had been parked right outside the new ice cream shop around the corner that we should have been standing in. If I hadn't taken the phone call that had delayed us by ten minutes, and if we had instead left on time to go and get ice cream, our bloody and disfigured limbs would have been among those blown apart and scattered across the street. So many people were killed, and many more were maimed by that bomb. Severed hands and feet ended up in doorways and lying on the street. The force of the explosion was so strong that the engine of the car in which the explosives had been planted was found on the roof of a building five doors down the road from where the car was parked.

Even parked outside my brother's house just around the corner, my car was covered with a layer of dust and debris from the bomb, with some damage from the shrapnel. Yet my car was a lucky survivor in the street that day. I quickly ushered my family into the car, as we couldn't be sure whether another bomb might be detonated at any moment. If nothing else, the police might now close the road to investigate. I didn't want to be trapped in my brother's house as I would be needed at the hospital to deal with the victims of that bomb.

As I began to receive news of the causalities, there was a name I recognised. Our Russian communist neighbour, who had attacked and tormented our family with lies and false accusations and had paid our other neighbours to lie about us in court many years before, had been injured. Her husband had been severely injured too. In the carnage of war and death, even the loss of life or injury of someone who has harmed you or your family leaves you with a grieving heart. They may have treated us badly all those years before, but not one of us would ever have wished this fate upon either of them. Forgiveness has always been at the heart of our values towards others.

★

All these events in my earlier years were God's way of preparing us for the extraordinarily distressing times ahead. All the people who tried to beat us down over the years failed in their mission to oppress and disempower us. Instead, they made me stronger; these experiences solidified my faith and increased my capacity to forgive. When I was a young child, I chose the human response, which is the normal way of this world. It took me years but, as I grew, I eventually learnt to choose the way of Jesus. Through the hatred and violence people used against me to take out their frustration for their own shortcomings, I was able to develop the strength to forgive people in this war. This isn't a strength we simply possess. It can only come from Jesus and we have to ask for his help to develop it, as it doesn't come naturally.

My prayer is that my son learns this lesson too. He needs to be able to develop and ask for the strength that Jesus gives to enable him to forgive in the battles he will face as he goes through life. I don't anticipate that Syria will be an easier place in the coming years. The years ahead may be even more brutal. This is a tradition that exists in our family, with the important messages of life and faith being passed from father to son and from generation to generation. This training was given by God from ancient times, teaching us to forgive those who hurt us and instead to accept, love and help them. This is what it means to be a child of God and a follower of Jesus.

Many people carry a grudge in their heart: a hurt that someone inflicted on them that they didn't deserve. My prayer is that every one of us will ask God for the grace we need to forgive all the people in our lives who have hurt us, including those who did it deliberately, deceptively and callously. This is what Jesus did when he hung on the cross. He had been betrayed by a friend, abandoned by his friends and followers, accused and sentenced by the religious leaders who claimed to represent God, and lashed until his body was so bloody that he was unable to carry his own cross. And as he hung, nailed onto his wooden cross, hanging by his wounded hands and feet, people hurled abusive comments and insults at him. At that moment he had the ultimate right to feel devastated, hurt and angry; instead he chose to ask his Father to forgive the many people who had degraded and humiliated him, and who would ultimately be responsible for killing him.

Jesus' obedience and forgiveness changed history for all of us. When we choose to be obedient and forgive, we too can change history for those around us and the people we encounter. When we forgive, we can change the future too, not just for the forgiven, but also for ourselves, for our children and for their children.

18

The War Against God: Being Prepared

'Happy birthday! Congratulations, you did it, A! You're about to be free!' It was beautiful to hear my sister's voice. I had not seen her since very early in the war, and I really missed her. Although I could now legally pay my way out of army service on account of my age, I couldn't yet leave my house as the paperwork wasn't complete.

She asked whether I would believe that their struggles in Europe had been harder than my own in the years that I'd been separated from society, and if I would give her the opportunity to explain, without competing for top place on the scale of challenges.

'As it's my birthday, I'll give you the chance, as my gift to you,' I smiled. 'You can speak, and I won't interrupt.'

One of their many struggles over the years was, bizarrely, their experiences of the medical system in a developed European country. My sister described how you needed multiple referrals just to get the right appointment, and how doctors were unwilling to make decisions outside their set protocols. The way you were treated felt deeply impersonal, almost if you were anonymous. The multitude of appointments her husband had had meant that what could have been resolved fairly quickly was now still unresolved years later. He had a rare condition and hadn't found a specialist willing to get to know him and find a solution to his problem.

I recalled how I had investigated her husband's condition in my fourth year of medical school. He suffered from multiple kidney stones and regularly went to hospital in pain. He had been told it was a matter of time before he would need a kidney transplant, or he would likely die. I did not accept his death sentence, and chose to fight instead. No doctors gave him any hope, so he decided to work with me to look for a solution.

I started researching renal disease, reading multiple books on the subject and reviewing medical studies and papers. He bought the books and we did the lab studies I requested. Although I found an obstacle in reaching a definite diagnosis, I chose a careful treatment plan. The result was that the fifteen stones he had in each kidney disappeared, leaving him free from pain or complications for the years he remained in Syria on the treatment plan. My brother-in-law is an atheist and thus refuses to believe in miracles, but even he said that his ability to live normally was truly miraculous. His doctor struggled to believe that a mere fourth-year medical student could have obtained a result like this.

His situation was fine until he arrived in Europe, where the medical system refused to accept the treatment plan I had given him for all the years he had lived in Syria. They began the laborious process of trying to make their own diagnosis. It took years, and when he finally arrived at the best specialist centre for kidney disease, their focus was on either making or excluding a diagnosis rather than trying to create an effective plan to alleviate his suffering. Once they had ruled out the possibility of properly diagnosing a genetic condition, they refused to give him the treatment that had managed his condition so well. He now continues to suffer recurrent, multiple kidney stones and excruciating pain.

This is just one of the many struggles they have faced having left Syria. It breaks my sister's heart. She cannot return to Syria for many reasons. Her children, raised in Europe, would struggle to accept the pattern of life in Syria now, and even for her it would be difficult to return to the life she had in Syria. Her husband is a journalist with opinions that are inflammatory to the Syrian situation, so it is unlikely he will ever return.

I felt she had lost herself in Syria, yet hadn't been able to find herself in Europe. As we talked, I really did feel she was in a worse position than me.

It is not always obvious who the victims are in a war like

this: the people who are killed or the radicalised people doing the killing; the people who stay or those who leave as refugees. What happened and is still happening here is a war against God. It is the devil's weapon, aimed at destroying Jesus in people's hearts. Love, joy, peace, patience, kindness, goodness, faithfulness, gentleness, self-control,[1] forgiveness and grace: what we have experienced destroys all of these qualities. Not one of the wars throughout history or any of those being fought today foster any of these virtues of God. On the contrary, they all destroy what Jesus teaches us.

Before the war, Syria was not a poor, primitive or uncivilised country, but an educated and progressive nation. We were advanced and civilised long before the West developed to a similar level. It's easy to talk about the superficial, physical changes the war brought, but people have lost their trust in each other. Too many people have disappeared from our lives. Death has enveloped us. Our homes, our buildings and our infrastructure have been destroyed. Yet it isn't just the buildings, the infrastructure and people's bodies that have been damaged or destroyed: it is people's souls.

The war has burnt up the wood, like fire, leaving nothing behind but the gold and iron. Our 'metal' has been purified in the process. Our community has been destroyed, but what is left is genuine. Now we can see what people are really made of, and their potential, because we can see who they are. This community is stronger now, and more active, because the fire has melded us together.

Jesus was with all of us in the middle of the misery. There were times and places when we managed to find comfort through his embrace, in the same way that when a child experiences pain they will run into the arms of their mother, flinging their arms around her. As she hugs them, everything else disappears and the child simply encounters their mother's embrace. We felt those all-encompassing hugs of Jesus in the middle of our crisis. Perhaps the first Christians might have felt this same joy when they went to their crosses and their deaths as martyrs, because they had refused to give him up.

Our community may be intensely damaged, but it is also very malleable to be reshaped and rebuilt. Before the war, people were less flexible and didn't accept new ideas. They were comfortable with their lives and traditions, and had no reason to change. They were taught by their grandfathers, who in turn had been taught by their grandfathers. Now people are more open to new ideas and ways, and they need something new in the rearranged landscape. However, this also makes people vulnerable to ideas that outsiders may try to push on them, which may be unhelpful. It is easy for outsiders to think they know what Syrians need, but they haven't walked this treacherous road with us. We need to rebuild our walls and temple now, just as Nehemiah, Zerubbabel and the Jewish people did, to be ready for the future. But just as the rebuilding in the Old Testament was done by the Jewish people, our rebuilding also needs to be done by our people, here in Syria, as we don't trust others much any more. My hope is that we will soon learn a way of living even more focused on God than we did before.

At the beginning of the war, my father said this was not a war against humans, but against God. It felt awkward at first as we saw people around us being killed, kidnapped and tortured. It certainly appeared to be a war against humans. His statement seemed bizarre, but my father has always been a wise man, filled with the Holy Spirit and experiencing many dreams and visions from God. As we watched the war develop, we began to realise he was right.

These radicals were not just trying to kill us. They were killing us, yes, but they were trying to kill God inside us: our faith. I cannot understand how anyone could kidnap a young girl, take her mobile phone and call her parents and family, then make them listen to her screaming and suffering while she is repeatedly raped. What would the perpetrators be trying to achieve? Those men are not just trying to please themselves. They are trying to kill the human feelings in people's hearts, to turn victims' families into monsters, making them want to take their revenge.

I have met people from both sides. Each says something against the other side and has a good reason to hate the other.

Both are victims of hate. There is a bigger plan to destroy the manners and texture of our community and the hearts of our people. Our country used to be very simple, peaceful and nice. Before the war we could knock on the door of any of our neighbours and say we were hungry, and it would have been their pleasure to empty their fridge for us. They wouldn't ask if we were Christian, Shia or Sunni. They would not care, and we would not feel embarrassed to ask our Muslim neighbour for anything. We lived in harmony and respected each other. We told them about Jesus, but we didn't hate them. They did not accept Jesus, but they didn't hate us. Overnight, everyone started killing each other.

It is like a game against Jesus, sowing seedlings of hatred. Jesus told us to love our enemies. How can a father who has listened to his precious daughter being raped again and again and again, for hours, forgive the men who did that to her? He can't forgive, let alone love them. Maybe this girl's family won't be able to take their revenge against the particular men who did this to her. But her brothers will search for someone in order to try to satisfy their fury and appease their broken and enraged hearts. They will feel they need to make *someone* pay for the evil that was done to their sister.

Sympathy, love and mercy have been killed in people's hearts. The perpetrators of these violent acts have sown seeds of wrath and hatred. They have planted a culture of darkness: one of killing, nastiness and bitterness. This is not just against us Syrians; it is against God. Jesus is love. He is mercy, forgiveness and compassion towards humans. When you force people to turn against these qualities, you turn people against God. It is almost impossible to forgive someone who does these depraved things on purpose. Maybe the person who raped your sister, or beheaded your grandmother and set fire to her body, was your friend, teacher, neighbour, work colleague or acquaintance before the war. Suddenly he has turned against you and started torturing you and your family. That is what happened to us, and the sense of betrayal and pain is overwhelming.

Many times I have heard people say that maybe we can forgive someone for the terrible things that have been done to us personally, but when a deliberate and heinous violation has been committed against your mother, your father, your sister, your son or your daughter, it is beyond your human ability to forgive. Only the power of Jesus can enable someone who has experienced this kind of atrocity to forgive.

A lot of people have lost their faith in God. A few people have learnt to trust God more. Our mission is to go to those who have lost their faith, or perhaps never had much in the first place, and try to heal the wounds in their souls by showing them the true love of God. We need to show them that we really care for them, by practising these acts of kindness, helping people get back on their feet by bringing them food, clothes and medical treatment and treating them as human beings. By showing them love, care and compassion through our behaviour, we are fighting against the plan to remove Jesus from his home. We are fighting for God in the war that is being waged against him.

Sometimes I have felt as though I could hear the devil taunting, 'Look, I'm destroying mercy in Jesus' home! No one will forgive their neighbour or love their enemy here now. I have destroyed everything he brought and all the seeds of love and honour he sowed here. People don't trust each other. Look how people are eating each other!' My heart felt battered every time I thought about it. He was right: too many people have lost their way and their faith. It is *our* mission to hold their hands while we ask God to rebuild their hearts again.

Because of what I have experienced, I feel burdened to warn people in the developed world to wake up. Life there is a dream. All the luxuries are a gimmick: nice cars, houses, indulgence, the latest trends, living by credit cards. This life is not about eating, drinking, accumulating possessions, making love, going on holidays, visiting spas or having a beautiful lifestyle. This life was never supposed to be a nice, luxurious experience. It was meant, from the beginning, to be the exam for humans to pass.[2]

When a true war starts, or when our lives are over, none of

these things are important any more. These are the things that draw people away from God. They are distractions and easily become idols, because the attention people give to doing and working for them takes the place of the attention we could spend focused on and working for God: for love, mercy, forgiveness and compassion. The early Christian converts literally sold their land and homes to follow Jesus. How many of us do this today? Are we as Christians truly following the mandate that Jesus gave us?

Spending our time, energy and life doing all these nice but superficial things will not help any of us to pass this exam. If we are not yet prepared, God helps us. The question is whether we are willing to forsake the easy and comfortable life and instead accept his road, which is difficult, painful and involves sacrifice but leads to eternal life.

When presented with the choice to enter or return to our war zone or to choose a safe life, how many of us would choose the war zone, and keep our family there? I chose Syria, while most people who could chose the safer country and moved their families out of the war zone.

Yet I believe this world is one huge war zone, and in this bigger war, between light and darkness, the weapons and methods of attack are different in every environment. Those who choose the safer country may not find their body and physical life under threat in the way it would be in Syria, but they will find their soul under a different kind of attack. These spiritual attacks may not be as obvious as the physical attacks we have suffered here, but they are more discreet, less tangible to most and even invisible to many, and lead us to focus on superficial and meaningless or even evil things, which distract us from what is truly important in our eternal lives. The distractions from God and his call are more dangerous for our spiritual lives than the physical threats we have faced in Syria. We were sidetracked by many of these superficial things before the war too, and some people still are, even after all they have seen and lived through. But I feel these distractions are an even bigger threat in the western world.

Are we able to say, 'Jesus, I give you my *whole* life'? If we can't say that to Jesus, we aren't adequately prepared for eternal life, just as I wasn't before. The only effective preparation is through a relationship with Jesus and going deeper into the Bible, not just reading and understanding the words, but actually *living* the events that happened. For me, many of the stories in the Bible changed from passages I had read to events that happened around me and to me. I have lived through many of the same experiences that Joshua, Solomon, David, Joseph, Jesus and the apostles lived. Maybe there were differences in the way the events happened or in our personalities or responses, but the basic encounters and lessons have been the same. As I read about events I had lived, I felt something in my heart jump in recognition. These passages are the events we will experience when we choose to truly give him everything and follow all his teachings.

It is an active choice to live out what is written in the Bible. Jesus *lived* the words of the Old Testament by applying those chapters to his life. He said it was written that he would be taken, tortured and given into the hands of people who would put him to death.[3] He then chose that path, in full knowledge of what he was doing. The question is, how many of us will *genuinely* apply these tough teachings to our lives when harrowing events surround us?

Jesus told us the servant is not above the master, so if we are his followers, we should expect to suffer what he suffered.[4] Applying the Bible to our lives is the only preparation. We should even be willing to sacrifice our feelings as a father or mother towards our children.[5] Every step I took in the direction of those medical centres in the areas of the worst conflict, passing the most dangerous sniper-targeted roads, applied unmeasurable risks to my life. I always asked, 'Who would take care of my family if I were to die?'

When the war came, I was not prepared. On some level I was physically. My medical specialities in emergency care, critical care and disaster management gave the best preparation anyone could have for an oncoming war, but that's not what

I mean. I had spent a big part of my life improving my skills and abilities, but only a small amount of time reading the Bible here and there, and I didn't apply the most challenging passages to my life. I would have been better prepared if I had, and if I had lived my old life with the knowledge I have now, spending more time with Jesus, focusing on him and trusting his radical guidance.

God gave us many examples of what we would experience when we apply the challenging parts of the Bible to our lives. He even showed us that when we are unable to carry our crosses to our own mountain of Golgotha, he will send someone to help us, as even Jesus couldn't carry his own cross to the end without help.[6] There is no shame in needing help. Simon was sent to help Jesus carry his cross, and God will send help to us when he sees that our strength is failing. Many people have helped me to carry my cross, by praying for me, gathering around me spiritually, sending encouraging words and Bible passages. This helped when it felt too heavy for me and when I was weak. I haven't reached the end yet, and I'm certain tough times lie ahead, but we must carry our crosses if we want to follow Jesus to the end.

As an ICU doctor, I treat people breathing their last breaths. Of course, we do everything we can to try to keep them alive, but sadly we see people who will die no matter what we do for them. At this sensitive time, I always look into their eyes. When I see the face of a dying person, I watch them reviewing their life. I have put myself in their position many times and asked myself, 'What do I want to feel in those seconds as I die? Would I be proud of what I have done in my life? Is there unfinished work? What will the most important thing be to me in that instant?' We should regularly think about that time in our own lives, because it is coming for every one of us. People usually avoid this thought, assuming it is a long way off, or live in denial that it will happen to them. But if we do that, we are wrong.

Having watched many people die, I have realised there is only one way to pass this moment in a fearless way. For the majority it is unpleasant, and for some, even terrifying. Most people face that time filled with uncertainty, and the only way to avoid uncertainty is if you know, with complete assurance, that you will rise again with Jesus. We need to prepare for that time, not only for death, but also to rise from death through Jesus. We must all consider what we need to do or change to rise up from the ashes of death to eternal life. Most of us, after truly appreciating this, need to go back and reprioritise our lives. Jesus is the way, the truth and the life, and no one comes to the Father except through him.[7]

It is our spiritual lives we must focus on because we know our bodies are going to die, whether tomorrow, next year or in thirty years. Death affects us all equally, no matter who we are, what we own, how much power we have or how much respect we command from others, however beautiful our lifestyle looks on the surface, or how good we feel we are or aren't. The only preparation for death is in having a close connection with Jesus as our Lord and Saviour. Only then have we gained the right priority in our lives.

We are all unique and face different issues and challenges. Jesus understands and will show each of us what to do to prepare. But it has to start with welcoming him into our hearts and living with him: speaking with him, eating with him, drinking with him and walking with him. When we read the Bible, we should let him take us by the hand and lead us through it – living the book. Everyone needs to give time to reading the Bible and understanding it, but the most important thing is to carry him and his word in your heart and actually *live* it.

We need to apply it to our decisions, how we handle situations and how we deal with people. It is so much more than just reading and understanding the words. When we *live* it, we stand with Jesus, seeing the fig tree on which he found no figs on, cursing it like he did.[8] We will find ourselves sitting with the woman by the well, asking her for water, drinking from it and saying that Jesus' water is better.[9] We will go with Jesus, as he enters Jerusalem on a donkey.[10] There is a big difference between learning Scripture by heart and living it by heart.

I reached for my Bible when my world started to fall apart, and I had to start praying. What else could we do when there was no ambulance to take an injured person to hospital? Or when there was no hospital because it had been destroyed or taken by jihadists? Or when there were no doctors in the remaining hospital because they had left the country? Or when they were killed or kidnapped? Or when no doctor would leave his house to attend an emergency because so many were being tricked and kidnapped in that way? How would anyone deal with this complete shift in mentality and culture without God's guidance?

The war against God in the western world is more subtle. Sometimes I feel it is more dangerous than the war we have faced here in Syria. Our enemies and threats became obvious. But in the western world I see dangerous things that take people's focus away from God and away from the life Jesus asked us to live – but people are largely unaware of them.

'Lifestyle' is a word that I have seen and heard more and more. Much of the media is devoted to promoting 'lifestyle'. But what is it, and does it matter at the end of our lives? Is the colour we paint our house important, or our style of furniture, or which gym we go to, or how many followers or friends we have on social media?

When I was a child, the houses in my village were built close together. Our homes were very tightly packed, side by side, like the cells in a beehive. There was a window in my grandfather's house next to the window of his neighbour's. They were so close together that they could pass things from one house into the other. If one family needed some oil, they could just pass it through the window. My grandmother used to shout through her window into her neighbour's house.

The whole village lived like one big family, and people lived simply. No one had many possessions or cared much about their interior decor. Everyone sat together in the evenings, laughing and chatting, and when it was time to go to sleep everyone would say goodnight and return to their own bed in their own home. We would help each other with our work, and regularly lend and borrow things. If one person visited another village or a city, when they returned everyone in the village would come to welcome them home. It would be a shame if someone didn't come to see them when they returned. There was sympathy and empathy and a deep trust between people, a sense of solidarity.

My father used to tell me how his family would suffer when it was raining because their house was built very simply from earth and clay. The roof was not watertight, so when it rained, water would simply leak through the ceiling. This caused a lot of problems because the floors were not tiled or wooden, but were an earth surface that would quickly turn to quagmire once it got wet. When that happened, they used to take their mattresses and covers and go to sleep in their neighbour's house, which was built from concrete.

My father always sounded so happy when he retold these stories. There was a twinkle in his eye as he described how the other family's mother would make food for them all and they would eat together, play together and sleep together. It sounded like a beautiful experience, and he always described the events with such fondness, not betraying any hardship. Listening to him talk, I almost felt as though he could still smell the food cooking and see the other children running around him. It wouldn't have been extravagant or sophisticated food – maybe just some bread and something to dip it in. But simple food shared among neighbours is always more delicious than an expensive meal eaten alone.

When it was cold, they would make a *hawash* in their home to keep warm. Unlike the more modern *sobia* heaters, they would dig a small hole in the earth, then place stones around it to build a fire. They had ways of trying to get the smoke out of the house, but they didn't always work. One night, one family would burn their wood. The other people from the village would come and keep warm by their fire and they would all sit and chat, telling stories in the evening. Then the next night another family would burn their wood and the other families would come and sit with them. It was more economical for all of them to share their resources. This is how families would pass on their knowledge and wisdom, and would teach their sons and daughters how to live, through human contact. They were happy and they were rich, not because they had a lot of possessions or money, but because they shared a lot.

Gradually, as we began to have more technology, people started to separate from each other. It started to divide people. Maybe we are communicating more now with people who live further away from us, but the result is that we are communicating less with the people we are physically close to. In the old days people barely used telephones. I can still remember when there was only one phone in the whole village, in the house of *al mukhtar*, which means 'the chosen one', the chief or head of the village. If someone wanted to communicate with the village, they would call *al mukhtar*, who would then ask the people concerned to come to him. That is how information was passed on. People simply shouted from their windows and doorways to each other. Life was grinding at times, but it was genuine, and people were happy.

Now, many people spend more time on communicating via technology than they do interacting face to face, and this has been exacerbated by the COVID-19 pandemic. Additionally, social media and the internet have the ability to spread ideas and concepts very quickly, some of which are dangerous and harmful, and many of which are untrue.

Social media played an enormous part in starting, fuelling and continuing this war here in Syria. The propaganda that has been circulated globally via social media has been overwhelming, yet its consumers have no idea that it is indoctrination. It can steer an entire generation of people in one direction or another, as can any kind of media that has the power to reach such a multitude of people. It is dangerous if not used with extreme caution.

In earlier days, life was simple, and so were our relationships. You could see things, touch them and smell them, and these tangible things were guaranteed to be real. Technology has created an entire parallel world within our world, which is different from the physical world that God created. It has also created a new way of having relationships that is far removed from the original relationships created by God that have existed between humans since the beginning of creation. Through technology, we can build relationships with people through talking with them via social media, yet this person or entity with whom we think we have built a relationship may not even be real. They could simply be a persona created by someone or something with a hidden motive, or a puppet for someone else's voice, yet we see their news and believe they are real. We have seen this happen many times in the Syrian war.

This is not real living. Focusing attention and energy on these kinds of relationships can very easily take us away from real life and relationships with the people around us and from a deeper relationship with God. Satan is very clever and has used this technology to create a new world where he is in charge. We cannot stop him in that world; it is his domain. It is filled with destructive messages and lies, and it is confusing to navigate what is true and false, and who we can and can't trust. The more people become wrapped up in this world of communication, the easier it is to let go of the more natural and personal ways of communication. Through this technology people believe fake things as much as they believe real things, and it is hard to distinguish which is which. Entire belief systems that have been in place for thousands of years can be destroyed so easily.

But the responsibility doesn't lie just with the founders and providers of this technology. It lies with us as individuals. The problems come from the way we consume media. It can be used for wonderful things too: to spread messages of hope and love, calls to prayer and requests for help. Much of the support made available for us here in Syria through Samara's Aid Appeal was initiated through social media in the early days. The prayer group scattered around the UK who pray for us and our work were connected by social media back then. There are also web apps, such as the Bible in One Year, which have been helpful to me in my journey of faith.

Social media makes many good and positive things possible. But it requires a significant amount of consideration and due diligence to use it in a responsible way, with close monitoring to keep that level of usage healthy over time. Yet it is extraordinarily difficult for most to achieve this within the framework of this world today.

True Freedom and Economic Crisis

The doorbell rang. It was the milkman. I always looked forward to seeing him, but when I saw his face, I knew something was wrong. Forcing a smile, he tried to pretend everything was okay, but when he spoke it was as if there was a pain in his heart. Although he looked embarrassed, I wasn't about to let him hide his problem.

'The cows are dying.' His eyes looked distant. 'A disease has been spreading among them.'

Not only were those cows his only means for survival, but the price of beef had also quadrupled because of the overwhelming economic crash that had hit us like an explosion over the last few weeks.

'People are hungry, Doctor. They can't meet their needs.'

His situation was manageable, but for hundreds of thousands, even millions, it wasn't. Even the rich were now worried.

'Is it linked to Caesar's law?'[1] he blinked, innocently. He had no idea what that was but had heard it on the street as the reason for our massive economic struggles.

Our chronic economic collapse was a culmination of notably significant issues; nine years of violent fighting together with hard-hitting financial and trade sanctions had already devastated our previously thriving economy. The noose had been tightened now through Caesar's law, designed to choke off the last sources of oxygen that enabled our people to take any kind of breath.

The unfolding COVID-19 crisis has also had an incalculable impact on our nation, first through our own lockdown and then through the global economic impact. If that wasn't already more than any small country could contend with, we were also hit by massive and rapid price increases for food and other essential items. This stemmed from an artificially inflated black-market exchange rate, shaking confidence over traders' abilities to replace stock for what they had originally paid for it. Almost overnight, prices of many things were multiplied by five or six, and many shops simply shuttered as their owners didn't dare to sell anything. Sales of properties and land stalled for weeks, and the prices of meat and dairy sky-rocketed so high that most people would have to go without.

My mother called later that day to ask if we should give more food to the orphans and widows we were working with. She had been working at our orphans and widows outreach centre and was also worried about COVID-19. One of the fatherless children attending our outreach centre had developed a fever and was coughing, and his family also had symptoms. Our teacher running craft sessions for the children was concerned as she had asthma and was worried about catching the virus from one of the children. She was one of the widows we had supported over the last few years and had joined the team, gaining employment as well as helping invest in other vulnerable children. Our music teacher's mother had cancer, meaning she was also nervous of exposing her through her work.

Everyone felt the risk, especially while there wasn't an appropriate medical system to support the sick. With no warning, the humanitarian system in Syria stalled because of the pandemic. People were hungry.

'God,' I found myself praying, 'there is no way to prepare for this, and even responding is a struggle. Only your mercy can help or change anything.'

Two days later, my mother came down with a fever, coughing and feeling unwell. She is in the high-risk category, as she has underlying health conditions. We closed the centre, using the break in our work to replace the plumbing, which was essential. My father developed the same symptoms and we all began to pray. We could not visit them; we simply had to depend on God to be with them. I wondered whether God had not yet released me from my captivity to protect me. I was reminded of Psalm 20:7: 'Some trust in chariots and some in horses, but we trust in the name of the LORD our God.' Thank God, both of my parents recovered.

★

During my captivity, I lost the ability to track time. A minute felt like an hour or a week. My memories began to feel like dreams. The future felt like the past. I couldn't recognise whether I was living tomorrow or yesterday. Everything felt the same. It is impossible to explain how desperate I was to get out of my 'prison' and how very, very low, tired and exhausted I had become. It was like being in a dream, where time was not real.

The freedom I longed for so deeply was to simply walk out of my house and to go to places, to do ordinary things and to work. I was afraid even to walk in the street in case someone saw me, as word travels quickly. I wanted to be a doctor again, to visit my friends and my village. I missed visiting my parents in their home. I missed my grandfather – he had been asking about me for all those years. When he was very sick, I couldn't even visit him, nor could he visit me, even though we were both in the same country. I missed my street. I missed walking among people. I felt so weary of being deprived of all these normal things. My heart ached for them.

Yet I learnt that none of those things is real freedom. True freedom was not to be able to leave my jail, but to be with Jesus. The thief crucified at the side of Jesus as he was hanging on the cross realised who Jesus was: the Son of God. Yet he didn't ask Jesus to free him from the cross. Instead, he asked Jesus to free him in the next life. I don't know whether that thief was a wise man or not, but in his dying moment this genuine wisdom came to him through the Holy Spirit. It is a lesson for us all.

The body each one of us lives in can be like a jail that prevents us from living a more beautiful existence in heaven with God, in the presence of Jesus, in his true freedom of eternal life. Even when my body was eventually able to leave the small prison of my home, I escaped only to the confinement of life in this world, which is a bigger captivity than my previous jail, even though it gives more worldly freedom. There is an enigma about liberty in this world, which many don't understand until it is too late.

Living and functioning in this world, within the society humankind has created, is the greatest prison of all. It has the appearance of freedom, but mainstream society and the infrastructure that exists to keep it running is a barrier to us all, preventing us from leaving everything behind to follow Jesus completely, unconditionally and with no reservations. How many of us who identify as Christians have truly followed his challenging calling: to sell *all* our possessions and instead to follow him? Jesus said, 'If anyone comes to me and does not hate father and mother, wife and children, brothers and sisters [in comparison to the love and commitment they have to me] – yes, even their own life – such a person cannot be my disciple. And whoever does not carry their cross and follow me cannot be my disciple.'[2] What a humbling challenge!

My father experienced his own prison, which was far more restrictive than mine. Western prisons and Syrian prisons are very different experiences. Locked in a cell, two metres by one metre, in solitary confinement, he had no one at all to talk to or to ask for help, except Jesus. He learnt to depend completely and wholeheartedly on Jesus. During that six months of torment, he had what most would call 'out of body' experiences, during which he would visit heaven and meet with Jesus. They were not visions, although he has had many of those too. He described those encounters as more real than sitting and talking with me in broad daylight. He described how, in his captivity, away from the busyness, noise and routine of life, he found *true* freedom.

Perhaps this is why Jesus called us to sell everything we own, give the proceeds to the poor and follow him.[3] He knows that everything else is excess clutter that slows us down and makes us less effective if we are aiming to be like the first disciples of Jesus and the first Christian converts, who literally sold their homes and distributed the money between them so no one had less than the others. Those disciples were effective in building

God's kingdom across the globe. If we would just be willing to give up the chains that tie us down, all the things that make us feel comfortable and secure, and instead depend on a different comfort and security (that which comes only through Jesus), making his kingdom and righteousness our greatest priority,[4] how much more could we achieve through our individual lives?

I learnt the hard way to recognise my true prison in this world. I believe each of us has spiritual walls around us, created by our desires and routines that chain us to worldly things with no eternal value. It can be so difficult for us to see the real freedom Jesus promised through the tiny windows of the prisons of our lives, unless we are willing to shake off the chains of captivity that our cultures create, and which we make for ourselves. That little window is provided through Jesus, through his Holy Spirit and through the Bible. There is a complete world and existence outside the daily, repetitive routine of the lives we live. Jesus is calling us to live *his* existence, not the one of this world.

Before the war, I was unable to see the real, unshackled world of Jesus outside the routine I was so absorbed in. I was busy being a doctor, building my life, seeing friends and going to parties. Those things were a continuous distraction from the true release that I had through experiencing captivity. God used it as a correctional facility for me, where I gained an enhanced ability to recognise the things that become walls around us, things that become chains around our hearts, diverting and preventing us from being released from the bigger, invisible jail in this world. I missed that bigger jail, but what I missed more was my eternal freedom with Jesus.

From the beginning of this war, everyone tried to categorise themselves and other people into different groups. Were you with the Syrian government, or with ISIS? Were you with the Free Syrian Army, or Al Nusra, Turkey, Russia, Iran or Israel? The question was always, 'Who are you with?' I have never been with any of them. I am first and foremost a normal person living my life, then I woke up one day and discovered that everyone around me belonged to something different from the life we lived before. At the beginning it was baffling for me to understand what was happening, and why.

The easy answer is to say, 'I am for justice. I am against killing. I am against violence and corruption. I am for equality. I am for freedom. I am with the ones who are supporting the people.' But when you go deeper, you find that everyone who says they are supporting people or serving honesty or freedom is aligned with one side or the other and will tell you that everyone else in that war is wrong. If I were to say, 'I'm with God and against evil,' every one of the people in this war would say they have their own god and their own perception of evil. I needed a compass in this war to direct me and stop me falling into the traps of the devil. Everyone fighting on each side has given a justification for killing someone on the other side. The question is, 'Who, in the bigger picture of life and eternity, are you or I really, truly with?'

When you are caught up in the middle of a war, you lose the ability to see the road ahead. There are many, many deceptive roads that appear attractive at first glance but take you to the wrong place. In war, people are under immense pressure to make on-the-spot decisions about which road to take. Making these decisions quickly can mean the difference between life or death. But in their haste, many take the wrong one. They don't have time to weigh their decision carefully. Time is life.

In war, you also lose your ability to listen. There are guns, bombs and other events that make people panic and cause them to make bad choices under stress. You lose your daily routine, your judgement and your way of making sense of the world. Everything changes and becomes bizarre. The right choices suddenly don't seem so obvious. It is very easy to become disoriented.

If anyone were to ask me who I am with or which side I am on, I would say I am with Jesus. If someone were to ask if Jesus were with any of these groups fighting on the ground in Syria, I would say I don't know or care. It's not something to argue about. As long as I'm following Jesus and the call he puts on my life (which he reveals to us as we seek him) to the best of my ability, this is the only thing that is important. Jesus is the only way, and his Holy Spirit is the only compass. He is the only one we should follow and align ourselves with, no matter where his road *appears* to lead us.

When we take his road, it may seem to others that we are doing something very wrong, because it's not what everyone else is doing. Perhaps it is the opposite of what everyone else is doing, and thus others inform us that we are doing the wrong thing. When they do, we must listen to Jesus instead of listening to them, and must do what he asks. We must walk on water towards Jesus. It's more rewarding than staying in the boat where everyone else is. But we will hear many sounds around us that will distract or confuse us.

When we turn away from our old lives and welcome Jesus into our heart, we become his sheep and he becomes our shepherd. Jesus said his sheep don't respond to the voice of a stranger,[5] as only his voice gives his sheep the feeling of safety. If we are committed to Jesus but don't feel safe with the voice we hear, it's not from Jesus. If we listen to his voice, he will comfort, guide and lead us along this very difficult road, through the rocks and mountains, surrounded by wolves who want to eat us. We can trust our shepherd, as he is so committed to us that he was willing to sacrifice his life to save each one of ours. He makes us feel comfortable to follow him even if we are going to an uncomfortable place. This is how we know if we are walking the right road.

Following Jesus doesn't mean only following him in the big, obvious events, because our faith is not made deep and true just by our big decisions. It is about the details of how we live our lives. If I were to ask every Christian and non-Christian where they stand on some of the biggest moral issues (many of which are detailed in the Ten Commandments), the likelihood is that the majority of people will agree on most of them. If I were to ask someone who is not a Christian if it is it okay to kill children, they would agree that it's not. If I were to ask them whether it is okay to steal money from others, most would say no. If, however, I were to ask them whether they love Jesus, they are likely to say no, they don't know Jesus. Perhaps they think Jesus is just like any ordinary person who lived in history or even in a fantasy book.

That is the difference between us and them, the difference between Jesus' sheep and the other sheep. We follow Jesus and accept him not only in big matters but also in those that appear small or strange to others. We read the Bible and take our wisdom from him because it is higher than ours. Being a Christian is not just about following the Ten Commandments, going to church and saying we love Jesus. It is about following Jesus in *every* detail of our life, both large and small, even when it looks bizarre, crazy or countercultural. That is what makes and shapes our faith. It's our commitment to the details and the little words he feeds us every day through his Holy Spirit and the Bible.

Imagine Jesus as an actual shepherd and us as real sheep, sitting around him on the hillside. Every now and then one of us goes and tries to get some grass from a field that's further away. He'll simply say, 'No, come back, not that way!' This is how he leads us. Those little prompts in our lives and how we respond to his guidance resemble actual sheep with a caring shepherd. This is what protects us and gives us the advantage as Christians. No matter how dangerous the place we are appears to be, we are protected, cared for and nurtured by Jesus. That is how I have survived this war; although I have been surrounded by bombs and enemies, I have listened to my shepherd and followed him in every step, not caring where he takes me, because I trust him and I know his voice.

I have been questioned, undermined, by so many throughout my journey, and many have tried to deter me from doing the things I have committed myself to. People asked why I was doing the things I was doing, and many thought I was crazy for the decisions that I made. A lot of people thought I was reckless for dealing with Samara. They asked me why I was working with her when she is English. But I heard Jesus say, 'Go ahead. You should work with her.' If I hadn't been listening to the voice of Jesus in my heart, saying, 'You can accept her; she is from my side,' we wouldn't have achieved any of the great work we have done together: distributing humanitarian aid to hundreds of thousands of people in Syria and giving medical care to more than 70,000, developing an outreach centre to serve orphans and widows and opening a permanent medical centre. We are now leading up to building a permanent Christian hospital, to demonstrate the love of Jesus for everyone, and have also started farming projects to grow food for our community.

If anyone asks whether I'm supporting one government against another, I will say that isn't my business, because I'm with Jesus and I will do what he wants me to do for him. It is what Jesus asked Peter to do, when they stood face to face on the beach one morning after his resurrection. Jesus asked three times, 'Simon, son of John, do you love me?' Each time Simon Peter answered that he did, Jesus instructed, 'Feed my lambs . . . Take care of my sheep . . . Feed my sheep.'[6] We are the sheep of Jesus, and we need to feed and care for each other. Jesus repeated this again and again. That's what I will always try to do: love Jesus, and feed and care for his sheep.

I felt in my heart that when I was free, I would face that bigger jail. I felt so happy when anticipating my freedom, but in my deeper consciousness I also felt a little afraid that I would be sidetracked by distractions and taken captive again in the bigger jail of the temporal world we live in. I didn't know how I would resist and fight the diversions that will keep coming in this different kind of war. This is one of the reasons I have written this book, because I wanted to document what I have learnt in these years. In the same way, I wish I could have warned my younger self of what was to come, so I could have lived and prioritised everything differently. I also wanted to remind my future self and to show my children what I have learnt in these years. I hope it will challenge and encourage all of us and our children, as well as remind me what Jesus has taught me, in case I start to become distracted and busy in this world again in the future. I wanted to write it while I was in my physical prison, while everything was so real in my heart and so fresh in my mind.

We should never forget the purpose and final destination of our journey on this earth, in these bodies. We are just here as passengers. This is not our home and it is not our world. There are many things in this world that can end up locking us into confinement, preventing us from going to our true home with God at the end of our lives on earth.

In my captivity it was easier to focus my time talking with Jesus. But negativity easily weighed me down. It came in waves, sometimes like a tidal wave. Yet during that time, I was trained to handle the spiritual battles involved in doing God's work. It was like putting a soldier in a training camp in preparation for fighting a real war. It was a focused training camp, to help me gain the spiritual skills I needed to go back to the real spiritual battle on the front line, but with a greater understanding and ability to break out of the bigger jail with all its distractions. In spite of the challenges of being confined, I felt spiritually stronger and more focused. I still had fears for the future, but I trusted Jesus.

Reflecting back over what I have read in the Bible, I could see how others who served God had their own time in captivity – whether it be the wilderness, exile or prison – before their ministry truly took off. Even Jesus himself spent time in the wilderness, fasting and praying and being tempted by the devil, before his ministry began. Elijah is a perfect example, with his time at Kerith Ravine before a true show of God's power.[7] Daniel was taken into exile in Babylon, before showing his amazing power in his life. Joseph was falsely accused and ended up in prison for years, then went from rags and weakness to riches and power, literally overnight![8]

Life for me so far has been tough, but I feel strongly that God has a ministry and a plan for my future. This tough time has been his boot camp for me and, however hard it has been, I am now stronger and better prepared for the future. I feel honoured and humbled that God would consider me worthy of this kind of discipline and training in my life and faith. Most of all, I feel excited and ready to see what God's plans are for the future. Most people feel their life belongs to them and they choose to spend it as they wish. The truth is that our lives do not belong to us because we did not create or invent them. None of us can choose the moment we are born or the moment we die. We cannot prolong our life even for a second. It is simply a gift from God to us. We should ask God how he wants us to spend it.

Developed cultures give people the illusion that they own their own lives, and I used to have that feeling about my own life. This war and my prison have humbled and humiliated me. I no longer have the attitude of my youth towards life, that I can do everything and anything I set my mind to. Instead of thinking about what I wanted to do and achieve, I started to ask a different question: what does God want me to do, and how can I help others? We all have a big responsibility. I'm sure at the end of my life he will ask me what I did with the gift of existence he gave me. Could I really spend it all simply trying to please myself and my family?

With the financial crisis we were facing in Syria, we decided we could save the equivalent of thousands of English pounds by making the furniture we needed to develop the services at the orphans' and widows' outreach centre we had opened that year. We needed storage cupboards for each room, tables and benches for the children to sit at and for the courses we were planning for widows needing support with their livelihoods. I brought a carpenter to my workshop, and he and I worked together to make all of these things while I was in captivity.

One day, he asked why I was bothering to use solid wood and proper joinery bonds for the furniture when poor orphans and widows wouldn't know the difference between these and cheaper alternatives. I said that even if they were the poorest orphans and widows in Syria, they still deserved the best. I just felt sad that I didn't have better, more expensive wood to use. I explained to him that we were making this furniture for God and should give him our very best.

He told me he had respected me before, but respected me even more for this. A carpenter's salary in Syria is very meagre, but at the end of that working day he collected all the portable tools we had been using, took them to be serviced and paid from his own pocket. Something in him had been moved, and he realised that he, too, poor as he was, had something to give to God, and to our suffering children and sisters.

We had many disagreements over the coming weeks about how to do this work in the best, most professional way, not just using hardboard backs or gluing instead of cutting joints. He was unaccustomed to working in this way, but I had taught myself a lot from the internet and refused to cut corners. I wanted furniture that would last and would look attractive for all our projects. At the end, he stood back and admired the beautiful cupboards we had created. 'Now that is how cupboards should be made!' he said with pride.

He was baffled, too, that a cardiac surgeon could turn his hand to carpentry. Usually in Syria you don't see doctors doing any kind of manual work. God had already humbled me in this, and I now saw the potential for the money that could be saved in furnishing our outreach centre and medical centre, and then also in building a new hospital, through creating and training our own carpentry team. We began to dream about working with some of the older, fatherless boys: running carpentry workshops and teaching them how to make furniture to the same high standards we wanted to use for all our projects.

*

It was never one of my dreams in life to write a book. My thoughts and ideas are personal, made for sharing face to face. In the past, the concept of selling a book with my thoughts and ideas felt like selling my children. But over time my attitude has changed. It is no longer about me and what I want; it is about God and what he wants.

Perhaps I haven't communicated everything perfectly, as I'm not a perfect person. I make mistakes, and will continue to do so. Other people will have their own thoughts about these issues and perhaps will be able to correct me on some of these things. Maybe people will like my thoughts, or maybe they won't. But these thoughts of mine have a presence now. Before, they were like souls with no body. It is my hope that this book will give my message a body which can then take on a life of its own, just as our souls live in our physical bodies during this life.

20

Healing

As I looked around the walls of my 'prison', I felt that they had not seemed as lovely to me over the previous few years when I had felt so oppressed. The modern, well-lit design and decoration and the large indoor spaces were a beautiful blessing, as was the solar-powered air conditioning. I had designed this building years before, and had always intended to establish a medical training centre on the ground floor for my work. But now I saw even greater potential to use it for demonstrating God's kindness, through serving some of the orphans and widows in this area as well as other areas we were working in. I could see that I possessed a resource that I could give to God to use for his kingdom.

One of the most frustrating things for the Syrian people is that we lived for all those years before the war totally unaware of what was coming. We were unprepared, oblivious and naive. The burning question is, 'What would we have done differently if we had seen this coming?' How would we have prepared if we had known that the 'biggest humanitarian and refugee crisis of our time'[1] would take *half a million* of our men's, women's and children's lives? And see *five million* of our friends and relatives driven out of our country as refugees? And more than *six and a half million* of us forced from our homes, some of us many times? How would our priorities have changed if we had known that genocide and breakdown of our society were about to engulf us? We could have made preparations on a physical level, but the most important provisions we could have made (the area in which we were most unprepared and had the greatest deficit) would have been spiritual.

I want to share my experiences not to overwhelm, terrify or burden anyone with sorrow, but because I care about humanity.

I want to give people access to the spiritual lessons I have learnt the hard way in this war. I don't want anyone else or their children to suffer what we have suffered. I wish I could have known what I have learnt during this war years earlier, as I would have lived my life so differently. Yet even if I had been warned, *nothing* could have prepared me for what was to come, or the impact it would have on our hearts, our souls and our nation.

I am not a holy man sent from heaven to tell people about Jesus. Nor do I feel like a prophet sharing a message about God. I'm just a simple, normal person who trusts Jesus and tries to live his way. I am passing through life on the difficult, narrow road that Jesus talked about, like many before me and many who will come after me. I'm just an ordinary person. Maybe God wants to use my story to show one thing: that whoever we are, when we stand firm for God and his values, he will stand with us. When we leave the comfortable option and instead go back to the battle, God says, 'I will fight with you.'

It is not who *we are* that matters, it is who *he is* that matters: God and his character. I am keen to show that I am someone who has a lot of faults, but I'm sharing my story to show that I am weak, isolated and broken, yet God has been able to do something good for and through me. The devil will try to make us feel that we are useless, but God doesn't use any of us because we are good or holy. He will use us because *he* is good and holy, and because we are willing, and in doing so he can achieve results through us that we couldn't achieve ourselves.

People search for safety. Our houses, our jobs, our routines, our breakfasts or our families give a false feeling of security. Our safety nets are often our biggest obstacles to living the fullest spiritual life we can in Jesus, and prevent us from seeing his power and glory demonstrated and his kingdom established. The only real safety in this world comes through being close to Jesus, trusting him and obeying him. He is the only thing we can truly keep in our hearts which no one on this earth or in life or death can take away from us. We can lose everything else, but if we have Jesus in our heart, we have everything: all our needs and our heart's desires.

I have learnt not to build my life on anything except God. As Jesus said, the wise build their lives on his teaching and will stand firm when troubles come, but those who build their lives on things that are unstable will find them destroyed when trouble comes.[2] Before the war, we built our lives on our careers, positions and status, infrastructure, hospitals and houses. In the blink of an eye, they were gone. Many of our friends and family disappeared, died or left the country. Even a husband, wife or children can be lost in a moment. The *only* thing we can have that will last forever, and which no one can ever take from us, is God.

If we find ourselves standing on a 'mountain', leading people, giving them advice and teaching them how to live faithfully, we need to be willing to accept being taken and losing everything we have the very next day. If not, we become hypocrites. I use the word 'accept' because Jesus accepted his painful mission. One day he was teaching and preaching and the next day he was taken. When Peter tried to protect Jesus from being arrested by soldiers in the Garden of Gethsemane, Jesus told him to put his sword away. He told Peter that he could ask God to send twelve legions of angels to fight for him, but he was going out of choice, so that God's will would be fulfilled.[3] He accepted, even though he had the ability to make a different choice. He didn't choose the easy way, but chose to be obedient in his difficult mission for God. That was his life's purpose here on earth. Because Jesus saw the bigger picture and was willing to obey, humanity can have hope through his act of sacrifice.

We are all put in the same position. God calls us to experience things which, if we follow him all the way, will be difficult too. Many will walk away from those challenges and choose the pleasant, comfortable things in life instead. Others will choose to follow Jesus to some extent but will stop short of following him all the way. They will go part of the way then continue with the easy version of being a Christian: the version that

doesn't involve life-changing, life-threatening, decisions or true
sacrifice. Others will like the idea at first but will back away at
the first sign of trouble or will get distracted. There are very
few who will choose to follow Jesus to the very end, sacrificing
everything, no matter what the cost.[4]

We all have the choice, but are we willing to go through the
full experience? If anyone is forced to do something, then they
have not made a sacrifice or done anything unusual. They are
simply a victim. Simon of Cyrene was made to carry Jesus' cross
for him, but it wasn't his choice. He did it because he was made
to. I am sure Jesus was grateful that someone carried his cross
when he himself couldn't, but we don't know whether Simon
did this willingly or begrudgingly. Maybe he even complained
to Jesus as he carried it, we don't know. Those accounts in the
Gospels don't show Jesus thanking Simon or promising any
reward for doing something he was *forced* to do.

★

That day, sitting in that luxury hotel with Dr Khalifa, I had a
choice. Instead of choosing the easier road, I chose what God
asked me to do, when it was the toughest of all the options. I
believe this is what it means to follow his will, to choose the
path Jesus chose. We all have the opportunity to decide which
road to follow: the easy or the narrow? We will always be in a
position to choose. Jesus spent thirty years preparing to make
that decision, then followed through with it.

This holocaust in Syria has taught me that to be healed, I
need to reach out and touch Jesus, just like the woman who
in her shame and desperation pushed through the crowd to
simply touch Jesus' clothes.[5] She needed him, and she knew
he was her one and only hope of being healed. With all her
other options exhausted, she reached out in faith and need,
and immediately felt his healing power flow into her as he felt
his power flow out of him. She came to him, trembling and
wanting.

I don't believe anyone in this world is better positioned than that woman was. We are all in the same desperate need of healing from him. Each of our sicknesses looks different on the outside, but we are all broken on the inside. When we ask for and receive his healing power, it changes us, and we feel a fresh and urgent desire to make his priorities ours, to make his desires ours, and his hope ours. I felt his urgent desire to continue every time I looked into the eyes of a mother as I told her I couldn't give her the dead body of her child, or that I was unable to take her child to the operating room because it was full, so I couldn't stop their bleeding and her child would die.

Sometimes people would tell me that a patient I was treating was a very bad person; maybe they had committed rape or murder. Maybe they were among the people who had abused me, my family or my friends. But that person, however good or bad, is still someone's child. Their mother feels the same excruciating pain that Mary felt when she watched her precious son suffering, bleeding and dying. When I helped any mother in Syria, whatever her son had done, it felt as if I was helping the mother of Jesus. I have felt that we have lived the experience of seeing Jesus crucified, again and again, through the events in this war. Perhaps we didn't see a wooden cross, but the pain of his crucifixion has been everywhere here.

The devil has been continually torturing, degrading and nailing people to the cross in this war. The people being crucified are divided into two camps: the thieves on the left and the thieves on the right. Some people, in their suffering, have asked God to forgive them. The others have had hard hearts and have mocked, saying, 'You have no power, Jesus, you couldn't even save yourself. How can you save me?'

Jesus rose from his grave and defeated death. Everyone who believes in Jesus and follows him has defeated death too. I have been delivered from eternal death because I trust Jesus, follow him and put my life in his hands. Anyone who doesn't trust in Jesus cannot survive the biggest war of all: navigating our bodies and souls through this life to safely reach the intended destination of eternal life.

Our brokenness and poverty are obvious here in Syria, and

we are desperately aware of our need for healing and provision. But around the world, many are blind to the pandemic of spiritual brokenness and spiritual poverty that is prevalent in developed countries. People have been deceived into thinking that they can gain freedom through the very things that render them spiritually broken and spiritually poor. The accumulation of possessions and dysfunctional lifestyle choices are not things that bring real freedom, but are rather the symptoms of spiritual sickness. Equally, no government can give or withhold real freedom. Real freedom is a gift that only Jesus can give.

Every time I left to go to one of those medical points or field hospitals, I didn't know whether I would return, as the sniper-infested roads were so dangerous. I had four young children and I didn't know whether I would be there to be able to continue to take care of them. But I still chose to go. Who is prepared to live the life I lived and experience all the things I have been through in this war? Who can drive their tin can from death to life? Who can rise up from the ashes to eternal life?

Once, Samara asked me about my hope for the future. Hope is a word that means so much to me. The first thought that came to mind was my old hospital. In my memory I saw the beautiful hospital that we had created, into which I had put all my hope before it was destroyed. I cannot erase the picture from my mind of that hospital reduced to nothing more than a pile of rubble. I had invested my hope in the wrong things, even though I was already a follower of Jesus. Is my hope to go back and rebuild the hospital that was destroyed, to turn back the clock and change history, or to look to the future and build another hospital? No. I don't want to go back and rebuild that kind of hope – it is destroyed too easily. Ultimately, it's the same old worldly hope: a hope that we create ourselves, in something we have created ourselves.

I heard Jesus saying to my heart, 'Do not store up for yourselves treasures on earth, where moths and vermin destroy, and where thieves break in and steal. But store up for yourselves treasures in heaven, where moths and vermin do not destroy, and where thieves do not break in and steal. For where your treasure is, there your heart will be also.'[6]

I want my hope to be in and for something beyond this difficult life and broken world. I can't keep my treasures here. The question is, 'How is it possible to have hope beyond this life, which can be taken from us in the blink of an eye?' How can I move my treasure from this earth, which is full of thieves, killers and unhappy events? The only way to avoid storing up treasure on earth and instead to build treasures in heaven is to give *everything* to God. In my mind I needed to transfer everything I have stored up here to Jesus, in order to have my treasure in heaven. In many ways, it is similar to transferring money from one bank account to another account in a different country, where we can't use or spend the money until after we die. Once we have finished these transfers, our bank account here will be empty. If we have any remaining money in our account here, we need to keep transferring it. We need to give everything we have to Jesus.

This is exactly what the earliest converts to Christianity did. The book of Acts describes how the first Christian disciples lived, detailing how miracles, signs and wonders were part of their ministries for God. Perhaps that is the difference between the lives of many Christians today and those early Christians. Those first Christians *literally* gave up everything to follow Jesus, and in doing so they saw the glory of God poured out through their lives. I feel that every one of us needs to ask ourselves, 'What are we willing to sacrifice?' A Sunday morning? Maybe another hour or two in our week for a prayer meeting, or ten minutes each day to pray? Maybe doing something nice for the homeless or another charitable cause once a week? Did we give up our comfortable home, our daily routine, our car or our lifestyle?

Now, it is not my desire to have a new hospital. It is not my desire to have properties, because they could so easily be taken from me or destroyed. I watched everything around me being obliterated, and everything I owned being taken from me. However, if God's will for us is to build a new hospital, then I will build it, but it will not be my hope, and I will not put my hope in it. It will be a way to introduce the love of Jesus to other people.

Somehow, as life developed over the ages, humanity lost the connection between healing and God. Now people simply go to doctors and hospitals for healing instead of going to God. However, in the Bible, people went to the temple to seek God when they were sick because God has the power to heal. Jesus was a doctor who had greater success in healing people through God's power than any of the doctors of his time had in trying to treat the same people.

On some level, hospitals are now providing some of the functions that temples used to, but in those days there were people in the temple who would guide people to God. Today, in our hospitals, we find some of the most arrogant doctors, who have no faith in God and no ability to explain Jesus to those who are in the greatest need of him. These hospitals miss the most important healing that people need.

In my earlier life I tried to be a good doctor and to build a good reputation for myself. God was very generous to me. But now, I'm not concerned about those kinds of priorities or with trying to raise my status among people. I am more concerned about showing people that this life is limited, temporary, and that it really matters what we do with it, as it will end soon. People who lived thousands of years ago are all dead now, whether they had hospitals, houses, possessions or not. So why build a hospital at all? Because hospitals are important to people.

Now, I want to build a hospital that is a temple. The only way to heal a person who is broken is to start with their soul. If you only focus on their body, you offer a temporary solution to a permanent problem, whereas the healing of a soul has eternal consequences. I want to see the healing of people's souls take place while we also try to heal their bodies. No matter what we do in our hospital, every person will die in the end. Even the nurses and doctors will die, so what is the purpose of only treating the body? Although we help patients, we can't prevent their eventual physical death. Maybe we can extend their physical life for days, weeks, months or years, but we can't stop the inevitable. We can only delay it with medical treatment.

After I stopped focusing on my success as a doctor, I was able to start shifting my treasure from being those things that are present only in this life, on this earth, to the treasure we need to store up in heaven. It is my heart's desire to convert everything I have here on earth to heavenly treasure. Death cannot stop us when our treasure is in heaven. Even if someone kills our body, they cannot kill our soul,[7] which we have confidence will be with God.

It is now my mission to help the broken souls around me to find the right path in their lives, as most have few worldly possessions. In spite of their worldly poverty they can still store up abundant treasure in heaven. In fact, they have the advantage over most of the wealthy people in this world.

21

The Ark for a Flooding World

Sitting at my desk, I did my daily checks, calling the teams of
each project. Focusing on the work to rebuild our community
was my way to avoid thinking about the fact that I still wasn't
free, two months after my period of captivity had technically
ended. My sleep had been more disturbed and my patience had
worn so thin. Lately, every day had felt equal to the whole three
and a half years I had been confined. I stopped daring to hope
I would ever walk free again, to protect myself from despair and
the tedium of waiting with such uncertainty. I focused on
everything except freedom.

The policeman's number flashed on my mobile. We had
been friends since I had saved his life years before. He
had sustained multiple gunshot wounds and the team in the original hospital had said he would die, and he suffered three cardiac
arrests. I had directed each resuscitation, then at my hospital he
had made a miraculous recovery. Recently his mother had
been paralysed by a stroke and had developed pressure wounds
which had become infected.

'I want you to come and examine my mother,' he said, when I
answered.

Having recently told him I was waiting for freedom, I replied
that his mother would be the first person I would examine
when I could leave.

'You are a free man. Go!'

It seemed impossible. I barely dared to believe him, yet I
knew he was honest and that, as a policeman, he could check
every document and assess my exact situation.

I sat and thought. Should I leave the house now or finish
what I was doing first? Could I remember how to drive? Would

my car still work? Should I check with someone else first, just
to be sure my paperwork was all correct?

I was no longer in 'jail'! I felt nervous as I thought about
stepping outside the front door I had closed three and a half
years before. Having been confined to one place for so long, I
was amazed how difficult it felt to leave for the first time. Would
the world I was returning to look anything like the one I had
left? The nature of the war had changed significantly during my
imprisonment.

★

The sun was setting on the seashore. As I felt the sand between
my toes on the beach, there was a surreal quality about the
moment, as the salty sea air filled my lungs. The warm orange
sun hovered just above the horizon, casting a streak of shim-
mering light across the ripples on the water. I dipped my feet
in the cool, gentle waves, letting them lap around my ankles.

'Thank you, Jesus!' I said, as I watched the boys splashing
and laughing in the shallow water. This was the beach where
Miriam and I had held our engagement party years before.
Tonight, the beach was empty. Everyone was afraid of COVID-19
and the prices of everything were thirty times higher than they
had been that evening at our party.

My first journeys out were an enormous culture shock as I
began to visit everyone I had avoided for years. I stepped out
into the pandemic which we had first watched spreading across
the globe, and which had been escalating in Syria.

When I visited a close friend whom I had known for many
years, he threw himself on my shoulder, weeping and asking
why I had returned to this awful place. He is a professional who
studied hard and is worthy of a respectable salary. When he first
qualified in his profession, he earned around $1,500 per month,
then more over time. Now he had a senior management position,
but earned just $100 per month. His wife had a similar profes-
sional role, yet their combined salaries could no longer cover
their rent and most basic needs. In this new economic crisis, they

now struggled to feed their children, yet they are educated professionals. There are too many others suffering the same fate.

I talked with another friend, one of the best cardiac surgeons I had worked with, who described how the economy and situation in the hospitals had deteriorated to such a low, he could barely earn his daily bread. Many doctors now were so desperate they were asking their patients to pay them with food instead of money. Money had lost its value, and few could earn an acceptable salary, but their families still needed to eat. The cost of buying materials and products had rocketed, meaning ordinary people couldn't afford them. Previously we had rich and poor, but now the middle classes and those who had been financially secure, even affluent during the war, could no longer afford the absolute basics for living. The despair across the country was unfathomable. People were desperate to rebuild their lives, yet there was nothing to rebuild with, and too many were struggling even to eat.

As I drove my car between the fields to my grandfather's house, I spotted a white-haired man sitting on an old wooden chair outside his house, watching people pass by in the street. I pulled up beside him with the window down and leaned across the passenger seat. 'Do you know anyone by the name of Abu Samir?' I called.

The old man rose slowly from his seat and peered through the open window. 'What do you want him for?' he asked, staring into the car. 'I am Abu Samir.'

His eyes grew wide and his mouth fell open as he registered my face. 'Are you A? Did you really come back?' he questioned in disbelief, as I broke into a smile at seeing my grandfather for the first time in years.

'Not yet,' I replied, getting out of the car.

He walked more slowly than I remembered, and his face shone with warm affection. We hesitated for a moment as we avoided the hugs and kisses we were desperate to feel after all these years apart.

'You should come quickly,' he said seriously. 'We need your help in the hospitals.'

My aunt arrived, a widow whose only child was now in Germany. She hadn't seen her for years. My uncle came too, whose oldest son was also in Germany. His younger son, he told me, was preparing to go as well. My other uncle on that side of the family had emigrated to the US with his family years before.

My aged grandfather sat on his chair in the street, counting all the people missing from his life and his village. 'Things are difficult, A,' he said softly, wiping a tear from his dark, wrinkled face. His eyes remained watery as he described how we had lost all our young men, and wondered out loud what we could expect for the future.

As I began to travel around, assessing the damage, I heard the voice of the devil taunting me. 'Welcome back, Dr A! Do you really want to come back to this? Your people are even more miserable than before. See how they are covering their faces with masks, afraid. Look how hungry they are. No one is smiling. Their eyes stare at nothing as they walk in the street. They are just shadows.'

I felt fear. It was as if I had been shut in a time capsule, preserved for years, while the world outside had changed beyond recognition.

I could no longer hear the sound of snipers, bullets or explosions like I had before. But I could see people dying for different reasons, with hearts more despairing than before. They had lost hope. Even during the worst years of war, we would hug, kiss and smile. In this new world I had stepped into people were afraid to be near one another. Everyone knew that if they needed hospitalisation, the medical resources in Syria were too scarce. Any shortages faced in the western COVID-19 crisis were multiplied exponentially here in Syria. Our war had not diminished; it had simply mutated.

Our medical infrastructure had been completely exhausted before I retreated, but what I returned to was unbelievable. As I visited the hospitals I had had partnerships in and had worked at before, I was deeply shocked to see that none of them had anything resembling a dependable ICU – none with any of the basic standards that I could work in. The ICUs in private hospitals were mostly empty: empty of patients, staff and equipment. Not because people didn't need ICU care, but because the hospitals' abilities to provide had crumbled, along with people's trust and their ability to pay for treatment. Confirmed COVID-19 cases were sent to a small handful of government hospitals to protect the patients in other hospitals, yet they too were struggling and had to send the majority of cases home.

When I withdrew from public life, I had to leave my main ICU in the care of another doctor. I had an uncomfortable sensation in the pit of my stomach as I worked through the handover with him that he was not experienced enough, yet there was no one else. I tried to keep in contact with him, but he became unresponsive and ignored my advice. Returning now, I found less than 10 per cent of the department I had handed over to him. Staff, equipment, protocols and standards: I could barely see anything left that I had established there years before. That day there was just one patient, without even a nurse in sight! Later, a nurse appeared, but no doctor was there. I would never have accepted leaving *any* intensive care patient alone, or even with a nurse and no doctor.

As I assessed the work that would be needed to revive that one department, I was overwhelmed by the enormity of the many tasks ahead, further complicated by the massive restrictions the COVID-19 crisis had brought.

As I started calling ICU doctors around the city, I felt their paralysis and desolation. No one knew what to do. 'We are ready, Doctor,' they said to me. 'Just tell us what to do.'

They, too, were afraid of getting sick. Doctors we all knew had already died from COVID-19, and those remaining knew that our medical system was too damaged to meet their needs if they or their families were to become sick.

I recalled sitting in a disaster planning meeting in Damascus, back in 2010. Influential people inside and outside Syria were there to prepare for the eventuality of a significant earthquake. The Minister of Health, Minister of Humanitarian Aid, Minister of Defence, Minister of Police, representatives of the WHO, Red Crescent and other large NGOs were gathered in this high-profile location as waiters brought us refreshments. I was there as a civilian consultant.

Syria sits on a fault line and has suffered a major earthquake every 250 years, devastating huge areas. We were due another and were planning how to protect people and respond to such a disaster. I mapped out places in each city that ambulances couldn't access: residential areas chaotically built by poor people who didn't follow building regulations. The roads were too narrow and illogically laid out, making ambulance access impossible. Many buildings had deep caverns underneath, making them unstable and dangerous. A major earthquake would bury the inhabitants in these areas, meaning rescue and medical workers would be unable to reach them. The only solution was to relocate as many of the inhabitants as possible and rebuild the substandard housing.

The head of one of the NGOs replied that it was impossible as it would involve evacuating too many people. 'Those issues cannot be corrected,' he said.

Looking him in the eye, I replied, 'Buying extra ambulances will not help if they cannot reach the areas where they are needed. We are waiting, then, for an earthquake to correct these problems.'

That day, I felt Jesus say, 'You should prepare, A; the flood is coming.'

The ark is a long-term vision, a vehicle through which a community can survive a 'flood' or disaster so devastating that it could obliterate all life not protected within it. Little by little, over these years, our ark has been growing and taking shape.

As well as the obvious humanitarian help needed to distribute food and clothes and to meet people's medical needs, our goal is to help people rebuild their lives with livelihoods and businesses to support themselves and their families. We have opened an outreach centre for orphans and widows, providing training to help with livelihoods, and a food bank for emergencies. We are refurbishing another building in which we are about to open a permanent medical centre to provide specialist services that many hospitals are struggling to provide. This will serve as the first phase towards building a new hospital, a new Christian hospital to demonstrate God's love and mercy to our whole community, whose plans have been drawn up and approved for construction. We are also undertaking a new initiative to grow essential foods needed to survive. The long-term vision goes further still, with a school and more.

While we were searching for land to farm staple foods, one night I had a dream. In it, I bought a piece of land, the purchase of which had gone so smoothly that I was surprised. Shortly after this dream, we were offered a piece of land in an area that generations before had been owned by Christian farmers. One day, armed extremists had taken the land by force and murdered the original occupants. When we were offered a piece of fertile land there with a well, for a very low price, land that hadn't been farmed in years, we felt that God was reclaiming it for his work.

The buying process dragged because of the economic crisis, and I became frustrated by how long it was taking. I felt ready to cancel, thinking we were being messed around, and called my lawyer. He was a close family friend and neighbour, and he encouraged me to wait a little longer. The night before, he had also had a dream about this piece of land, that once we began to farm it, it became very fertile, with tall crops producing far more than anyone had expected. I recognised that the devil has ways of trying to undermine the work we do for God, one of which is by destabilising relationships, so I waited for the purchase to be completed.

The most essential part of the ark is to nurture a church. Not a structure with walls where people meet every week, but a body, a community of believers who love and serve Jesus and everything he stands for, who pray for and support one another. That is the true meaning of a church. My new priority is to show people a different reality. Our reality since the war began had been thoroughly exhausted. We all needed a revolutionary solution to our problems, far more than anything our community had so far. We needed to pump fresh, oxygen-ated blood into this system. People needed something different in order to start thriving. It's like adding yeast to ordinary flour, which on its own is inedible; the yeast turns it into fresh bread that is delicious and nutritious. People's hearts needed restoration.

We can't create a new reality for everyone, but if we do it for a few, then they can support others, and this new reality can grow. I feel as though even the people helping us from outside Syria have become weaker and more vulnerable. COVID-19 has shifted reality for most people on this planet. As I have watched the global situation deteriorating, my eyes have opened and I have seen that the concept of the ark is not limited to Syria. The whole world is entering a period of increased turmoil. Every country and community needs its own ark to survive the future. The concept is for everyone who shares the same vision as us, and the same love for Jesus and his teaching.

As I drove back from the hospitals I had just visited, the volume of work needed for each one of our projects was on my mind. Nothing was functioning in Syria. The country had already been through lockdown at the beginning of the COVID-19 emergency, but now the government was allowing people to work freely, as the alternative was that more people would die from poverty-related issues if they couldn't work than they would from COVID-19. But people were so fearful that they were restricting their own activities. The country had slowed to an unofficial pause and it was hard to find people willing to work or even to meet, even though I was ready.

As I drove through the city, I saw the gaping hole where my dream hospital had stood. I drove past my old house and my old school, remembering the old Dr A. My chest felt tight. I left the city and drove along the highway, seeing more devasted remnants of buildings.

The phone rang. It was Samara. 'Have you seen the news?' An explosion the size of a nuclear bomb had just decimated the port of Beirut and surrounding areas. 'It was huge, A, bigger than any of the bombs in Syria.'

My stomach felt tight as I pictured the dead bodies, blood on the ground, the destroyed hospitals. I could almost hear the crying, terrified children and their injured mothers. As we talked, our hearts were resolute. The ark was our priority.

We need to keep our fires burning, and to use sparks from our own fires to keep others burning. Today I am strong and maybe you are weak, so I can help put fuel on your fire or reignite it when it goes out. But perhaps tomorrow you will be strong when I am feeling weak, and your spark will help relight my flame. This way we keep each other sustained and burning brighter and stronger. On Palm Sunday in Syria we each take a candle in our churches and make a circle. Sometimes a gust of wind or a sudden movement might extinguish some people's flames. But they can simply turn to their neighbour, whose candle is still burning, to help them relight their flame. This is how we need to help one another.

My feeling now is that this war has spread, and the damage we have sustained in Syria is seeping out into the world. Maybe not by guns and bombs, but by other weapons: COVID-19, economic crisis, massive global tensions between nations, racial tensions and other religious, social and ideological tensions. In the developed world, people are losing their businesses, jobs and homes, not because of rockets or fighting but because they can't cover their costs. Watching these events unfolding around the world makes the reality here in Syria even darker. The tidy-looking lives our people were watching outside Syria, which many were dreaming of, suddenly don't look as tidy.

We are waiting, preparing for the next big explosion, the next stage of the flood. We don't know what it will look like or when it will come, but we know we need to be prepared. We are focused on establishing the ark to protect and preserve our community in Syria, and to resource and restart the next generation. We are aiming to supply our needs and continue this work of mercy, compassion and preservation. We are building it day by day, and the vision for it grows as we build it.

As I was driving into the city one morning for meetings about the hospital, medical centre, farming projects and outreach centre, the police suddenly stopped the traffic from every direction at a junction where five or six roads meet. It wasn't obvious why, so with all the other cars I slowed to a stop, but a policeman singled my car out, telling me to continue. There was nothing different about me, so I stopped with the other cars, as the lights were red. The policeman approached my car, leaned in and told me to go. I asked why, as no one else had been allowed to move. He replied that he just felt I was someone he should allow to pass. Maybe he knew I was a doctor, as we were always given priority. I handed him my ID card.

'No, I don't care about that,' he said. 'I just felt in my heart that there was something about you, and you should pass.'

Leaving all the other cars behind, I drove off, feeling that this was a tiny sign that God will open the path ahead of me to achieve everything he has put in my heart, to serve his kingdom and people.

I drove to the plasterboard factory to negotiate the best price for the walls we were buying for the medical centre. Plasterboard is not yet a common finish in Syria, but I had calculated that it would save money and give a nicer finish than concrete. When I walked in, I realised it wasn't the plasterboard factory, but I was intrigued as it was selling wall panels. It was making PVC panels, which could be manufactured to the exact lengths we wanted, saving time on installation and negating the need for decorating. They would also give a superior finish for a medical environment as they are easier to clean and sanitise than plaster. The factory offered a significant discount and confirmed it would be cheaper and quicker to install, with a more hygienic result. My 'wrong turn' was in fact a huge blessing, which would also help with our new hospital once we started building.

The medical centre building had been fraught with many challenges over the months, and every day seemed to bring a new problem or a reason why the tradesman couldn't do the work. I was increasingly frustrated by people's lack of urgency and the complications we were facing. During this period, there was a terrorist attack on a gas pipeline which was supplying fuel to the power stations producing electricity for Syria. Suddenly, most of the country was suffering electricity outages, and the PVC factory couldn't supply the panels when they had agreed as they didn't have the electricity to manufacture them.

Samara asked our prayer supporters to pray and fast with her as the problems and delays were escalating daily. Lots of our supporters took our prayer requests to their churches and prayer groups, and we could visibly see and tangibly feel the dynamics improving each day. Once the factory began producing again, however, we soon faced another problem.

We had suffered fuel crisis after fuel crisis during the war because of the sanctions, but the reduced electricity supply from the pipeline explosion exacerbated the shortages. We would queue for an hour to buy petrol, and sometimes I would arrive at the pump only to be told they had run out. People abandoned their cars in queues at fuel stations that had no petrol, and many of those cars' petrol tanks were completely empty. The queues tailed back for kilometres. There were queues like this at every fuel station across Syria.

The only way to continue without electricity was to run a generator, which needed fuel. The large generator I had put there, capable of supplying all the needs of the centre, wasn't cost-effective to use for cutting the metal pieces needed to build the frames for the PVC panels. Not only was it expensive to run, it was also wasteful, given how difficult it was to source fuel. It was especially frustrating as I had a smaller machine operated by solar power which would have been perfect for this job, but it had broken more than a year before.

At the time, I had spent weeks trying to source the spare parts to fix the machine, but they could not be found anywhere in Syria. I had contacted suppliers in every city, but none could help. One supplier suggested using a different part to replace one of the missing parts, but it didn't work. Trying to source

spare parts outside Syria can become more expensive than
replacing the whole machine, so I eventually left it as I had
already spent so much time trying to fix it.

On the day we were trying to work out what to do about
the generator, the carpenter, who had been making furniture
for our new centres, came to me with some parts in his hands
which he had just found in the drill bag while tidying the
workshop. 'Aren't these the parts needed for the broken machine?'
he asked.

'It's impossible,' I replied despondently, as I had spent weeks
the year before searching for them and had been unable to
find them anywhere in the country. They certainly wouldn't
have been in the bag for the drill we had been using every
day! It had been empty, except for the drill, when we had
used it the day before. No one else had used my carpentry
workshop except me and the carpenter, who was a poor man
with very limited resources and who hadn't even known we
wanted those parts.

I eyed the parts in his hands, as they did look remarkably
like the ones I had searched for so extensively the previous
year. To humour him, I took them and walked to the broken
machine. We both stared with intense concentration as I
attempted to fit them to the broken machine. Not only were
they a perfect fit, but the machine sprang into life once I
flicked the switch. Neither of us could believe our eyes and
ears! We laughed with the excitement of children with a new
toy as we started trying the machine out, watching it cut
everything we put into it.

I had searched the country to find those elusive parts and had
not been able to get them anywhere. To suddenly find them in
a bag we were using daily, where they hadn't been before, *on
the day* we needed them most, was astounding. What an amazing
and mysterious gift they were! God in his generosity had provided
what we needed when we were at our most desperate. We
couldn't explain how it happened, but I felt so encouraged. The
recent months had been tough and exhausting, and this was a
massive boost that lifted my spirits as I continued working.

When I was first introduced to Samara, I told her I didn't want any money or aid; the only thing I wanted her to do was to pray for me, and for all of us here. The power of prayer is far greater than the power of money, especially in a place like Syria. You can have all the money you want, but it can't buy you the people you need with the attitude you desire or the results you want. Only prayer can achieve that, and we desperately need the prayers of faithful supporters: people who pray with sincerity from the deepest parts of their hearts and souls.

A day or two later I was struggling with the air-conditioning for our medical and outreach centres. We had agreed a price for the units and accessories, but the prices quoted for installation were too high. The supplier gave me the number of a man in the same city as our centres. When I called, he didn't want to budge from the 25,000 Syrian pounds per unit I had been quoted, and we needed twenty-seven units to be installed.

As we were talking, I felt the sound of the Holy Spirit in my heart. 'I feel I know you,' I suddenly found myself saying to him. I couldn't have said why.

'How do you know me?' He sounded a little bored.

'I feel that you are my neighbour,' I said, for some inexplicable reason.

He seemed more amused now, asking where I lived.

I found myself saying the area where I *used* to live, from which my family and I had been forced out nearly ten years before.

'Which building?' he asked, now focused.

I told him the building, and he asked which floor.

'The fourth floor,' I replied.

'No way! I live on the second floor, but I have only recently moved in.'

I explained that I hadn't lived there for years but still owned the empty property.

He paused before saying, 'Then we can't have met there. How can you know me or know that I live there when you haven't lived there for years?'

Somehow, I just had a sense in my heart. I felt the Holy Spirit put the right words into my mouth. 'So, we are neighbours!' I smiled at the end of the phone. 'Now are you willing to help me with the price for installation?'

He considered my question for a second before telling me to name my price, saying he would do it for whatever I wanted.

A week later, I was struggling to find a reliable team for our farming projects. Time was running out to ensure the produce didn't spoil in the fields. Having finally found a group of twelve workers, I received a devastating call on the morning they were due to start. The day before, they had gone to clean their old house, in a post-siege area, and they had been planning to return. When the siege was broken, the jihadists had riddled many of the homes with landmines and explosive traps before they were evacuated. Although the army try to clear these areas of unexploded devices before civilians return, sometimes a couple are missed. One of the workers was killed by a landmine that had been planted in his home. With a very heavy heart, I went with my own family to harvest the produce myself.

★

The work now, and that which lies ahead, is enormous and challenging. Without the miraculous answers to prayer that God so graciously gives us in our testing moments, which encourage and lift our spirits on this difficult path, we might not have the strength to continue. But through the love, support and prayers of many faithful hearts, in Syria, in the UK and around the world, we are certain that God will provide everything we need, at exactly the right time, through the right people.

This isn't the end of our story: it has barely started. There is still much to be lived and to be done, and more to be written. We need to walk together now, side by side, hand in hand, carrying our candles and lighting new ones as we walk. We need to light as many candles as we can, to illuminate the darkness in this fractured world. We need to build beacons to guide the way for each other, so that should my brother's or my children's candles ever grow dim, your child's candle or my neighbour's candle will be there, ready to relight them.

As we survey our damaged cities and villages, we are searching the rubble for survivors, ready to take them by the hand, encourage them, pull them up and help them to rise up from the ashes, from death to life, from this life to the next.

Endnotes

Foreword

1 'Dr A' is a somewhat unimaginative pseudonym that we began using at the start of our working relationship to enable supporters to pray for him and understand the challenges faced in Syria, without compromising his safety.
2 Intensive care unit.
3 Matthew 20:20–8.

Introduction

1 Quoted in a press release from the United Nations, 15 March 2016. https://www.unhcr.org/news/press/2016/3/56e6e3249/syria-conflict-5-years-biggest-refugee-displacement-crisis-time-demands.html (accessed 21 October 2020).

Chapter 1: The Carrot and the Stick

1 Matthew 10:16.

Chapter 2: Early Years in the Promised Land

1 Matthew 10:28.

Chapter 3: Growing up in Syria as a Christian

1 A loose-fitting, full-length robe.
2 A red-and-white checked head covering used by certain Arab and Bedouin groups.
3 A thin black rope wrapped around the head to secure the headdress.

Chapter 5: Becoming a Doctor

1 Medical students are under the authority of the Ministry of Health, so any pathway deviating from the standard pathway needs special permission from the Health Minister.
2 Cardiopulmonary resuscitation.
3 The insertion of a tube into an unconscious patient's body to enable them to breathe.
4 At this point I was still classed as being in training, as a newly qualified doctor completing my residency, therefore this commercial company could not deal with me directly without permission from the Health Minister.
5 Azrael is the name used for the angel of death in Judaic, Syrian, Aramaic and Islamic culture. He is understood to have Hebrew origins.
6 Critical care comprises emergency and intensive care services for people with life-threatening injuries and illnesses.

Chapter 6: Fleeing Back to Syria, Early in the Conflict

1 Luke 22:42.
2 A temporary hospital that treats casualties in hard-to-reach, dangerous or strategic areas.

Chapter 7: Losing It All

1 The name of a ruling system under Islam dating back to Mohammed.

Chapter 8: A Cup of Tea and a Baptism of Fire, During the War

1 Red tea is a very popular drink in Syria, usually boiled up with cinnamon and a lot of sugar and taken without milk.
2 Luke 10:19.

Chapter 10: Fighting for Our Inheritance

1 Matthew 5:17.
2 Matthew 6:19–21.
3 Matthew 21:13.
4 Also known as a central line, this is a thin tube placed into a large vein.
5 A thin catheter inserted into an artery.
6 Zechariah 4:6.

Chapter 11: A Broken Cry for Help

1 Matthew 14:30.
2 Matthew 7:15
3 Matthew 7:20.

Chapter 12: Renewed Faith and a New Vision for a Church

1 Electrocardiogram, which records the heart's rhythm, rate and electrical activity.
2 John 2:1–12.
3 John 8:7.
4 Matthew 16:18.
5 Mark 6:5–6.
6 Matthew 7:3–5.
7 Matthew 26:39.
8 John 14:23.
9 John 14:26.

Chapter 13: A Narrow Escape and a New Trust

1 An open-air courtyard in the centre of a traditionally built home in Syria, often with plants and trees.
2 2 Corinthians 12:9.
3 Proverbs 3:3–6.

Chapter 14: Breaking Down Idols

1 Matthew 19:16–26; Mark 10:17–31; Luke 18:18–27.

Chapter 15: The Milkman, the Carpenter,
the Fisherman and the Thief

1 Cream.
2 Genesis 3:19.
3 John 14:6.
4 See Matthew 16:24–6.
5 See John 12:24.
6 This applies to biological children, adopted or fostered children,
   and even those with whom we have contact in day-to-day life.
7 John 18:36.
8 2 Corinthians 12:9–11.
9 Matthew 26:35.
10 Luke 23:39–43.
11 Matthew 10:33.

Chapter 16: Praying and Worshipping in Spirit and in Truth

1 Matthew 11:25.
2 A free Bible commentary app with readings by Nicky and
   Pippa Gumbel from Holy Trinity Brompton in London.
3 John 14:26 (ESV).
4 Matthew 4:4.

Chapter 17: Lessons in Forgiveness

1 Matthew 5:40–1.

Chapter 18: The War Against God – Being Prepared

1 See Galatians 5:22–3.
2 See Psalm 11:5; Zechariah 13:9; James 1:2–3, 12; Deuteronomy
   8:2–3; Exodus 16:4; 1 Peter 1:7; Job 7:17–18; 23:10; Malachi 3:3.

3 Luke 18:31–3; Mark 8:31–9; Matthew 16:21.

4 John 15:18–25.

5 Luke 14:25–7; Matthew 10:37–8.

6 Matthew 27:32–3.

7 John 14:6.

8 Matthew 21:18–19.

9 John 4:1–26.

10 Matthew 21:1–11.

Chapter 19: True Freedom and Economic Crisis

1 The Caesar Syria Civilian Protection Act (Caesar's law) is United States legislation that restricts governments and entities around the world from dealing with the Syrian government. It imposes heavy penalties on entities supplying fuel, helping to rebuild or providing other services needed for the country to function. This law, however, affects anyone outside Syria attempting to deal with anyone inside Syria, and has a significant negative impact on every citizen in Syria.

2 Luke 14:26–7.

3 Luke 18:22.

4 Matthew 6:33.

5 John 10:3–5.

6 John 21:15–17.

7 1 Kings 17–18.

8 Genesis 39–41.

Chapter 20: Healing

1 Filippo Grandi, cited in 'Syria conflict at 5 years: the biggest refugee and displacement crisis of our time demands a huge surge in solidarity', UNHCR, 15 March 2016, https://www.unhcr.org/news/press/2016/3/56e6e3249/syria-conflict-5-years-biggest-refugee-displacement-crisis-time-demands.html (accessed 21 October 2020).

2 Matthew 7:24–7.

3 John 18:10–11; Matthew 26:52–4.

4 Matthew 13.
5 Luke 8:43–8.
6 Matthew 6:19–21.
7 Matthew 10:28.

Read Samara's story in

REBUILDING THE RUINS

Following God's call to serve Syria

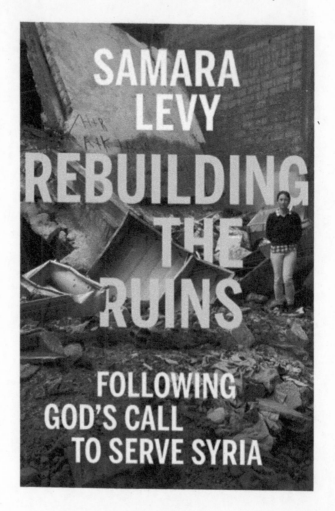

978 1 529 39077 3 | £16.99 | Hardback

C000003645

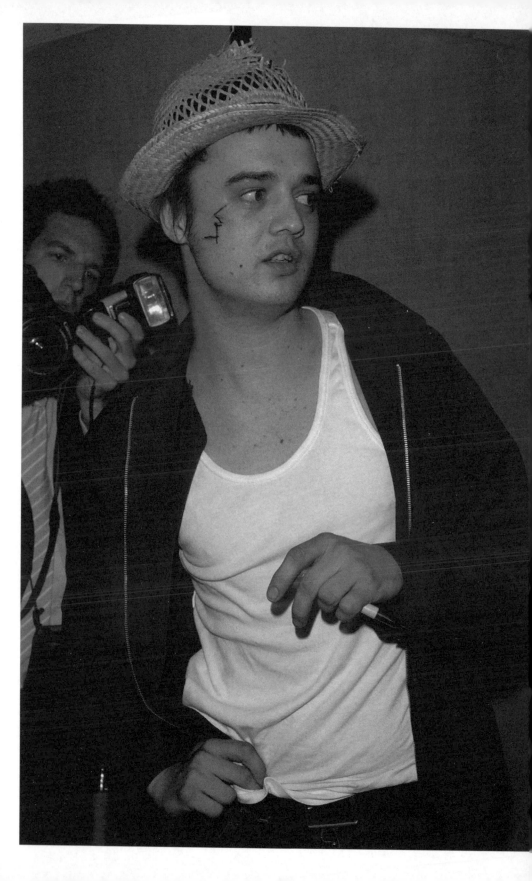

CONTENTS

PETE DOHERTY *Talking*

When literary critic Clive James, 65, told a theatre audience of greying 50-somethings that Pete Doherty, 26, had to "get in touch with his inner adult" – and the audience laughed in recognition – it was clear that the former Libertines singer had transcended the pop market and graduated to a wider stage. Certainly, the tabloid-reading section of the British public had received its fill of Doherty-related news over the course of 2004 and 2005. But that coverage was rarely thanks to his musical exploits – it was his status as boyfriend of top model Kate Moss and his occasional shambolic public performances they zeroed in on.

Introduction

The defining moment came when, in July 2005, he made a cameo appearance during Elton John's mini-set at Bob Geldof's Live 8 concert. Dressed in quasi-military dress uniform a la *Sgt Pepper* – coincidentally, the song that opened the show courtesy of Paul McCartney and U2 – he shambled through a version of T Rex's 'Children Of The Revolution' that was arguably the musical low point of the event. Yet his four minutes in the spotlight generated almost as many column inches the following week as the once-only, bill-topping reunion of four feuding middle-aged paunch-rockers who once called themselves Pink Floyd. Had he remained a member of the Libertines, the band he formed with songwriter and sometime soulmate Carl Barat, the best he could have hoped for was a spot down-bill between Keane and Stereophonics. Yet the music he made with Barat and bandmates remains the most convincing so far of his short career. While some critics wrote them off as an ersatz Clash (encouraged by the presence of that band's guitarist Mick Jones, in the producer's chair), there were signs that they had the talent to blow the inoffensive likes of Keane and Coldplay out of the water with a musical Molotov cocktail of incendiary melody and incisive lyrics.

Signed by the legendary indie label Rough Trade at the end of 2001, the Libertines made an immediate mark the following year when their debut single, the swearword-strewn 'What A Waster', received a blanket radio ban. But the word was on the street, and the presence of producer Bernard Butler, lately of Suede, helped them make the cover of *New Musical Express* in record time. They'd jettison Butler for Mick Jones, an even more iconic figure and a fellow supporter of Doherty's beloved Queens Park Rangers football team.

The first Libertines album, Up *The Bracket*, elbowed its way into the public's consciousness in the late autumn of 2002, and provoked comparisons with Blur's similarly ill-mannered arrival exactly a decade earlier. "Genuine talent of indisputable class" purred *Mojo* magazine... though the UK dates that promoted the release were described as "the worst drug-fuelled debauchery (I'd seen) in 22 years" by a road manager who left the band's employ at the end of it and – a recurring theme – spilled the beans to the press.

INTRODUCTION

Pete took his first spell of French leave in early 2003, exiting the band bus at King's Cross and going missing, assumed on a quest for drugs. But by the time second album *The Libertines* had been released in August 2004 – an immediate chart-topper, compared with its predecessor's number 35 peak – the bus had moved on and cut one half of their singing and songwriting talent adrift in a very public act of tough love. At the time of writing (late 2005), he had yet to mend those fences.

Freed for better or worse from Barat's influence, Doherty produced an autobiographical album in the form of 2005's *Down In Albion* released under the band name Babyshambles. There was certainly much to write and sing about. Jailed for breaking into Barat's flat, arrested while on tour for drug possession, seeing his supermodel girlfriend shopped to the tabloids for cocaine abuse, failing to show at a number of gigs for a number of stated reasons... After the previously mentioned Live 8 performance, Pete even found himself lampooned by the Little Britain comics on the cover of *New Musical Express* where once he'd stood as a Libertine.

There were as many convinced that Doherty was a likely saviour of British music as there were those who believed he was one step from a James Dean-like martyrdom. But as Clive James' audience appreciated, like him or loathe him, no-one could ignore Pete Doherty. Child of the revolution or misguided junkie? Read his words and decide for yourself.

Growing Up

"I had a crush on one of my teachers at school. I was about eight and she took advantage of it actually. It's a bit dark, really. She stole my innocence. She taught me to read and write, amongst other things! In fact that's probably the most rock 'n' roll thing I've ever done, snogging my science teacher when I was eight!"

PETE (2002)

"(Dad) was a grafter, really. After 36 years he's managed to climb through the ranks from Private Doherty to Major Doherty. But he's still like a soldier's man. I idolised him as a kid. I've got good memories of him taking me to football. He took me to Queens Park Rangers, all over the place." PETE (2005)

"The British army is a very masculine environment. It was a bit of a shock to my dad to get a son who immersed himself in books, and flowers and petals." PETE (2005)

"The only life I knew was moving on, changing schools. Rootless? Particularly from 13 to 16 I was pretty much alone, living dreams, kicking footballs against walls all day long. There was no nest to fly but wandering was my nature. I was a fanatical journeyman – devoured literature, lived inside books and so on." PETE (2005)

"I think I took a couple of bad blows to the head, and ever since I've suffered bad hallucinations from an early age." PETE (2005)

PETE DOHERTY *Talking*

"My Dad told me I'd broken my Mum's heart. He said I represented everything he hated about humanity: a liar, a thief and a junkie. That really got to me. But after five minutes – five days, maybe – I cut myself off from him completely. We hadn't spoken for years anyway." **PETE (2004)**

Describing the demons in his head:

"Digits in the face. Horrible. I'm shivering now, thinking about it. It like distorts your relationship with the walls. Colours and numbers crawling up in your skin, and stretching you and crushing you. They're the things that were haunting me since I was a kid. Hallucinations or something. Long before I took drugs. I didn't take drugs till I was quite old. I used to get nightmares. Christmas nightmare, I used to call it. Not a nice feeling."

PETE (2005)

"(My father)'s disowned me. He's not having any of it." **PETE (2005)**

"I used to steal Django Reinhardt records from the local library when I lived in Finsbury Park." PETE (2005)

"The idea of being on stage playing guitar just never seemed possible. I was never a bedroom guitarist. I learned to play on the kerb, while trying to chat up birds, eating bad speed." **PETE (2005)**

"I was working in a bar, selling drugs, working on a building site. Writing poetry in the graveyard shift at the Kings Head."

PETE (2005)

"I never had guitar lessons but I used to learn a lot from other people, just sit and watch them play." **PETE (2005)**

"(Dad) was away a lot... he was in the Gulf and Bosnia." PETE (2005)

"My Mum would probably want me to be, I don't know, on a desert island wrapped up in cotton wool. She says she blames the parents." **PETE (2005)**

"When I was a little kid I chewed the vacuum cleaner cable. That's why I've got this grey hair. I don't remember things cos of what happened then and subsequent hospitalisations and shit. Between the ages of two and 11 is a blank." PETE (2005)

"The fascination for London did extend to Liverpool as well, spending summers up there with my Nan.**" PETE (2005)**

"It was weird, I was on the dole and I got to go to Russia to do this performance poetry thing, at their millennium festival. You know when you go to the Job Centre, and they look on the computer for relevant employment. Cos I was quite happy claiming the dole money, I said 'poet', knowing they'd be nothing for me. And he tapped it in and went, 'Oh, I think we're in luck'." PETE (2005)

"I think my Mum's ambition for me would probably have been to be someone like Fred Astaire or Ginger Rogers. I was dressing up in Brownie uniforms when I was young. I went pretending to be my sister's cousin – I got the uniform and everything.**" PETE (2005)**

"I fell in love with a girl called Emma Frogg with two g's. I was in Liverpool and I used to play football with her all day – she was wicked but she had no teeth." PETE (2002)

"When I was 12 years old I was coming home from a school disco, a real innocent school disco, drinking lemonade. And when I got in, (Dad) followed me into the kitchen and I was drinking water really fast because I was so thirsty. And he said, 'You've been drinking.' And I literally didn't even know what he meant. I said, 'Yeah, I'm drinking water.' And he said, 'You've been drinking, haven't you?' And I was completely paralysed, completely in awe, and I started crying. And he stands me in the middle of the room and tells me to walk in a straight line. And I can't.**" PETE (2005)**

GROWING UP

Family Matters

"It's bizarre – I look at his body and wonder where did my little boy go? He's not my Pete – my son wouldn't do anything like taking drugs." MUM – JACQUELINE DOHERTY (2004)

"I don't fear death for him. At least he wouldn't be in this living heroin hell he is now. I'll always be there for my son, but he's broken my heart." **JACQUELINE DOHERTY (2004)**

"(Sister Amy Jo) is great. She respects me and understands me better than anyone. She knows that a lot of things reported about me are exaggerated. She's very protective of me." PETE (2002)

"Between me, Banny (Poostchi, former Libertines manager) and Pete's sister Amy, we called his Mum over and I drove her to that little hotel in Paddington where he always stays. We'd slowly been trying to talk him round into getting some sort of treatment, which he seemed to be going for – that was two weeks before I was due to have our baby." **EX-PARTNER LISA MOORISH (2005)**

"I'm more terrified for others – my mum and friends who are worrying themselves over me. Sometimes I'm convinced I do want to be free from the drugs – but I don't feel a lot of people's worries justify it. I know people who take more drugs than me and they're still here." PETE (2004)

"I am his biggest fan and watch him everywhere. He's absolutely top class but it's a real shame he's living with that bird (Dot Allison) these days. She's definitely not the best influence on him." **UNCLE PHIL (2004)**

"I nearly lost everything – my parents, my son, my life. Something Mick Jones told me, it's about self-control. You can't play Russian roulette with yourself. With needles. Stop all that." PETE (2005)

"I'm well into my drugs and music, and that, but – then, at 15 – I wasn't... I had no interest in it. I was from a working-class family, but not a working-class family that was into drugs. Well, apart from the Liverpool side of them." **PETE (2002)**

"Peter called me after he walked out of the Priory to tell me he was on his way to Thailand, I hoped the Thai clinic could help him, but again it was for all the wrong reasons – he was trying to please me." JACQUELINE DOHERTY (2004)

On being in Pentonville Prison:

"I'm determined to stay clean. Six days without heroin hasn't been as bad as I expected. I've been through the worst of the detox and I want to prove to my mum above anybody else I can do this. I also need to stay clean for the sake of my band mates and all my fans." **PETE (2005)**

"Pete told me they are still very much an item and in love. He is just sex, drugs and rock 'n' roll, that's why Kate (Moss) likes him." UNCLE PHIL (2004)

"Maybe it's better if they (the Libertines) go their separate ways and get on with their lives. There is too much stigma surrounding the Libertines, Pete and drugs. It would be good if he had a clean break and started again." **JACQUELINE DOHERTY (2004)**

FAMILY MATTERS

Pete & Carl

❝I liked (Pete's) drive and persistence. I was secretly envious of some of his character and I think he must have been of mine.❞

CARL (2004)

❝Carl is a lot less confident about his own ability sometimes, and also a lot more private about his ideas.❞ PETE (2005)

❝I went to Brunel (University, West London) to study acting. University disappointed me. But there was one girl who saved me. She lived in the same residence block as me. That was Pete's sister. Pete was a year younger, he was still in their hometown, in Nuneaton near Coventry. But he was into coming to London. She'd go home for family things and tell him little stories about how great I was. She thought we were quite like-minded.❞

CARL (2004)

❝We didn't really get on. But I was fascinated by ideas he had about himself and the country. I'd never met anyone like him. It was riveting. Despite everything, you knew there was goodness there. Something to believe in. Something which is good, pure and untainted by anything.❞ PETE (2003)

❝Pete neglected to mention I'd been to see him on consecutive days in the Priory. He wants to be a victim sometimes.❞ CARL (2004)

❝I remember once Carl giving a grand and a half away to a tramp in Brick Lane. I gave 800 quid to a tramp on the Charing Cross Road.❞ PETE (2005)

"Pete's helped me with my demons in the past, and I'd love to help him with his. But he has to let me in. It breaks my heart, all this, every day. Breaks my heart." CARL (2004)

"Carl says that I'm the only one he can actually discuss ideas with. He often resents it when I write songs with other people – like a lot." PETE (2005)

"I used to drink too much and come in pissed all the time, and would wind Pete up cos he was in the house sober." CARL (2004)

CARL BARAT

"Carl has his moments when he's really enthusiastic, really wants to get things done – but putting them in practice?" PETE (2005)

"We were still living in this skanky little basement, absolutely hated by the people who lived above. Even the woodshed had been rented out. Our ambition was not to be in the same position in 30 years' time. Our mission was to just get paid for doing music. We held some of the best parties Camden has ever known." CARL (2005)

"He (Carl) became a bit disillusioned with me and the path I was taking. He wasn't staying in tune to what we'd always believed in. We couldn't get on at all, couldn't be in each other's company without bickering." PETE (2005)

"Pete was into Chas 'n' Dave, Lindisfarne and the Smiths. I'd grown up with the Velvets, the Jam and Buzzcocks. The Doors were also a big influence." CARL (2005)

PETE & CARL

❝I was getting a band together one way or another, with or without him (Carl), but there was this nagging thing in the back of my mind that it had to be this fella.❞ PETE (2005)

❝Pete was in London for the weekend. There was an audition for the theatre society or something, and I was really rubbish. And he (Pete) got up and auditioned and got the part! (Then) he told them he wasn't a student and they were pissed off.❞

CARL (2004)

❝I'd just taken my first job after leaving school as a gravedigger. I needed saving, I was in a bad way. Carl came and saved me, he took me under his wings really, turned my life over.❞ PETE (2005)

❝You've got to bounce off someone to work with them, haven't you? Otherwise you'd just do your own thing.❞ CARL (2004)

❝Carl wanted us both to kill ourselves together at the same time. Get shotguns and shoot each other or jump off a high building.❞

PETE (2005)

❝We've evolved into best mates in a natural way. When I first met Carl, I think I was about 15, around the time I was at a place called Ainsworth Close, which was an estate my Nan was living in; he had a cousin living there. I didn't really know him – but I didn't want to know him, because Mum always said, 'Don't hang around with them lot.' But then he started going out with my sister, so I sort of knew him; he didn't like me, and I didn't like him. But I knew he could play guitar. We went from being two people from completely different groups, different worlds...❞

PETE (2002)

❝Straight away we were asking competitive, searching questions of each other. We had the dictionary out, seeing who knew the most words, and arguing for hours.❞

CARL (2005)

"All those early meetings were filled with spite and tension. It was fits and starts, boozy encounters in smoky little cellars, violent parties. He was just this wild fella, completely out of control which kind of drew me to him." PETE (2005)

"Pete was intelligent and witty. I felt I had competition, for once. Somebody I could spark off. We just clicked. Then he moved to London and kept hassling me to write songs with him. I didn't have any confidence really, and he had no talent for the guitar, he was completely out of tune, but he had all the confidence in the world. It really inspired me." CARL (2004)

"When I first met Carl he was a heavy drug user and I wasn't. I saw through that and I believed in him." PETE (2004)

"There was one point where I very, very nearly, just to be close to him, started taking full-on heroin. It was actually Alan (McGee) that saw it and nipped it in the bud." CARL (2004)

PETE & **CARL**

PETE DOHERTY *Talking*

"Look at him. Look at him. He's a clever thespian. Look at him. You know what? His dead uncle is Basil Rathbone. He's very well known, apparently. He played the finest Sherlock Holmes and then the family fell into poverty and Carlos was born in a fucking kitchen sink." PETE (2002)

"Carl did promise me years earlier that the day we got signed he'd roll me a massive booner, which was what we called a spliff with heroin in it – whee, everything in it all at once. I think he's still making it." PETE (2005)

"Carl ended up in this posh upper-middle class Notting Hill house (of girlfriend Vicky). He just crashed there now and again, made her come, and her mum fed him up. I went round to see him one time with Francesca and absolutely disgusted him by fucking in the front room... I got him evicted, I think." PETE (2005)

"We realised we were in it together. I'd done two years of drama, he'd done a year of English. I'd blagged every grant going just to stay alive. We'd beg, borrow and steal. We moved in together at the Holloway Road end of Camden Road, it was a guest house type of place, every kind of fucked-up weird you can imagine. At this stage, me and Pete were sharing a bed, a flea-bitten mattress, top to tail. It was a proper hovel." CARL (2005)

"I'd never met anyone like him (Carl). It was – what's the word when you can't take your eyes off someone?" PETE (2003)

"Pete started doing the brown (heroin), all the brown people used to come round. And being with brown people is no good."
CARL (2004)

"I was completely devoted to him (Carl). It was us two against the world." PETE (2004)

In The Beginning

Doherty remembers Barat being depressed at trying to get a record deal:

"Carl just reaches this point where there's no talking to him at all. It took media hyperbole and fans' adoration to drill into him that, yes, you can play guitar. Yes, what we're doing is good." **PETE (2004)**

"It was bit like finding a manhole cover and lifting it up and then going under. We came out of the manhole the day we signed to Rough Trade." PETE (2003)

"We had this early song 'You're My Waterloo', he (John Hassall) played bass along to it right away. You've got to remember I wasn't from a musical background. Jamming? I'd twitch if someone used that word." **PETE (2005)**

"Money didn't really figure that much. As long as we had enough for a packet of Benson and Hedges, a couple of drinkies and to take a bird to the pictures." PETE (2003)

"The plan was to get a load of money but it was frustrating when, in reality, it didn't materialise." **PETE (2005)**

"It was the Strokes, I suppose, who pissed us off in the first place really by coming to our country, wearing our clothes, having our audience with our women and our excitement!" CARL (2005)

PETE DOHERTY *Talking*

66I got into every fad possible, buying the most absurd things – like one of those ridiculous metal guitars, for no reason, and never playing it. Pete would buy all manner of junk and call it 'comfort shopping'.**99** CARL (2005)

66Our old drummer used to have a friend who worked in an old peoples' home and he asked if we could go and play for them. So we did all the old musical numbers. It was really amazing. A woman died during the show actually. These were old, old people and we played a few of our own songs and that's when she copped it. They loved it. Some woman kept shouting out (Pete imitates Barbara Windsor) 'I saw you at the Palladium in 1949. You haven't aged at all'.**99** PETE (2002)

66Anyone who could play in time and in tune to a song I'd written just blew me away.**99** PETE (2005)

66Before we got signed to Rough Trade, times were pretty desperate. We were both homeless and Carl owed the County Court £230. That doesn't seem like that much now, but back then it was like 'Where the fuck are we going to get that from?' We signed a special agreement with Banny (former Libertines manager) who said: 'I'll pay you £230 if you sign this contract.' We didn't think about it; we just did it, because she said she was gonna get us signed to Rough Trade eventually.**99** PETE (2002)

66It was just a case of let's get the best looking people and be as much like the Strokes as possible. That was the idea at the time.**99**
PETE (2005)

66What you have with us is some people who can write some songs and, in the process, create another land. We have a romantic vision. We have a dream and, much to my surprise, it seems to be coming true.**99** PETE (2002)

"When I was 16, 17, I started drifting away from everything else and picking up a guitar, and it was like, 'What are you doing? You can't sing and you can't play a guitar,' right up to the day we got signed by Rough Trade. And then it was like, 'Go on play us a song,' whereas before it was, 'Shut up, fucking racket'." **PETE (2005)**

"What kept us going was strong ideas and passion. We were angry at this stage as well. Sick of it. Carl was really down on his luck, kipping on sofas, split up from his missus. Fucked off. Lads coming over in American bands and sweeping up." PETE (2005)

"We spent the summer (of 1999) in Odessa Studios in Hackney with Gwyn, this Welsh fella who used to keep this eyes open with matchsticks – a proper old school engineer." **PETE (2005)**

"We didn't have a drummer. So this Welsh fella (Gwyn) says 'I know this old geezer who'll play the drums for you for 50 quid,' and half an hour later Mr Razzcocks walked in the door. We did our first demo, a song called 'Pay The Lady'." PETE (2005)

"Our proper gig was at the Hope & Anchor on Upper Street (Islington) on 11 September 1999. We were like the Bootleg Beatles with a 70-year-old drummer and a fucking weird cellist." **PETE (2005)**

Signing to Rough Trade:

"It wasn't the most money but we were under the impression we were going to have artistic freedom and they'd (Rough Trade) appreciate us as artists." PETE (2005)

❝We went in and demoed 17 songs over two weeks, it was incredible – looping drums, and even Carl playing a bit of drums. Gary came in and did a few bits and bobs.**❞ PETE (2005)**

❝James Endeacott (of Rough Trade Records) said he was going to take out a full-page advert in *NME* with just the lyrics to 'What A Waster'. I thought it was the greatest idea I'd ever heard.❞

PETE (2005)

On the choice of producer:

❝All I can say, really, honestly and with clarity is Mick Jones is a Libertine and Bernard Butler isn't. Mick makes you want to go in to the studio and record your songs. The other fella made me want to sit in a cupboard and smoke crack. I threatened to knock him out a few times.**❞ PETE (2005)**

"I was completely wrapped up in the songs and particularly the words, how people were going to interpret the words, and how important it was to get it right." PETE (2005)

LIBERTINES
Line-up: Carl Barat (vocals/guitar),
Pete Doherty (vocals/guitar),
John Hassall (bass), Gary Powell (drums)

"I approached (Razorlight's) Johnny Borrell and asked him to play, told him I was putting down the guitar. He was a friend but I don't think he had a great deal of respect for our friendship. He was arrogant, and that's not me bitching." PETE (2005)

"At the end of the album recording Carl turned up absolutely fucked. He'd been on skag and bone all night. He cracked his head on a mike and fell asleep – halfway through a song."
PETE (2002)

"They (Pete and Carl) were alive, alive to a degree that you just don't see. They were hilarious, entertaining, jumpy, songs coming out of their ears." ROUGH TRADE BOSS GEOFF TRAVIS (2004)

"As of right now, our lives are much like before, except that now we live them in front of other people. But we don't yet know what kind of effect all of this will have one us. Maybe, it will consume us, and it will be the beginning of the end." PETE (2002)

"Obviously he (Liam Gallagher) pretends he can't spell but I made him read a dictionary and explained to him that a 'libertine' is actually a man who, rather than going by anyone else's idea of what liberty is, does so within himself as an individual." PETE (2005)

"I just got the royalties through from the second Libertines album – the other three got ninety-five grand and I got eight hundred quid! Not sure where it went..." PETE (2005)

IN THE BEGINNING

“Apart from the Sex Pistols, the Libertines were probably the most manufactured band ever. Me and Carl signed to Rough Trade as songwriters and then pieced together a band from the miscellaneous. I mean, John (Hassall – Libertines bassist) had left the band the year before we signed because we were getting nowhere, but we swallowed our pride and asked him back.”

PETE (2005)

“I sometimes get a feeling when I play with the Libertines that we are playing beautiful songs that feel just perfect, and then I feel like I have got it. Success is when, despite all the hurdles, we can make something beautiful together.” PETE (2004)

“Sandra The Wood Nymph used to play with us quite a bit. She was a French dancer, who used to crawl out of a plastic egg with fire around her. Was it any good? Well, it was a woman dancing out of a plastic egg, so it was OK, I suppose.” **PETE (2002)**

“I think it's going to turn sour and then we'll get back together. But you know as well as I do that we disagree on some major issues.” PETE (2002)

“I think (the cover of The Libertines) is absolutely horrendous, it scares me. It looks like, 'Oh look, it's Carl and his junkie mate'.”

PETE (2004)

“Mick Jones had a baby around the time of *Up The Bracket* and he had another little girl around the time of The Libertines. That's two Libertines babies. So I'm saying this to the world: you want another Libertines album? Then get Mick Jones' missus to eat some fucking oysters or something!” PETE (2004)

“'The Ha-Ha Wall' dates back to the very first night Carl and I, having met and having seen through maybe a year of animosity and standing-off, the first night we actually sat down as friends with guitars in about 1998 in Mortlake (West London) above a furniture shop.” **PETE (2005)**

"He (Carl) was really proud of his Union Jack tea towel and this old guitar he had, and the first song we wrote together became 'The Ha Ha Wall'." PETE (2005)

"Primarily, we're about establishing the Arcadian dream. That statement might make people laugh, but that's the bare bones of it; that's what we're all about. For three minutes inside a song I can live in Arcadia.**"** **PETE (2002)**

"Our first manager, Banny, introduced us to different press teams, and different photographers. The infrastructure that stands today as being at the Libertines' roots since entering the industry is the one that Banny brought together – it's her legacy." PETE (2005)

"We're not part of this punk revival; all the best punk bands were pop bands anyway. The Ramones, the Sex Pistols – all pop.**"**

PETE (2002)

"There's been a lot of violence directed at us. In Wolverhampton a bloke head butted me for no other reason than I was wearing nail varnish, which I thought was a bit harsh, but understandable. This fellow tapped me on the shoulder and I thought he was gonna shake my hand and say 'Nice gig'... but he butted me in the face."

PETE (2002)

IN THE BEGINNING

"We're being chucked in with the Strokes and the Vines by people that we don't give a shit about. If we worried about stuff like that we'd go mad. You've got to remember that it's the way we've always been doing things.**"** PETE (2002)

"Me and Carl got done actually by one of their (Strokes) security guards – got a bit of a clip round the ear for trying to nick their guitar pedals." PETE (2005)

"I remember telling Carl that I wanted him to sing 'What Katy Did', and he thought I was winding him up. I said, 'I don't want to end up out the band again, with you going round the country and on TV doing these songs and I can't play them,' and he said, 'No, we are in it together—you've got to believe.' So I did, and it was great and I threw myself into it. We had our fallouts, but we made the record. I feel a little bit duped because I want to do those songs. They're not anti-Libertines songs, but they were never written for the Libertines to sing because the words, the things we're singing about, they were feelings that had been stifled by the Libertines, and those songs were a way out.**"**

PETE (2004)

"After the signing (to Rough Trade) everyone went to see British Sea Power, I think, at the Water Rats (London bar), but we lost each other. But at about three in the morning Carl and I both happened to be at the same place – Percy Circus – at the same time. So, we'd both come from different directions and bumped into each other, and then we saw this tramp on a bench. We hadn't said anything to him, but he just came up to us and he went, 'It's the worst thing that could happen to you.' It really freaked me out." PETE (2002)

"We started playing to fair-sized audiences all the time and me and Carl entered into this strange world of paranoia, feelings of paranoia and over-analysis." PETE (2005)

"Mick (Jones) is very direct. He comes from another decade, a less absurd one, while Bernard Butler came from a more recent decade. It seems there are two ways to do things: to either follow something along the same direction or follow another path. If we get led along two different paths, tough – we get lost."

PETE (2002)

"It's always been really important that support bands, and bands we go on tour with, are good people." PETE (2005)

"The Libertines is an ever-changing, swirling unpredictable monster of a band, and line-ups change as often as I do brogues... not every week but 'don't ever get too comfortable if you're not Carlos or myself', basically, is the rule of things. The boys are not playing Libertines gigs; they're doing their best not to get Banny sued for breaching European gig contracts."

PETE (2003)

"The Libertines is more than a four-piece band you read about in the *NME*. Just as *Up The Bracket* is more than a Rough Trade album. It is a now eight-year-old blueprint for life, and an uncustomised illegal/illicit manoeuvre in the Arcadian hinterland. We have been forced to operate in this manner in order to grab your children's attention, in order for the real show to start, in order for justice to be done. There is no such thing as a backstage pass or hospitality tent in Arcadia. Do not be conned. Music is free; come and get it. Roll up, roll up, donations welcome..." PETE (2003)

"My brother (Carl) and I are not rivals. We are shipmates and best friends and the greatest songwriting partnership in the world."

PETE (2004)

IN THE BEGINNING

PETE DOHERTY *Talking*

2002 DEBUT ALBUM *UP THE BRACKET*

'Vertigo'

"I like the line 'Was it the liquor? Or was it my soul?' It's when you can't work it out whether it was genuine or whether you just got caught in a debauched outside influence. Is it a Hitchcock reference? Well, there's a hit and there's definitely a cock, but that's nothing to do with the film director." PETE (2002)

'Death On The Stairs'

"That song's a cry in the darkness. But not from us – it's when you're in the darkness and then you hear a cry." PETE (2002)

'Horror Show'

"I think heroin is mentioned on this and a few songs – heroes and heroin, soft drugs and hard drugs, days by the sea. But it's quite an upbeat song and if you've been down on the brown the last thing you want to do is thrash about. You'd much rather lie down somewhere or spew up. Dangerous territory, really. You'd think in this day and age it wouldn't be, but you've got to be careful."

PETE (2002)

'Boys In The Band'

"Everyone's been singing along to it, they love it. I always find it a bit weird singing 'They all get them out/For the boys in the band' and seeing all the girls singing along. But it doesn't matter – it is a bit of a singalong number. It's not actually saying 'Get your bangers out for the boys!' It's more like 'Roll out the carpets! Get out the drinks!'" PETE (2002)

'Up The Bracket'

"That's me screaming at the start. There was all this fucking about in the studio. It was frustration. I can still see Mick (Jones) with his can in his hand going, 'Right lads, no more fucking about!'**"** PETE (2002)

'The Boy Looked At Johnny'

"Ah! That's one of my favourites. It's a blatant singalong. It's got this amazing riff on it – you're going to piss yourself with pleasure or laughter when you hear it. It's restored my faith."

PETE (2002)

'The Good Old Days'

"That's a call to arms really. It's not nostalgic at all. It's saying there were no good old days, stop going on – these are the good old days, probably.**"**

PETE (2002)

'Can't Stand Me Now'

"I wrote that in Whitechapel with Mark (Hammerton) – well, he wrote a bit of it.**"**

PETE (2005)

2004 ALBUM THE LIBERTINES

Recording The Libertines

❝I thought it was a sick joke when (our manager) said not to show up because the band would not welcome me.❞ PETE (2003)

❝That's not my album. I've been packaged by it and advertised by it and had strategies weaved around by it. It's nothing to do with me. The cover with me looking like a very handsome boy's junkie mate? Come on, man. It's not the Libertines.❞ **PETE (2005)**

❝Are we making an album? Either way I'm gonna make some records this year, with or without (the Libertines).❞ PETE (2004)

❝I don't know if the Libertines would want to carry on. I can't see why they'd want to prolong the agony. For them. For the British public.❞ **PETE (2005)**

On why a bouncer was assigned to the recording studio.
"To get us there, to stop fighting, to stop drugs coming in, and to stop (the) hard-hitting pipe posse turning up. To stop unpaid-drug-debt people turning up." CARL (2004)

"When I think about it. I just feel like putting a bullet through my head.**"** PETE (2004)

"It's turned into a soap opera. And besides, all the shit that people are romanticising and embellishing, it's all on the record."
CARL (2004)

"Things were as they'd never been before. I was making a big effort to be with him (Carl), to show my love for him. All right, I wasn't squeaky clean, but I had nothing but love for him and I was trying fucking hard.**"** PETE (2005)

"I feel a bit disgusted and disturbed by the way someone, other than myself, has done the artwork, the inlay, and how my songs haven't been credited." PETE (2004)

"They should change their name and do their own songs. Carl's going around saying he wrote '(What Became Of) The Likely Lads'. He knows that's not true.**"** PETE (2004)

"I knew I had a better album than *Up The Bracket* in me and I wanted to record it. But I was told we've got to keep touring, keep promoting. That was the first time I realised we were on a conveyor belt." PETE (2004)

"My nightmare is to be kicked out of a band, then have all your songs and artwork taken out of your hands. Oh no! That happened, didn't it? But what can you do but keep going, keep fighting?**"**
PETE (2005)

IN THE BEGINNING

Falling Out

Libertines Statement

"Peter is unwell and the band are very concerned for his well-being, They have told him out of concern for his health that he needs to get better before he can rejoin them. They also want it to be known they fully support him through this difficult time. It was an extremely difficult decision for Carl, Gary and John to continue with the tour, but they decided they would proceed so as not to disappoint their fans, who they trust will understand the adverse situation they are in." (2003)

"In the end, I just got better conversations out of the needle than I did from Carl." PETE (2004)

"Back when we were on the dole, or working in the theatre, we'd fall out and then that would be it. (Carl) would fuck off for a couple of months and everything would be at odds. I'd just be pressing on with the band on my own." PETE (2005)

"I'm getting on with things without any of them, though God knows I love him. It's not happening anymore and that's the way it is. Fuck 'em. And fuck all you who sit back typing, self-preening, running me down. Carlos asked me not to play, that he didn't want me, so that's that." PETE (2003)

"Pete didn't turn up for the tour over a misdemeanour, but there was obviously more to it than that. He said it was because I didn't come to a shitty gig he organised on my birthday." CARL (2004)

PETE DOHERTY *Talking*

"It's not going to be like the traditional band split cos it's never been a traditional band." **PETE (2003)**

"That (the tabloid press) is the only way to communicate with the Libertines. Carl doesn't answer my calls, doesn't call me. It's a way of saying, 'Hello? I'm still around'." PETE (2004)

"I really felt like that people thought I was a villain last year when I was doing the gigs (as if) I'd sneakily ripped them off, kicked Pete out and abandoned my mate. But now, everyone's involved. And the fans do have a part in it. There's always been an intimacy with our band." **CARL (2004)**

"All he has to do is come and talk to me. If he came round and said 'Stop taking smack, stop taking crack,' I'd do it. I'd do anything he wanted." PETE (2004)

"The one true horror is that if I was to be true to myself as an artist, as a man, as a Libertine, I would not work with the band as it stands any more. The release and the liberty of the other path – in other words Babyshambles, Peter Doherty solo, whatever – is immense. I can feel it from this side of the barbed wire, like in the cell in Wanno (Wandsworth) last year. Like a weight off me poor old bony shoulders." **PETE (2004)**

"When all of this past and all of this chaos is out of the way, and we sit down together, there's still a truth there, in our connection and in what was there on the first day we met. That's why it's so sad." CARL (2004)

"I need to speak to the boys before I go nuts. Maybe I don't know what I'm talking about. Maybe they know how I feel but are holding out at whatever cost. We have a good thing going etc, etc – but fuck me, he's (Carl) a difficult man to love and he gives me nothing." **PETE (2004)**

"Alan McGee's (Libertines manager) got them on a conveyor belt. We would only have signed a deal that allows freedom. As individuals. As Men. As Libertines. But maybe that's the attitude that gets you kicked out of the Libertines. It is, actually." PETE (2005)

"We wrote (the second album) together. On the record it says Barat. It was always 50/50. That was their idea." PETE (2004)

"You can't be in a band with people who've done that to you, man. I give them my fucking songs and they kick me out of the band. There's eight or nine songs I should have done as Babyshambles. I was duped over those songs." PETE (2004)

"Pete has not been kicked out of the band. I think it would be irresponsible to play with Peter when he's in this state and I don't even know if he could handle it himself right now." CARL (2004)

"Peter's got to clean up. Then he can come back to the band and we can have a friendship again. It's the hardest thing, making him understand." CARL (2004)

FALLING OUT "

PETE DOHERTY *Talking*

"I go through each day and am twisting up. When I finally, fully unwind it will be furious, disastrous, dangerous, spectacular.**"**

PETE (2004)

"Apparently Carl wants to talk to me; he was sending texts to a number that doesn't even exist. For fuck's sake man." PETE (2005)

"It's got to the point where Carl and I don't speak except on stage. It breaks my heart. He treats me badly and every time I come running back like a battered housewife. I feel like I'm seeking the ghost of a former friendship but Carl gave up on me years ago. He did come to see me in the Priory but I hardly remember his visit.' **PETE (2004)**

"Timeless boo-hooing about Biggles (Carl Barat) not being my mate. Never does 'owt to reach out to me, loves me but doesn't like me. No birthday pressie or even message or anything since I left (the) dressing room at Brixton on Sunday. But this is normal, and so why now let it upset me?" PETE (2004)

Libertines Statement

"It is with regret that Libertines announce they are to continue without singer and guitarist Peter Doherty due to his well-known addiction problems, specifically with crack cocaine and heroin. Peter is and always will be a Libertine – and when he cleans up from his addictions he will be immediately welcomed back into the band. This decision is made with love and with no disregard to Peter and his problems. The other members of the band – Gary, John and Carl – have come to this conclusion after three recent failed rehab attempts, all of which the Libertines have funded. Peter's erratic mental state worries us greatly and having him on tour would only compound his problems. We aim to complete all existing tour commitments without him. The Libertines are not splitting up and their future is secure." **(2003)**

"**If (Carl) comes to Paris and grabs me by the hand, maybe we can reclaim the empire together. But for now I'm out of the band. Surely no one wants to see me trapped in this cage that is only making me miserable.**" PETE (2004)

"Being a Libertine is supposed to be about freedom – but I don't feel free at the moment." **PETE (2004)**

"**(Seeing Pete earlier this year) was reassuring. We're not ready to work together again right now and I don't know what Pete would say. But there's someone in there I love very much as a friend and will do until my dying day. I'd quite like to think that it's reciprocated.**" CARL (2005)

"We worried about the magic being lost in periods when we couldn't be in each other's company for months at a time. Back in the days when we had nothing, we still turned on each other. But we'd come back and we'd find ourselves in the same place and carried on. If you know you're gonna hurt someone and you love them, and you know you're gonna keep hurting them, then surely the good thing to do would be to stay away from them. But that's the mystery of love and that's the fatality of it as well."

PETE (2003)

FALLING OUT

"They (the Libertines) can't play a gig without me. He (Carl) knows what's going to happen if he does. He promised me that would never happen again and I believe him, because... I'll fucking kill him. I'll stick a 1957 Epiphone (guitar) down his throat and rip out his guts... Or something down those lines." PETE (2004)

"Over the years it's always been the same. We'll have a little fallout. Sometimes it'll last six months. I'm not going to sit at home like a wife like I used to back in the day. Like when he was out gallivanting round town and I'd be sitting at home sticking chords together." PETE (2003)

"Most people fancy Carl more than they do me. For years I've been in his shadow – but now the worm has turned and I'm getting all the quotes." PETE (2002)

"Me and Carl were arguing about a digital recorder. Someone said, 'What's going on?' and Carl said 'Nothing he just can't handle the brown.' I went absolutely mental. I jumped across that glass table and started leathering him. And I would have fucking killed him an' all, but the guards dragged me off him. It was like Baloo the bear and Mowgli. He had me by the back of the shirt and I was flapping about. Carl was a bit surprised because traditionally he's been harder than me, but since coming out of prison I had a lot of bottled-up aggression." PETE (2004)

"The driving, aggressive stuff that I like is the English punk and the New York era. Carl's more the metal side of it – he was into Rage Against The Machine and Iron Maiden when he was a kid."
PETE (2004)

"Of course, the official reason I'm out of the band right now is because of drugs. But part of the reason I've been made unwelcome by Carl is that I've been writing songs with other people, and doing Babyshambles with as much, if not more, passion than I was doing the Libertines. The Libertines has just become a big blow-up doll. If it's not me and Carl together, then it's not the Libertines. It's just a big con." PETE (2004)

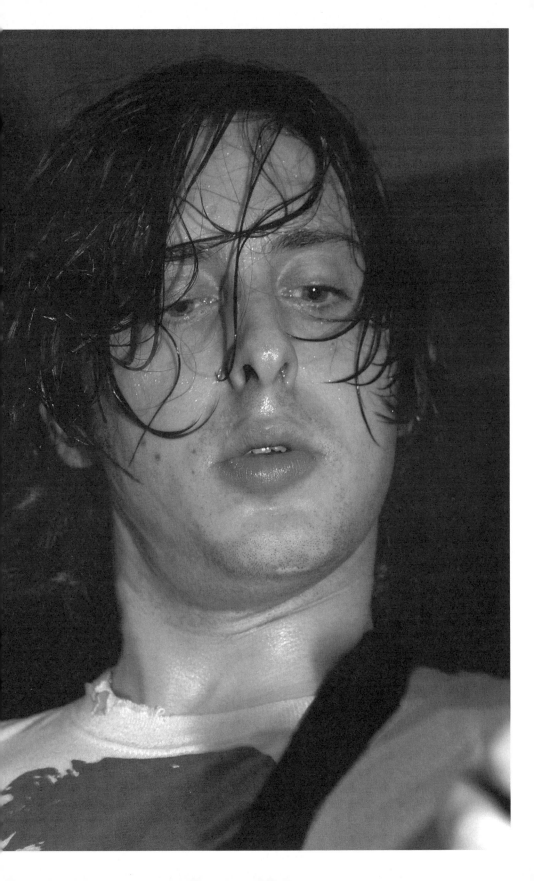

"Things like being kicked out of the band, going to prison, are so horrendous, I think it's gonna take me some time to talk honestly about how I feel about it. I'm managing, so far, to shut it out pretty well. I've never been to prison. I've never been kicked out of the band, never been in a band called the Libertines. That's the way it has to be." PETE (2004)

"It had taken six, seven years for him to say it, to say the truth: 'Can't stand me now.' He sang it to me and I thought, 'You're right. We've used each other, got here, but underneath it all, you're not my mate.' So I kicked his amp over, smashed his guitar and cut myself up."

PETE (2004)

"I was removed by force from my flat, or somebody else's flat, and taken, again by force, to a so-called safe house to stop me going to the (Carling) festival."

PETE (2005)

"He (Carl) does not want me to play in my current condition. I'm not sure what he means but he's deadly serious and it's settled."

PETE (2003)

"I can see it from their point of view, Gary, John and Carl have worked like martyrs and I just expect to show up when I choose." PETE (2003)

"I can't just swan up and plug in and scream it all out any more. I don't want to be in that position any more, I don't want to have all of them relying on my whims." PETE (2003)

❝I'm not comfortable with the line-up and over the months have repeatedly tried to explain to Gary and John that I don't want to be in a band with them.❞ PETE (2003)

❝My capriciousness deters them from taking me seriously but that is the way it is. My new songs are all I have, along with my liberty, and everything has to be just right from now on in. I need to start singing my new songs, and I want to play with other people.❞

PETE (2003)

❝I respect someone putting their hands up and saying, 'I was out of my mind on cocaine and whiskey, and I've made the wrong decision.'❞ PETE (2005)

❝What I've heard from a few people is he (Carl) thinks he's made a mistake. He thinks he's made the wrong decision and he hasn't got the backbone to phone me and say, 'Come on, let's get on with it'.❞ **PETE (2005)**

FALLING OUT ❞

Baby-shambles

❝Maybe for the first time ever I'm going on stage and feeling like I'm completely part of a band. More than the Libertines.❞

PETE (2005)

❝When I asked Gemma (Clarke, drums) and Drew (McConnell, bass) to join the (sic) Babyshambles, I myself was under no illusions. I said to Drew, 'This is exciting – we could do a few gigs, we could put a single out, but it could all fold tomorrow.' I'm being honest with you.❞ **(GUITARIST) PATRICK WALDEN 2005**

"I had an outlet for my songs. The Libertines wasn't an outlet." PETE (2005)

"I can tell you it's all done. We've got a load of songs, about 30. It's sounding good. You'll like it, there's a couple of surprises on there, a couple of brand new ones we wrote when we were in there.**"** **PETE (2005)**

"I suppose the key difference (between Babyshambles and the Libertines), and you might notice it at first, is that, if you look closely, I'm not the Libertines." PETE (2005)

"Babyshambles started in Teesdale Street with the Wolfman (Pete Wolf) and a digital recorder.**"** **PETE (2005)**

"Babyshambles is a benign dictatorship! No, It's a democracy! What Drew lacks in songs he makes up for in looks, so we have that barter. Sometimes Pat will come up with this riff and you just can't ignore it, like in 'Fuck Forever'. It has to be used."

PETE (2005)

"I'm so tired, man. The original idea (was to), get some kip, to be on the ball for the interview. So much for that. I'm like a bag of potatoes.**"** **PETE (2005)**

"We might call (the album) *Up The Morning,* maybe, but we don't know yet. Same with the Libertines, it's always (decided on) the last day when we have to get the artwork sent off. But I like 'Up The Morning', that's one of my favourite tracks on it, it's a new track." PETE (2005)

"(The songs) are like children; you shouldn't really have a favourite. Unless one of your kids develops into a pervert.**"**

PETE (2005)

BABYSHAMBLES

❝'Fuck Forever' will be the next single and then
followed by 'Albion' after that. The lyrics go, 'What's the
use between death and glory, I can't tell between death and
glory, what's the use between death and glory, I still can't choose
between death and glory. But they, they have a way, a way to
make you pay, and to make you toe the line.' We've been playing
it live since the gig at the Shepherds Bush Empire.❞ PETE (2005)

❝I'd like to go to a residential studio where we can just go and hide
and cocoon ourselves away. There is talk of Mick Jones producing
the album at the moment.❞ **PETE (2005)**

❝I wouldn't like to continue playing live unless this band were
better than the Libertines. Better than anything I'd done before.
Ever.❞ PETE (2005)

❝It took me a year to listen to that first Libertines album. I listen to
it now, and I love it. But I couldn't listen to it like I can with this
(Babyshambles album). I don't feel like such a fraud, you know
what I mean... like the second Libertines album was nothing to do
with me at all. By the time it came out it had nothing to do with
me, the artwork, nothing – I just wasn't in the band. It was quite
strange.❞ **PETE (2005)**

❝The hardest part was getting the line-up together but it's the best
when the trust is there. It's a real unit now. We've got songwriting
aspirations and like the marriage of melody and noise.❞
PETE (2004)

❝I've been in a band with Patrick (Walden) before. So I've known him
for a long time. I always knew he was a brilliant guitarist. He's got
so many ideas and a real talent. I think he's a genius actually. In a
way there are similarities to when I met Carl from the Libertines, in
that there is this huge untapped resource of creativity that's never
been given the opportunity because he's quite shy.❞ **PETE (2004)**

"I think 'Fuck Forever' is one of the best songs I've ever written. I was singing it last night over and over again – trying to work out if I really like it or if it was just signifying something – but I really do like it. I'm extremely impatient to get our album done." PETE (2004)

"Even though Babyshambles are singing quite a lot of sad songs, it's positive – we've got a group mentality. There's a lot more openness and trust (than the Libertines)." PETE (2004)

"Do you know when I first met Pat? He was playing in a band called the Hamstrings or something... This is true; he was lying on his back for the first few songs and halfway through the third song he sort of levitated and rose straight up, played the solo and then went back down. And then this girl came on and started kissing him." PETE (2005)

"It's the best record I've ever made by a long shot. Always in the past, in every album review or single review, they've never ever discussed the songs or the music. I don't think they will this time." PETE (2004)

BABYSHAMBLES

"For me, some of the album's terrifying. There're a lot of really sad songs on it, so it's quite hard mixing it, listening to those voices again and again and hearing those lyrics, but it's too late to turn back." PETE (2005)

"There's never been a band good enough to make me give up crack. Babyshambles are better than crack. Otherwise I wouldn't be doing it. I'd be too busy doing crack." **PETE (2005)**

"It was just getting everyone in the same room and pressing 'record'. Well actually, pressing record was easy, it was just a bit of an obstacle course getting to the room. We had to get over mountains to Wales, through security guards, over to Henley and then Metropolis (studios). It was like leapfrog." PETE (2005)

"I was pretty gutted the way the first Babyshambles single ('Babyshambles') was handled, the fact that Rough Trade only released 4,000 copies when they knew very well it could have sold ten times that. They sold a lot less records than they could have." **PETE (2005)**

"Carl didn't like the (Babyshambles) name at all. He told me he thought it was shit, that the whole idea was a shambles as far as he could see. I wanted a name that was a bit different, and that's what I came up with, and it stuck. I liked it then and I still do."

PETE (2005)

"I know for a fact they (Babyshambles) must believe in the music, because we're not making any money out of it. Music must be their motivation, unless they're just masochists. They've got a lot of freedom as musicians." **PETE (2005)**

Making Music

"Songwriting is a part of me. Just when you think you've dried up and you'll never write another good song, you sit down with a guitar and have another go... it's one of my major sources of happiness." PETE (2005)

"If they (the Libertines) are so important to all these people, they should take time to listen to the lyrics. It's an explosion, right? With the songs... romantic and the low moments and the highs... it was pretty much a cry from the darkness, a lot of it. Why carry on celebrating that? 'Time For Heroes' should have been the last single." PETE (2005)

"On the demo of 'Can't Stand Me Now' it's just me singing it to myself but basically I got turned on I think by the idea of putting the words in his (Carl's) mouth, making them so personal, so he's singing them back to me. It was difficult on my part, not to sing the line, 'You twisted and tore our love apart'." PETE (2005)

"I had complete faith and belief in him (Alan McGee), complete trust, and I liked him. Carl got on with him very well – they're both as insane as each other." PETE (2005)

"(The Libertines) wouldn't have stuck together and recorded another album if it hadn't been for (producer) Mick (Jones). It just wouldn't have happened, we wouldn't have pulled it together."

PETE (2005)

PETE DOHERTY *Talking*

"The whole world's a circus, and I'm the ringmaster."

"I was completely devoted to him (Carl). It was us two against the world."

"In the words of Dr Johnson, the law is a pain in the arse."

"Kate's my rock – not my rock of crack, though!"

On the Babyshambles website:

"I don't even have the internet myself, but people aren't putting stuff on the net the way they said they would." PETE (2005)

"Now and again I will turn around and say, "Yeah, I am a fucking brilliant songwriter," and I'll put it into practice as well. I'll write songs and I'll be desperate for people to hear them, and love them and want to record them and release them." PETE (2005)

"'Skag And Bone Man' stands out because we wrote and recorded it all in a day. Just being able to take what was around me, all my feelings, all my emotions about everything and put it into a song, whip the band into shape and give Carl his little 30 seconds for his solo and just BANG! It was there and I was happy, I was proud." PETE (2005)

"I'm proud of the (Libertines' first) album but there was that sense of coming in, plugging in, heads down. Here (Babyshambles) it's a little bit more fluid, you know what I mean? The work is the life and life the work. It's very natural." **PETE (2005)**

"The songs have come from me and in a way I've been mugged of them." PETE (2005)

"When I heard 'For Lovers' (a single he recorded with Wolfman) was nominated (for an Ivor Novello award) I thought Wolfman was lying, to be honest. For me, being a songwriter is really exciting. Out of everything that's ever said or written about anything I ever do, it's never about the music or the songs or the lyrics, so it's nice to be here. It's a lovely change. I'm really proud of myself, and Wolfman as well." **PETE (2005)**

"Once upon a time there was a part of me that wrote about things that some people might see as destruction, but actually they were the things that saved me from destruction. Words and music." PETE (2005)

MAKING MUSIC

"I'm quite disappointed that I wasn't asked to write the QPR anthem. I'm doing my best for them. I've got a picture of the missus (Kate Moss) in the Rangers shirt inside the sleeve of the new Babyshambles album, *Down In Albion*. Now that is fantasy football." **PETE (2005)**

"The day I realised that I wasn't going to play for QPR was the day I started writing melancholy songs." PETE (2002)

"When inspiration and emotions are sudden, and you can truly capture something, then, yeah, of course it feels good. But when you're stunted, and you're having trouble expressing yourself, then obviously it doesn't. So it's never constant." **PETE (2005)**

"I wrote 'Time For Heroes' after (the) May day (demonstrations) in 2001. At the time it was one of the most exciting days of my life. Everyone said, 'Oh, it was rubbish, we got penned in at Oxford Circus,' but we didn't. Quite a lot of people got penned in, but some of us made a break for it, and that was a great feeling. It was quite a peaceful protest up until the police attacked. But I like the fact that when the police kicked off, and it wasn't justified, a lot of people stood their ground. And it felt quite good to be fighting for a cause. I felt like there were so many things wrong, and I didn't know where to channel it, and for that moment it felt like I was with a lot of people who believed in the same thing, and we were all channelling it together. If there had been more, we'd have gone to Parliament – that was the dream."

PETE (2004)

"There were running battles with the police and I was part of that. I ended up with a scarf wrapped round my head and I did get hit. I think the policeman thought I was taking the piss – I was doing my hair by looking in his riot shield and he clumped me round the side of the head." **PETE (2004)**

"We're amazed really, it's our first single and we didn't expect it to do so well. I heard 'I Get Along' on the radio, it took me half a minute to work out who it was. Then it hit me like a kick in the face. I'm as happy as a parrot, really." PETE (2002)

"If I wasn't doing music, it wouldn't be me, would it? I've always been into music. But maybe I would've concentrated more on writing, as in creative writing. I'd just immerse myself in my imagination. But like, starting to learn the guitar, getting together with Carl, writing songs, getting out there, getting Babyshambles together, I've been given the opportunity by life; the chance by fate, the kind lady. She showed me a bit of leg, didn't she? She's allowed me to, rather than sit in – which I'm not knocking – rather than sit in and reside in my imagination I can actually live out any of those things I dare fucking dream or fantasise about. I can live them out." PETE (2004)

"'Cunt' as a word has almost become meaningless... You say it enough times and it doesn't have any effect. I played that song ('What A Waster') to my Dad at Christmas, worried about what he may say, even though I knew he swore, because he was in the army and all that... and something really weird happened in the room. He just started eating my cigarettes and saying, 'You cunt, you cunt – that's amazing; you've gotta release it.' Funny, as it started off as a ballad, originally." PETE (2002)

"You can't get that feeling anywhere else. (Performing) is communion. It's like being washed away in the ocean, carried aloft on a wave."

PETE (2003)

MAKING MUSIC

PETE DOHERTY *Talking*

❝I'm not one of these people who doesn't care what people think, otherwise I'd stay in and play for the bedroom wall. But you can't force people to like your music.❞ PETE (2003)

❝'What A Waster' was probably the most self-explanatory song in the history of pop.❞ **PETE (2002)**

❝(Single 'Don't Look Back Into The Sun') is a beautiful song. When we wrote it me and Carl knew it was a special song and we both fucking love it. I've heard him singing it in his sleep.❞
PETE (2003)

❝I like to think, and I do believe – maybe it's wrong – but I do believe with all my heart that someone who's gonna pick up on the lyrics and be interested or inspired by them, like straight away. That's gonna nullify anything else anyone would ever say about me or the music. Because the lyrics are very honest about lots of things that are talked about in interviews. They're quite clear as well in how I feel about it.❞ **PETE (2004)**

❝I was living in this basement with Carl. He came in that night when I'd finished writing it and straightaway he came up with the 'bom bom bom bom bom,' you know what I mean? It was perfect; he came up with that, that riff, but the song was mainly mine. It's a very old song, 'Music When The Lights Go Out'. It used to be the staple song in our set. It used to be the... well, not that we had a crowd, but the crowd favourite – the one man and his dog favourite.❞ PETE (2004)

❝Once you realise that what I'm saying is true and comes from the heart, then it's easy. But if you see it all as a facade and just a presentation of affected emotion, then it's not so easy, it'll just confuse you.❞ PETE (2005)

❝Rough Trade – like 'bum deal kid', it's an old-fashioned expression for working-class male prostitutes. It's also the name of a record company.❞ PETE (2005)

"You always see lists and polls about the 50 most influential people in music, and it's always quite hip artists or talented rappers, but they're not the most important people in the music industry. They might be in terms of the music itself, but unfortunately the music is often dictated by who owns it, which isn't the artist. It's the boss of Time Warner, it's the boss of Dreamworks. It's not the kids – they're just pennies for the slot machine." PETE (2004)

On Franz Ferdinand

"'Take Me Out' – that's Ringo Starr, isn't it? It's exactly the same riff. What was it Oscar Wilde said? Amateurs borrow but geniuses steal." PETE (2005)

"'I Get Along', I wrote with Carl. He came up with the phrase 'I get along, I get along...' and that's quite poppy and optimistic. Then I wrote the verses and the 'Fuck 'em' bit. I was saying 'I was really fucked up. You saw me there. I don't know what to do...'"

PETE (2002)

"Primarily, we're about establishing the Arcadian dream. That statement might make people laugh, but that's the bare bones of it; that's what we're all about." PETE (2002)

"Being in studio should be free – not financially, but spiritually and physically. You should be free to experiment with ideas. There is no regime. Okay, you might be recording a single, in which case you get that done, but it's gotta be a fella with a paintbrush, not like some anal designer who's all rigid." PETE (2003)

"Is 'Down In Albion' death-fixated? 'Knocking On Death's Door', yeah; 'A'rebours'; 'Sticks And Stones' yeah; 'Killamangiro' yeah; 'Eight Dead Boys' yeah; 'Pentonville' erm, 'Back From The Dead' yeah... I dunno. Probably less than the Libertines albums. Maybe I'll look back and think, what a morbid album." PETE (2005)

"If a feeling is real or anything is real then the last thing I want to do is fucking shout about it. But by putting it in songs you end up shouting about it..." PETE (2005)

MAKING MUSIC

Past Loves

LISA MOORISH

"Low self-esteem. As you get older, you grow out of it. If you've been out with a so-called bad boy and you've been damaged, you can't have those kind of relationships any more because of the battering you take emotionally and mentally."

KILL CITY SINGER LISA MOORISH, MOTHER OF DOHERTY'S SON ASTILE (2004)

"He got under my skin. I knew it was a bad idea. We were ultimately friends; we tried embarking on a relationship but it wasn't meant to be... I was careless and (the pregnancy) happened. I couldn't get rid of it, I didn't want to, even though there were a million reasons not to have it. I thought, 'I'm going to get it in the neck for this but I don't care'.**"**

LISA MOORISH (2004)

"I wouldn't want (Pete) around my son like that (stoned). He's not well, he needs to get well and he needs to be there for my son. But not right now, definitely not. He has seen him and been in his life, but obviously as things get worse, it's been less and less. Now's the time to say we've got to cut this off until hopefully he sorts himself out." LISA MOORISH (2004)

"Peter certainly wasn't a star when I got pregnant by him. I couldn't have predicted in a million years that he would be – and I hate it. I wish they (Doherty and Liam Gallagher, who fathered her other child) were anonymous people. Of course, I've always found it sexy that they were leaders in some way, but that's got nothing to do with fame." **LISA MOORISH (2004)**

"I didn't plan it that way, it happened. I'd love 2.2 kids and a white picket fence. I wouldn't advise anyone to do it the way I did. But it happens, not just to me, to other women. What I wish was different is the fame thing. It's just made it a million more times more difficult." LISA MOORISH (2004)

PAST LOVES "

And Then There Was Kate...

66It's been the best week in a long time because I've really found love with Kate (Moss).99 **PETE (2005)**

66**I think it will last... she is good for me because she has a beautiful soul and I think I can trust her. I believe her when she says she loves me and I know I mean it when I say I love her.**99

PETE (2005)

66My life is going up and up. It's like I'm reborn with Kate, my life is complete. I'm on top of the world and can't wait to settle down and have kids. We're already trying for a brother or sister for (Kate's daughter) Lila. I just can't help talking about her, I can't hold it in. I'm just so happy.99 **PETE (2005)**

66**A lot of people basically are obsessed with the missus and I don't know (why) really... she's just a bird from South London.**99

PETE (2005)

66I'll do anything to stay with Kate. I'll give up the drugs. She's the woman I want to marry. I think the reason (we split) was she was getting a lot of pressure from her family.99 **PETE (2005)**

66**I went out for Sunday lunch with (Kate's friends) and they nicknamed me the Crackhead.**99 PETE (2005)

PETE DOHERTY *Talking*

"They (Kate's family) think I'm bad news, but I'm not after Kate's money and I'm not interested in her fame. I don't know what's going on with the relationship right now, who knows what the future holds?" PETE (2005)

"She's beautiful and amazing and I want to marry her." PETE (2005)

"Yes, it's true, I have asked her to marry me – and she's agreed. I told her that if we were to continue going out with each other then she'd have to marry me." PETE (2005)

"She assured me she doesn't trust me an inch – and I'm a bit paranoid and insecure – so we make a right pair. But she's one of the most beautiful women in the world, so who wouldn't be insecure?" PETE (2005)

"Liam (Gallagher) cornered her at some party the other week and he was going: 'You and me, man, we're meant to be together.' She (Kate) went 'Fuck off mate, even in your prime I didn't want to sleep with you.'" PETE (2005)

"I told her to put him (Liam) on the line. And he began going: 'Nah you're cool man, fuckin' love your band. You're not a puppet, I'm a fuckin' puppet.'" PETE (2005)

On Liam Gallagher's attempts to woo Kate

"I said we should go for a coffee. It turned out to be a whiskey."

PETE (2005)

"I just miss her. She says she just wants to be with me. She says she doesn't know why I love her, I don't know why she loves me, but that's just the way it is. Yeah, but no, but yeah... maybe she just wants me to go through it because she's been through it." PETE (2005)

"Kate's been there for me. She's my rock – not my rock of crack, though!" PETE (2005)

"It's not about whether I'll make an honest woman of her, it's about when she'll make an honest man of me. I've written numerous songs about her. She gives me inspiration. She's everything to me. What else can a man ask for?" PETE (2005)

"The only thing I have a problem with is anything that mentions my lass (Kate). I get it in the eye. She was reading something out the other day and she ripped it up and said, 'You're so vain! You just want to read about yourself!'**"** PETE (2005)

"For some reason, no matter how hard I punch a wall, it doesn't hurt. But the idea that I might be using (Kate), or fucking her over, that sets me off. I will run a million miles from her if there is the slightest indication that I am doing that. And I know I'm not." PETE (2005)

"It was get an implant or die. I was fixing up, shooting white, shooting brown, and then entering a relationship. I mean God knows, Kate saved my life.**" Pete (2005)**

"A lot of people are against us. I'm not saying who. It does my head in, being in love. But I'm still in love. Once you're in love, you're in love – whether you like it or not." PETE (2005)

"We are madly in love with each other and can't stand to be apart. We are still planning to get married later this year – a small ceremony with close family and friends. Nobody can split us up.**"**
PETE (2005)

"I said to Kate, 'I've run out of cigarettes,' and she said, 'Oh, we've got some rolling baccy,' so I rolled this roll-up with great care and affection – lovely rollie – and I lit it, and the smell really reminded me of prison (Pentonville), and I just turned to her and said, 'You know, I think roll-ups are really romantic,' and she went, 'I think they're disgusting.' My romantic moment destroyed." PETE (2005)

"I've got a little K tattoo on my arse, she's just got a little P there. And it doesn't stand for Pirelli.**" PETE (2005)**

AND THEN THERE WAS KATE...

Trouble
Ahead

On the sale of footage to the tabloids
that revealed Kate's drug dabbling

"Kate is devastated. There were only a few people in the room at the time – all supposed to be our friends. I will be able to work out who is responsible. There will be blood on the carpet when we work out who betrayed us. I will seek down and kill the person." PETE (2005)

"She's (Kate Moss) doing really well. I shouldn't say really. She wants me to go to this (rehab) place in Arizona straight after her and do it." PETE (2005)

"Each man kills the things he loves. I recognise that in myself – in relationships or even with guitars, or beautiful things that I've had, then wilfully destroyed." PETE (2004)

"I never know where I stand with her. It's either a black eye or a love bite. It's like being in Afghanistan with her. I wish I could find some middle ground. I spoke to Kate about 30 minutes ago. She shouted and screamed at me. She threw her mobile at the wall. She's furious." PETE (2005)

"Everyone believes (Kate) went in there (to rehab) to beat her own cocaine addiction. That's wrong. She did it to save her career. Having said that, she came out saying it really works. But she is terrified of her will power failing. She's petrified of being caught again. She knows if she ever went back to drugs she would have to be more discreet." PETE (2005)

"Kate can't come back to England because of her situation with the police. She's too scared to come back. We had a secret rendezvous in Paris. She slipped away from her people. They don't want me near her." PETE (2005)

TROUBLE AHEAD 99

Drugs

"Yes I'm a heroin addict, yes I'm addicted to crack cocaine, and I don't know what to do. I'm all cut up, unsure. I don't know what I'm doing. I need a good kicking and I need some help."

PETE (2003)

"It isn't drugs that I need to get rid of; it's the demons that fill my head. Once I have come to terms with my demons, maybe I'll be able to get clean." PETE (2004)

"There are three things that I know a bit about in my life and that's QPR, my guitar and drugs. I know Queens Park Rangers are the best football team in the world, my guitar is the most beautiful thing I own and that I don't take enough drugs to kill me."

PETE (2004)

"If I want drugs, I don't have to do a gig to get them. I do a gig when I feel shit, because I need to be playing. There's no drug in the world that can compare with playing music." PETE (2004)

"I still hadn't smoked coke, that was to come later. But I did have a rock, having scored on the street in King's Cross... I ended up with this rock of crack but I didn't know what to do with it. I just had it in my little tin." PETE (2005)

"You've got to understand the amount (of drugs) I was taking... when you come off it, it's poison, effectively. It's difficult. And anyone who knows anything about it wouldn't believe me if I said, 'Oh, I've knocked it on the head.' But I don't want to do it any more. This is it." **PETE (2005)**

"History has shown that there's only one conclusion, and that's the blackout. The great void. Which is worse, maybe, I suppose. I'm not a nihilist and I don't want to die, so that would be the worst thing." PETE (2004)

"I value my creative talent and to destroy that is a terrible thing. I know where the self-destruct button is – I just have to resist the temptation to push it." **PETE (2004)**

"I'm not scared about death. I don't care if everyone says I'm going to die if I carry on taking drugs." PETE (2004)

"It is impossible for things to go on as they have done. I will end up six feet under, particularly with the crack. It just spirals into the darkest, saddest melody." **PETE (2004)**

"There is something irresistible about it, something like waiting for the perfect wave that never comes. But it is awful if it destroys anything that is good." PETE (2004)

"It's of no interest talking about drugs. You do them or you don't do them. I wouldn't encourage anyone either way. Choose your own path. But tread carefully on this drifting ice. Because any one of us could go under at any point. I ain't going down like that."

PETE (2003)

"When I first took heroin I didn't think of it as smack. I had this romantic image of it as like opium. Poets have always taken opium." PETE (2005)

DRUGS

"Drugs have never been the driving wheel. They're just part of creating music. I just want to play, so I take heroin to enhance my creativity. A lot of my songs are heroin-related, but they're never a celebration of it." PETE (2004)

"(Crack addiction is) like you're in love with someone. You never really stop loving that person. It's like a family member who's a bit troublesome, but you love them anyway because you know they're all right, even if the rest of the world can see the truth – ie they're not all right. They're in your blood." PETE (2004)

"The first time I had heroin, I was 21, walking round the streets of Whitechapel on a Sunday, smoking brown my dealer gave me and thinking I was cool. I've no idea how much I took that first time or how much it cost. He gave it to me free. As it got into my bloodstream, I noticed it exaggerated parts of me that were already there: solitude and loneliness. Then I started getting all these creative thoughts." PETE (2002)

"What's the worst situation I've woken up in after a heavy night? Oh God! Under a taxi with no clothes on... I ended up knocking a cyclist out and nicking his bike." PETE (2005)

"I think some people's lives would be ruined with drugs and some would be dramatically improved with drugs. Anything that's going to move them from the fucking middling state they're in, whether it's a cup of coffee or a snowball up your jacksy." PETE (2005)

"I don't know if taking drugs would make you feel glamorous, maybe the opposite. It might make you feel dingy or sordid. Or maybe for a split second you might feel elevated or glamorous, but I would never say drugs are glamorous or made me feel glamorous." PETE (2005)

❝I feel guilty about so many things. I don't feel guilty at the point of taking drugs, no, otherwise I probably wouldn't take it 'cos the negative things that came at the moment would outweigh any of the joys.❞ PETE (2005)

❝**Drug-taking affected my creativity in that it'd distract you from picking up a pen or a guitar.**❞ PETE (2005)

❝Each man kills the things he loves. I'm not a nihilist and I don't want to die.❞ **PETE (2005)**

❝**I think a lot of the kids that come up to me or write to me aren't bothered about drugs. I've yet to have someone come and ask me for my drug dealer's number.**❞ PETE (2005)

❝I had this amazing china white heroin which you don't get in London. This fella I knew had smuggled it back from India up his arse.❞ **PETE (2005)**

❝**Crack's gorgeous. But I want to get clean for Kate.**❞ PETE (2005)

❝I've had it. I've done it (drugs). Sporadically, always, for the last couple of years. When I hit it I hit it hard, but I'm not like this drugs monster that people make me out to be.❞ **PETE (2005)**

❝**Me and Wolfman were off to bury the stuff by my grandfather's grave in west London, to draw a line under our drug-taking days (when we got busted). We were just unlucky to be pulled over. Kate doesn't know I've been arrested, and only got out of the nick at 6am.**❞ PETE (2005)

DRUGS

PETE DOHERTY *Talking*

Rehab

"People in the Libertines' camp think I've wasted all this money and time on rehabilitation but it's not true. The time in the monastery (in Thailand), the time in the Priory, were times of being clean, so it's not a waste, is it?" **PETE (2005)**

"You learn about your strengths and you learn about your weaknesses. Any effort you make... you can't knock someone just because they don't last the distance." PETE (2005)

The Priory

"I'm fine... they've whacked me on loads of medication. 16 different colours (of) pills like hundreds of thousands of Bassett's jelly babies." **PETE (2004)**

"If I can't even go 24 hours without having a hit... then I'm never in reality going into rehab voluntarily." PETE (2005)

"I've got to start getting clean straight away. But I can't do it in the Priory or places like that. I have to do it in the environment I live in because I am always going to be surrounded by drugs when I'm making music. I've just got to find the inner strength to control it." **PETE**

"It's the only time I'll have fucking voluntarily gone into rehab."

PETE (2005)

❝(I went to the Priory) to show them I was making an effort, because I know they don't like those things (drugs). Even though I feel I'm in control.❞ PETE (2004)

❝**Carl came down and brought me some QPR trunks and said, 'Come on, let's go swimming.' But the swimming pool was closed so he went home.**❞ PETE (2005)

❝I was told I was allowed no visitors, and all of a sudden Carl comes in. I didn't want to see him, I wanted to fucking get clean, and do it and make him proud and that's the reason I was in there, for him... then he came in and I just felt really dirty.❞ PETE (2005)

Thailand

❝**I'd only come out of the Priory a couple of days earlier so I'd been through all the shakes, vomiting and (sleepless) nights with cold turkey. Foolishly I didn't do any research about Thailand before I went, and it was hardcore.**❞ PETE (2004)

❝To get the most out of that place (Thailand) isn't to approach it like, 'I'm going to recover from a drug.' It's to enter on a spiritual journey within yourself to find that precious thing you might call a soul. All I could think of, though, was songs.❞ PETE (2004)

❝**I had a breakdown at one point. I said 'Let me go.' They said, 'We don't think that's a good idea; the head monk is dying, he's very ill, it's a very bad time at the moment you can't go without his permission'.**❞ PETE (2005)

❝On the third day, I left and went to Bangkok. I booked into a hotel where they offered room service of heroin with my bacon and eggs. I told them I didn't have any money but they said I could have it on a tab. I notched up a £280 bill in three days. If I'd done the same amount of brown in England it would have cost me thousands.❞ PETE (2004)

REHAB

"They (the monks) thought I was some millionaire rock star who was going to invest in the monastery." PETE (2005)

"They were expecting me to be a gibbering wreck. I was sleeping, and eating, I was all right – it was psychological. I couldn't stay in that place. I thought I was going to be isolated but I wasn't. I had monks coming up to me with photocopies of *The Sun*.**"** PETE (2005)

"(I have a) very deranged and murky recollection of the last few days. A gaggle of nurses around my crinkly bed, they all jump as I wake up and yelp something about jelly. Then I notice a needle sticking out of my arm and spots of blood. What the fuck is going on? Vomit and shrieks, some girl warbling down the corridor in a towel. At least my laptop is here still. The only one who ever stood by me." PETE (2004)

"Thamkrabok was a wake-up call. I was getting stronger and learning how to deal with something that had overtaken me at the time. I discovered things about myself that I didn't like. It was part of the process of spewing up poison. One of the monks was convinced that the demons coming out of me were the scariest he'd seen. It frightened the fuck out of me. But it let me know that that dark energy is there – and when I've developed as a human being I'll try and confront that dark side.**"** PETE (2004)

"I was cut off (in Thailand) from my immediate surroundings in this room with 12 or 13 mattresses, bunks and lots of people who looked like they hadn't slept for a long time." PETE (2005)

"(Arriving in Thailand) reminded me of certain times in my life when I've arrived in a new place completely alien, like moving to England when I was very, very young.**"** PETE (2005)

Escaping from the monastery in Thailand
"With the help of this bloke from Manchester I managed to get out." PETE (2005)

Arizona

"With the amount of coke Kate was taking, it was amazing she got through rehab. I don't know how she stuck it for five weeks because I was bored senseless. I thought I'd be able to do five weeks. But if I'm honest my head would have exploded. I only stuck at it because she (Kate) paid." **PETE (2005)**

"**I had to share a room with two people. There were lots of strange people in there. It was like a prison.**" PETE (2005)

"They made me carry a teddy bear to show I had lost my inner child. A light came down from the sky. It was like a vision telling me to pull my finger out – pull my finger out of my crack pipe. I really wanted to do well in rehab to be strong for my family and Kate. But I missed London and my friends." **PETE (2005)**

REHAB

PETE DOHERTY *Talking*

On The Road

"You certainly find out who your friends are in times of trouble, and right now it's clear there are many who just can't wait for me to fail and appear a flaky junkie, unreliable and fucked up on drugs." PETE (2004)

"On stage every night I feel really quite exposed. Just like a little boy, a rabbit caught in the headlights. It's like a dream. It's annoying that you can't read everybody's mind in the audience and know exactly what they're thinking and feeling." PETE (2005)

"There was the point when we went out to Philadelphia and I sat at the back of the minibus blowing fumes of crack into the back of Gary's head. You could have cut the atmosphere with a fucking cake knife." PETE (2005)

"We haven't rescheduled it (the 2005 Babyshambles tour) yet, but we're going to. It was a bit scary. We were in the tour bus and they (fans) were actually rocking it. What's funny was, I was looking out of the window at all this craziness and the riot police and I looked down and Pete was sleeping. I was laughing most of the time but I felt sorry for our tour manager when he had to go and announce on stage that we wouldn't be appearing. He got a hail of about 500 bottles thrown at him.**"** **PAT WALDEN (2005)**

"It's happened so many times, waking up in the wrong town, and not making the gig. It's never a deliberate 'fuck the gig' thing. I was gutted the other day when we got out of the police station in Shrewsbury (after being arrested for alleged drug possession) and I found out they cancelled Norwich. How far was it away? Three hours, four hours? Yeah, we could have done it. It's a shame, especially in situations like that, when you know in your heart that going to the gig and playing music would have been the best thing for us." PETE (2005)

"I remember in Switzerland we ended up in a state-sanctioned brothel, and it was a Rolling Stones-themed brothel. They'd only play the Stones and there was this big fat mama who ended up chasing us out.**"** **PETE (2005)**

"By the time they (Chas 'n' Dave) played with us at Brixton I was getting stuff in the post from them, invitations to go down to their gaff, communication with one of their daughters and getting a bit of support as well." PETE (2005)

"I remember fucking this girl in the toilets, on the floor, proper sort of sliding about the tiles and Carl came in with another girl, just as cool as you like, and bent her over the disabled toilet. So there were those intimate, tender, romantic moments...**"** **PETE (2005)**

ON THE ROAD

"I remember, we supported the Strokes, and I was walking down backstage past their dressing room, and I hear this voice 'There goes Pete, trying to be Julian (Casablancas).' But that's just them, you know? I don't care really." PETE (2003)

"There was one lad who was really not very friendly. He was preaching really seriously 'Libertines! You've got to get back in the Libertines!' and trying to grab my microphone." PETE (2005)

"The gig I played with Babyshambles in Manchester was the most extreme collection of hooligans and geezers that I've ever seen since I stood on the Shed at Chelsea when I was about 10."

PETE (2005)

"I felt differently about myself and my life after prison. I can't emphasise enough what sort of torments Carl and I went through before going on stage – proper heebie-jeebies, running the gauntlet, everything turning inside out, and then all of a sudden it wasn't like that any more." PETE (2005)

"(2002's Up The Bracket Tour was) not a really happy time. The camera didn't lie, but you laugh and joke and can still be unhappy. We were battling so much with each other, and with the world." PETE (2005)

A 2005 Babyshambles gig:
"It was a self-aware Manchester crowd, girls as well singing, 'Oh Manchester is wonderful, it's full of tits, fanny and United, oh Manchester is wonderful'. I was scared until I realised they were having a good time." PETE (2005)

"That's what we were after. That's the thing we wanted: a fucking riot with people singing our words. That's what makes everything, the unity of the crowd, that's the buzz. The mob. If it's a harmonious mob, it's all right." PETE (2003)

"The crowds we'd had before were a little more edgy, a bit more quirky, and reaching out to different sections of the society. I'd say the crowds we were starting to get then were a little more mainstream, and a bit more homogenised.**"** PETE (2005)

"I get the heebie-jeebies and fidget and pace before a show. It's not nerves, it's proper terror. It's like a little kid about to go into confession." PETE (2005)

"Who's that fella who rolls the boulder up the hill? Sisyphus? Touring is like that. You build it up one night and then start again from scratch the next.**"** PETE (2002)

"I remember Carl, he picked up a couple of brasses (girls) and he gave me the one he didn't really want, but I ended up being sick on her tits in the hotel room so she ran off. I had to listen to all night to his bed squeaking." PETE (2005)

ON THE ROAD

"A tour routine developed – we'd both sleep whenever we were on the bus, wake up, stumble out and be forced into an interview, then be forced on stage." PETE (2005)

"I felt like the only one on stage who was playing properly, with commitment and concentration, and I felt detached from the rest of the band who were a bit sloppy, to be honest." PETE (2005)

"In Italy we met some very serious girls. They told us we were deluded. That we were stuck somewhere between passion and the *New Musical Express*. They said they followed the original Arcadian dream... which is rural. Whereas we've got this tin-pot ideal of Arcadia based on the Celtic tradition. They'd stolen some icons from a church and they gave us one each."

PETE (2002)

Arriving for the Dave Letterman Show

"I remember having a hat on and a pair of sunglasses that I'd found and pretending to be Marilyn Manson's brother. I just happened to fall out of a car with black-out windows and there were hordes of kids down there going, 'Are you Marilyn Manson?' because I had a guitar, and I go, 'Yeah, I'm playing guitar with him today, I'm actually his stepbrother man,' and, 'Man, I'm buzzed out,' and there was a furore." PETE (2005)

"We'd been up all night, bombing around Tokyo, breaking into bars. We found this funny complex where the lifts went up to different bars and we found ourselves on this level where the bar was actually locked so we bust open the door and the pair of us stole bottles of gin and an umbrella." PETE (2005)

"The other night in Barcelona we finished the gig and no-one was dancing afterwards. So we just put 'Dreaming Of You' on and started jumping around. Once they saw that we wanted to have a good time too, everyone joined in.' PETE (2002)

"At *Top Of The Pops* **you make your own amusement, running around the corridors. Mick Jones came down and it was drinks all round. We met the Cheeky Girls' mum. Busted were there too."**

PETE (2005)

To fans on missing a gig

"I apologise to all those who lost out but, given some of the reactions, I'm glad that a few of you have been inconvenienced. In fact, I'll eke out all of the gits until I can be sure I'm playing to a crowd who trust me, believe in me, and don't turn on me at the first chance they get. You want clockwork, amoral live music? There's plenty of that about. What I did I did for you... and the response is quite heartbreaking." PETE (2004)

"Within five hours of being in New York (for the American tour) I had a homeless crack bum living in my hotel room, washing-up, these twins, a couple of Sixties freaks and the daughter of a politician – all in my bed!" PETE (2005)

"I wasn't lost for words and I wasn't out of it on drugs. Just before I went on stage (at Live 8) Peaches (Geldof, Bob's daughter) squeezed my bum hard and whispered something rather suggestive to me. It left me in such shock I didn't know where I was." PETE (2005)

"Bob Geldof has organised this amazing global event (Live 8), I was facing 210,000 people, the cameras are rolling, and fucking Elton John is duetting with me. And Bob's daughter has secretly made a pass at me. It's all I can think about. It did my head in. I didn't think Bob would be very happy." PETE (2005)

ON THE ROAD

" The (Babyshambles') secret gigs aren't really secret.
It's just that the only way of communicating with people is
through the internet, and it's normally a last-minute decision
to play. I'll have a new song, and I'll think, 'I want to play it,'
so I whack it on the internet. But generally I'll just do it in a local
pub or my front room or something, because I know it's going
to be a last-minute terrorist gig. There's never any hassle, the
neighbours are normally all right, and the police have got better
things to do, I'm sure. " PETE (2004)

" (Live 8) is the biggest crowd I have ever performed in front of.
I enjoyed it, but everybody has been knocking me and that's put
the dampers on it a bit. I didn't turn up late at all and I wasn't all
over the place on drugs. I may have been slightly agitated, but
I wasn't on drugs. " PETE (2005)

" Playing to 4,000 people in Birmingham was the most astonishing
thing, but people didn't seem like they wanted to dance to songs
they didn't know, which I can never understand. So I thought that
maybe they didn't dig it. Ideally, I'd really want people to come
away thinking 'Wasn't that
really good fun, jumping up and
down for half an hour?' I want
movement in the crowd. I think
that, up until now, people that
would want to dance have
been put off because they've
been looking around at the
audience and seeing nothing
but a load of industry
scum. " PETE (2002)

" There was one gig where I'd
had enough and I tried to
explain it to everyone but
no one was really
listening. " PETE (2005)

Heroes & Role Models

"Imagine a relationship that went wrong but you held on in there for years: that's what it is like supporting a football team. Your loyalty to a team can never die. Ties are stronger than they could ever be with a woman. If she goes and sleeps with your best mate, it's over. If the Rs' boss, Ian Holloway, slept with my best mate, Queens Park Rangers would still be my team. Even if many of the things that you loved about going to matches have gone – terraces, team shirts without sponsors and being able to smoke at grounds – you still stick with your team." PETE (2005)

"You could sit at his (producer Mick Jones) feet and listen to stories about the Clash. We didn't know that much about the Clash and we learnt so much. Something as simple as Mick giving Carl a DVD, and Carl really treasured that, still does." **PETE (2005)**

On topping the *NME*'s 2004 'cool list'

"Moi? You can't take these things too seriously, but then who am I to argue? It's probably one of the most uncool things that can happen to you – I was 'Git Of The Year' last year, I think, and I haven't changed that much..." PETE (2004)

"When people say, 'Oh Pete, you make me want to play guitar,' that's the dream. Just keep it going, because that's our culture really." **PETE (2004)**

PETE DOHERTY *Talking*

❝Playing with the Strokes was almost the ideal. I first bumped into them through this lass I'd been Bonnie and Clyde-ing with for a few years called Francesca.❞ PETE (2005)

❝I believe that at the core of everything I do there is an innocence. I don't care how soppy that sounds. There is a belief in dancing and unity through music, and fuck everything else. Everything else just upsets my Nan.❞ **PETE (2002)**

❝Wolfman (Pete Wolf) is a talented fella, you know. Songs like 'Cyclop', 'The Delaney', 'Back From The Dead', they've all had input from Wolfman.❞ PETE (2005)

❝Ian Brown's made probably my favourite LP. They always say he can't sing. But people don't credit his lyrics. That's the best thing about him. His writing.❞ **PETE (2005)**

❝You only have to look at his (Shane MacGowan's) lyrics and they are so historical, magical, emotional and gentle...❞

PETE (2002)

❝Was I always into music? Not into chart music and bands. Just into songs.❞ **PETE (2005)**

❝I was always sung to and read stories from an early age, which is very important for a child and their creativity.❞ PETE (2004)

IAN BROWN

❝That's what music is all about. Music isn't a mouthpiece, it's a vessel.❞ **PETE**

"The only person I really wanted to reproduce (on guitar) was (the Smiths') Johnny Marr, and I couldn't – no matter how hard I tried, I couldn't. It wasn't until five years later that I realised you could play the same chord in a different shape..." PETE (2005)

"When I was a boy, I couldn't imagine anything other than going and living in Ellerslie Road or on the White City estate, near Loftus Road, where Rangers play. That's how central to my existence QPR was." PETE (2005)

"I used to write a QPR fanzine, *All Quiet On The Western Avenue*. I was brought up in lots of different places, so there was a rootlessness to my life and the team gave me an identity. Playing football brought people together – we'd play against any brick wall, on any kerb, or see if we could put the window through in the art department." PETE (2005)

"He (Suede guitarist Bernard Butler) took us shopping for proper guitar strings; he comforted us, calmed us. I went in with an open mind and he was wonderful. He's still so young-looking."
PETE (2002)

"My fondest memories involve things that happened off the pitch. I would climb into Loftus Road in the summer when the stadium was empty and sit there with my little book and pen, smoking a spliff behind the goal. One time, my girlfriend and I got into the dressing room and I stole a pair of shorts. That was one of the most romantic days of my life – snogging in the dressing room at QPR." PETE (2005)

"I think a lot of the kids that come up to me after gigs or write to me aren't really bothered about drugs... they are quite clued up, they don't take their inspiration from the drugs." PETE (2004)

HEROES & **ROLE MODELS** 99

"There were certain things I could romanticise about other people's lives. I might perceive certain things and think, 'Well if they did it, it must be all right.' Take (QPR footballer) Dennis Bailey, for example. He scored a hat trick on New Year's Day in Old Trafford, right, 4-1; it's before Sky took over English football, the halcyon days you might call them, but he was a born-again Christian, and he made me turn to Genesis. I wrote to him, and he wrote back saying I should read the Bible. He made me open the pages of Genesis." PETE (2005)

"I heard the Smiths and a whole new world opened up. I suppose obsessed would be the right word – not in a morbid way. It broke my heart when I realised they had split up 12 years previously. After discovering the Smiths, I followed the trail back to the Buzzcocks and I was well into the Only Ones – melodic bands who had a bit of a dirty sound. And then the New York Dolls. I fell in love with them... and the Stooges." PETE (2004)

"I never like to be disrespectful to the elderly, and she (Sharon Osbourne) is knocking on a bit, despite all that surgery."

PETE (2005)

"I was obsessed with certain writers, certain styles of film. Those kitchen-sink films, like *Billy Liar*, hit me right in the heart. I suppose I did live inside those films for want of a better place to be. The films I watched were about a pride, a dignity and a respect for people who you feel you belong with – a community and a mutual respect." PETE (2004)

"I must have been 17 or 18, living in Whitechapel, and me and three mates went to a Morrisey Battersea Power Station gig. None of us had been to a gig before. Morrissey was like something weird, from a different world. We didn't know what to do. We knew it wasn't like a football match. I remember a lot of animosity. Then the music started and that was it. It was wicked." PETE (2003)

❝In 1998 someone spiked me stuffing and I missed a Tony Hancock Christmas special.**❞** PETE (2002)

❝('I Started Something I Couldn't Finish' by the Smiths) changed everything for me. I could live in that song. It was like a drug trip, even though I wasn't taking any at the time, and I understood at that very moment that I had to start creating. I understood that, in three minutes you could save the world or find a girl, become anyone, do anything. You could climb mountains or go down sewers. You could drown yourself in your dreams and believe in them. Music made real what I felt deep down in myself without managing to define it, to express it, it was possible. Real.❞ PETE (2002)

THE SMITHS

❝I was a bit of a late starter with bands. It just passed me by, even though when I was at school bands like Nirvana and Oasis were around. Looking back, I remember people being into them, but at the time I was in another world.**❞** PETE (2004)

❝When I went to shake (Morrissey's) hand, he sort of did a rude boy shuffle. Apparently he said the Libertines are better off without me. How does that feel? Horrid. Next time I see him I'll boob him one on his hooter.❞ PETE (2004)

HEROES & ROLE MODELS

PETE DOHERTY *Talking*

Others Have Their Say

"The Libertines? I looked it up in the dictionary and it said 'Dissolute'. So I looked up dissolute and it said 'lacking in morals.' Albion – I looked this up in this Victorian Collins Dictionary and it said 'England: a phrase used in poetry.' So there you have it. The Luvverly Libertines – long may they reign."

MICK JONES (2002)

"Did I talk to Pete Doherty and warn him about Kate? Jesus. That never happened. I've never met him. I like him in that I like his music very much. I think he has a great talent and it seems to me that he and Kate could be great together because she's a great girl. She's got a great brain on her and I think she's a good mummy." JOHNNY DEPP (2005)

"Carl is probably the one that you can get on easier with, but I love them both for what they are, they're both very funny. They would antagonise each other quite a bit, shall we say..."

LIBERTINES PUBLICIST TONY LINKIN (2005)

JOHNNY DEPP

"Listen son, you wouldn't last a fucking rehearsal in Oasis. You'd be injecting washing-up liquid into your sphincter within half a fucking hour." NOEL GALLAGHER, OASIS (2005)

"We went to see them rehearse and it was love at first sight. I didn't need convincing at all – it's nice when that happens.**"**
ROUGH TRADE RECORDS GEOFF TRAVIS (2005)

"Peter's got a really unique style; he's a much better guitarist than people take him for. I was amazed when I first sat down with an acoustic guitar with him – he's really different. He plays a lot of jazzy fingerpicking kind of stuff, and it's not sloppy like the live shows at all." BABYSHAMBLES PAT WALDEN (2005)

"The first time I came across them (Pete and Carl) they lived above me in a flat on Holloway Road.**"**
ROGER SARGENT (BAND PHOTOGRAPHER) (2005)

"I'm not into smackheads. Smackheads need slaps. So what does the word Libertine mean? What does it mean? Freedom? He's fucking in the corner doing smack with a helmet on his head! There's nothing free about that. It's nasty, innit? If the kids like them, fair enough, but they're nowhere near like us. The music's rubbish, for a start." LIAM GALLAGHER, OASIS (2005)

"The pair of them (Carl and Pete) together have got such a sense of humour; they're like brothers, like Liam and Noel (Gallagher), in that way they can argue a hell of a lot then make up.**"**
TONY LINKIN (2005)

"He used to come into my shop, the Soul Kitchen on Bethnal Green Road, fairly regularly just after he got his deal and he must have bought five or six Sixties' re-conditioned battery-operated record players, for over a ton a time. He was really polite, really cool."
ACID JAZZ RECORDS EDDIE PILLER (2005)

OTHERS HAVE THEIR SAY

"It's difficult to get Peter to sit down, to sit still and talk to you – there's lots of jumping around and clowning around."

TONY LINKIN (2005)

"I was disappointed (about his no-show supporting Oasis at Southampton's Rose Bowl, summer 2005) because I convinced Liam to get Babyshambles on because I'd seen them at Brixton and I thought it was amazing. And Liam was going, 'No man, I'm not having any of this shit,' and I was going, 'Fucking trust me man, it's great.'" NOEL GALLAGHER (2005)

NOEL AND LIAM GALLAGHER

"We weren't furious, it was like, 'Oh, he's got to do a fashion show,' and it was like, 'Well if fashion shows mean more to you, good luck to you.' He should change his name really, I think he's living up to his name as Babyshambles." **NOEL GALLAGHER (2005)**

"Can you imagine if he goes on *Celebrity Big Brother*? It just seems like the most ludicrous thing ever. Most people who are in that position have got really minor talent. Hank Williams got married on stage and charged people money. I can see Pete doing that."

GEOFF TRAVIS (2004)

"He thinks no one understands him but of course we all do. You're just being a wanker. Go home."

CHARLOTTE 'VOICE OF AN ANGEL' CHURCH (2005)

"Peter, I remember, kissing me the first day (of meeting Pete and Carl) and being very charming. We just hit it off immediately. I thought they sounded great – they were great."

TONY LINKIN (COALITION PR) 2005

"I'd just had the baby, which he turned up for and was, well, I won't say fine but it was what it was. It was great he was there for the birth but at that point he was really low, he was really bad."

LISA MOORISH (2005)

"They're the most extreme band I've ever worked with. It's sort of not rock 'n' roll. I don't know what it is. Mental illness, probably." ALAN MCGEE (2005)

"Addiction is a horrible thing, it's nothing to be laughed at. I look at Pete Doherty and I just want to put my arm around him."

ELTON JOHN (2005)

"It's really sad. He's so young I don't think that he's going to listen to anybody. I don't think the people around him set a good example, which is a shame. I have to be very discreet what I say, but I just think he was really nervous on the (Live 8) day. But, you know, he had his chance to do it and he came on... at least he looked great!" ELTON JOHN (2005)

OTHERS HAVE THEIR SAY 99

"Fucking Babyshambles. I don't want to fight them, I don't want their fucking birds, I don't want to shoot their dogs, don't want to stand on their hamster's head and I'm just not into their music."

LIAM GALLAGHER (2005)

"The boy's gone through hell. It's his second implant and it's gone septic... he's gone through it, he's suffering... You think crack and heroin are hardcore? Try not sleeping for five days. That will fuck you up... After two days I need to get some kip, but Peter and Patrick have an ability to stay up for days." DREW MCCONNELL (2005)

"There is only one British hero right now: Pete Doherty, lead singer of the Libertines and Babyshambles." **LIAM GALLAGHER (2005)**

"It's inspiring (being in a band with Pete) but it's tiring because he's so prolific. The reason he does his music is because he has to. He writes constantly. He'll stay up writing for three or four days, like an obsessive." PATRICK WALDEN (2005)

"He lives the rock 'n' roll life – he's understood everything about that side of things. He doesn't give a monkey's about anything, does exactly what he wants to do. I admire his decadence. I completely recognise myself in him." **LIAM GALLAGHER (2005)**

"I think Doherty and Elton were fantastic (at Live 8). I know there's been a lot of criticism about Pete forgetting his words and stumbling around the stage, but it was undoubtedly a very memorable performance." BOB GELDOF (2005)

"I mean, with someone like Pete from the Libertines, who I have never met, God, it's like a biography that you have read 10 times before. It doesn't have to be that way." **FOO FIGHTER DAVE GROHL (2005)**

"I'm not one to preach to anybody. I've had my share of fun, too. But music is such a beautiful thing. I would hate to see it suffer to something like drugs. What a drag. What a waste. Such a bummer." DAVE GROHL (2005)

PETE DOHERTY *Talking*

"In a way it is almost glorified, you know. 'Wow, he must be a bad ass, he is living the life.' To me it just seems like, 'God, don't do it.' It's such a clichéd dead end. But at the same time I don't mind drinking half a bottle of whiskey every now and then with some friends." **DAVE GROHL (2005)**

"Pete Doherty's behaviour is like the crying of a baby and we all have to go through it. It's just that some people go through it up to the time of their memorial." BILLY IDOL (2005)

"I don't know Elton what was hoping to achieve by doing a duet with Pete Doherty at Live 8. It was almost like it was Doherty's duty to be wasted and stumble about on stage. He's a very intelligent man. It's sad to watch his heroin addiction being glorified. He hasn't written a memorable pop song. (Kate Moss) didn't deserve all the flak she got because she doesn't court publicity. But the press was doing her a favour in the end because she has a child – and you can't hang around with heroin addicts and dealers when you are a mother." **GEORGE MICHAEL (2005)**

"It's a shame that some people who write good songs feel they need to submerge themselves in that gunk. I got caught up in it myself but it doesn't need to be done." BILLY IDOL (2005)

"I think two years ago, if you thought of Pete Doherty, he was kind of untouchable. Now when you think of Pete Doherty you think of that guy who's always in the background of that picture with Kate Moss. And if he wants to go out like that, then each to their own, and I'm sure he's having a great time but, y'know, are you gonna be remembered as Kate Moss's boyfriend or a fucking artist?"

NOEL GALLAGHER (2005)

"He needs to go through some hardcore rehab. That will strip him of any notion of celebrity. They should be telling him, 'You're the same as everybody else. You're a fucking addict.' It's his only chance of survival because I'm terrified the poor little thing's gonna OD. Now he thinks this is a part he has to play, it's become like a character to play out. People want to see that."

SHARON OSBOURNE (2005)

"Pete, if you wanna do some good, tell the world that being on drugs is a fucking waste." **JOHNNY BORRELL (RAZORLIGHT) (2005)**

"He's got the X Factor, hasn't he? He's magic to watch. You can't learn that." ROGER DALTREY (THE WHO) (2005)

"What's so disarming about Peter is that he pretends he's in control, or he thinks he is. But if he's up to everything (with drugs) people say he is, he cannot be in control." **ROGER DALTREY (2005)**

"He is a genius. But I've known many people like that and they're all dead." ROGER DALTREY (2005)

"All I can say is good luck to him. It's a hard life anyway."
JOHN LYDON (SEX PISTOL JOHNNY ROTTEN) (2005)

"In six months, if he's not put a record out, it's gonna smack of the emperor's new clothes, all of it." NOEL GALLAGHER (2005)

OZZY OSBOURNE

"I just hope he gets it before he dies." **OZZY OSBOURNE (2005)**

"He's made a decision to play this drugs game. But I haven't seen many survivors. And I don't want to see him become another stupid rock death. Pete – calm down a little and start checking yourself. You're not impressing anyone. You're depressing."
JOHN LYDON (JOHNNY ROTTEN) (2005)

"I don't know what all the fuss is about. Pete's just a junkie, a useless waste of space. We supported the Libertines once when they were at the height of

OTHERS HAVE THEIR SAY

their powers. But they seemed to get worse and worse from then on. He's so unreliable. He's always late or not even bothering to turn up for gigs. **" JUSTIN HAWKINS (2005)**

"My opinion of him hasn't changed. His heart's in the right place but the people he's around are not that good for him."

NOEL GALLAGHER (2005)

"I don't know what Kate Moss sees in him.**" JUSTIN HAWKINS (2005)**

"I'm the last person to give advice and I think he should make the most of everything and have the best time he can. But I just hope he quits before it's too late." OZZY OSBOURNE (2005)

"Pete Doherty is a brilliant songwriter. 'Fuck Forever' is a real anthem. I was really impressed with him when I saw him in Paris.**"**

FRANZ FERDINAND'S ALEX KAPRANOS (2005)

"The (Live 8) concert was all about raising awareness, but Peter looked like he was having trouble raising his own awareness. He looked wasted. With Africa we're talking about a nation battling through immense poverty and hardship, and he can't quite get it together to sing a song. When you look at what they're faced with, it kind of makes his drama and what he's faced with seem trivial."
MURDOC (GORILLAZ BASSIST) (2005)

"The fact of the matter is, I would never lash out at Pete Doherty like that. Are we really listening to cartoons now? What next, Homer Simpson for President?**"**
BLUR'S DAMON ALBARN (2005)

DAMON ALBARN

"Pete Doherty? Well he needs a bleedin' good slap, that's what. He needs locking down in rehab for a couple of months."

SHARON OSBOURNE (2005)

"Y'know, every so often I'll get off my face, but I look at someone like Peter and I just think, 'You're a fucking moron because your music was so much better before you started doing that.' Y'know, it's working in the sense that people want to come and look at the car crash. But, although last night was a bad fucking night for me, I am not a fucking car crash. I am here to make music!"

JOHNNY BORRELL (2005)

"Pete Doherty needs to ditch the hangers-on and find someone who really loves him enough to tell him the truth. And the truth needs to be told to his face. There's nothing harder to take than the truth. It's not hip to be in that state he's in. It's not cool, it's pathetic." SHARON OSBOURNE (2005)

"He didn't display the self-obsession that is a hallmark of addicts. He was courteous and solicitous... Doherty appears younger than his 25 years, but he's also pretty savvy and the Byronic image is not an accident." **BBC NEWSNIGHT INTERVIEWER KIRSTY WARK (2005)**

"(Pete and Carl) will be talking only from their individual standpoints with respect to their relationships with each other and that's fine, that's between them. But y'know, if they start talking about the band, then that's when I'll have to get involved." GARY POWELL (LIBERTINES DRUMMER) (2004)

"It would be good if people just started concentrating on the music instead of the thing with Pete. Without wanting to blow our own trumpets, we're kind of an OK band and the band is four of us, not just Pete and Carl. I hope people realise that. I love Pete, Carl and John equally and as far as I'm concerned we're all the sum of our parts." **GARY POWELL (2004)**

OTHERS HAVE THEIR SAY

❝It's not as bad as the press make out. The majority of Peter is this little lost boy. He's very thoughtful. I had flu on our first tour, and Peter was always bringing me honey and tea and fussing over me like a nurse. On my birthday he arranged to have a big cake come on stage with the band singing 'Happy Birthday' to me. He's a sweet guy.❞ FORMER BABYSHAMBLES DRUMMER GEMMA CLARKE (2005)

❝I'm not sure he can cope. There's a desperation to him. I sense he's on thin ice. It's all very giggle-worthy for *NME* to report two hours after a gig that he's in a crack house in Glasgow but I don't find that amusing.❞ **MORRISSEY (2005)**

❝He should learn from the mistakes we made and the major mistake for us was to get involved in drugs. He should remember that drugs destroyed our band and killed Phil (Lynott).❞

SCOTT GORHAM (THIN LIZZY) (2005)

"It's obvious he's very insecure. He's not confident because he wouldn't do it if he was."

SHARON OSBOURNE (2005)

"Our drug addiction was never a conscious path taken, it was a trap we fell into. It wasn't premeditated. We did lots of drugs and became a big time party band. I'd advise him and anybody else right now that it doesn't work."

SCOTT GORHAM (THIN LIZZY) (2005)

"I've never met anybody as charming or charismatic as Peter. He's a very talented poet and a really lovely man. Give him a phrase or topic and he can produce a great song in five minutes. I'm in total awe of him when he's creating."

JAMES MULLORD (BABYSHAMBLES MANAGER) (2004)

"Pete is a huge, soulful, musical talent but it is getting to the point where I feel like I'm managing a tabloid pin-up like Jordan. I don't recognise the portrait of Pete as a bug-eyed lunatic. We need to get him into the studio, and then we will be able to reply to all this trash with the power of song."

JAMES MULLORD (2004)

SHAUN RYDER

"Pete's a young lad, he takes drugs, right? I think everyone's done that from John Lennon to Paul McCartney to fucking Brian Jones, y'know what I mean? Everyone's been a young kid that's got fucking stoned and a bit of their head and caused a few hassles, y'know?"

HAPPY MONDAYS' SHAUN RYDER (2005)

OTHERS HAVE THEIR SAY "

66Addiction is different with Pete Doherty. He's different and we live in very different times. It isn't the Sixties any more. People don't have to die because of their addictions – they get clean. It's not as if people haven't reached out to Pete. And I'm not being funny, but there's a sense of his addiction being quite pretty. You know? He stays up all night off his head and then the next day at midday he goes down to the beach with a supermodel wearing a silver ball gown to shoot tin cans off a wall. It's appealing. My addiction did not look like that. I'd end up with any old idiot who'd talk shit with me till the early hours. That wasn't pretty.**99** ROBBIE WILLIAMS (2005)

66I think the Libertines are pretty special and I think Pete Doherty's a great singer and a great artist all round. Don't take crack and smack is probably the best advice. But hopefully he'll come through it because it'd be a waste of real talent. But it's his demons, not ours. It's not for us to talk, really.**99** **PAUL WELLER** (2004)

66Pete Doherty got up with us on stage at the Forum. It was jam packed with young kids, all singing our songs. That was some buzz. Well it's rock 'n' roll, ain't it?**99**

DAVE PEACOCK (OF CHAS 'N' DAVE) (2005)

PETE WITH WOLFMAN

66He turned up the other day and moved all his stuff in. He won't leave me alone. It's like having a really needy little brother. He wants me to be his Bohemian trinket. He doesn't want me to do well. He wants me to do all my songs with him. My lyrics are all over those records.**99**

ONE-TIME CO-SONGWRITER
WOLFMAN (2004)

"What can you say about Pete Doherty? If you have to take heroin to be famous – well, I don't get it. Will Pete be a Kurt Cobain or a Jimi Hendrix? Never in a million years. He hasn't the talent to tune their guitars." SUPER PRODUCER PETE WATERMAN (2005)

"Is it difficult dealing with drugs in the band? I wouldn't say difficult. It's sometimes a challenge to pin people to commitments." ADAM FICEK (BABYSHAMBLES DRUMMER) (2005)

"I'd say firstly (Pete) doesn't do rock music, and secondly, he only sells records because people are curious as to what a junkie sounds like. I think that's really wrong and really irresponsible... I think he's a talentless waste of fucking skin!"
JUSTIN HAWKINS (THE DARKNESS) (2005)

"You wouldn't mind so much if the bloke had written a song that was good enough to justify all his publicity, but he's not got a good song in his body. I would like to smash him in the face really hard. I hate everything about him." ED GRAHAM (DARKNESS DRUMMER) (2005)

"He (Pete) should be on a plate. Served up on Sunday, with a selection of veg.' ED GRAHAM
JUSTIN HAWKINS REPLIES: 'You wouldn't eat that. You wouldn't put that fucking poison in your mouth would you?" (THE DARKNESS) (2005)

"He's a distinguished musician and brilliant at playing the guitar. It's a shame no one has shaken him and said, 'Wake up.' I feel sorry at the glorifying around him. He needs help." CRAIG DAVID (2005)

"It's a waste of a life really, because he's got talent. He seems to be feeding off it, now he's become infamous for his drug addiction he seems to think, 'That's what I do so I've got to do it.' It's very sad." ROGER DALTREY (2005)

OTHERS HAVE THEIR SAY

Taking On The Tabloids

On a recent Channel 4 documentary

“I thought it was a disgrace. Two things, I didn't go out with that girl, Katie, who said she was my girlfriend for two years, and I didn't go to private school. He (film-maker Max Carlish) did suffer for it, and then I suffered, and then everyone else had to suffer it. Did you see that bit with, 'In Pete, On Kate, Under Pete...?' It was disgusting. I may make one of my own (laughs) 'My Struggle'.**”**

PETE (2005)

“I've never been open with the press. Or I would be assassinated. It's not what the people want to hear. They wouldn't even be able to hear. Their earmuffs would blow up. Fucking cunts.” PETE (2005)

“Rough Trade own the *New Musical Express* anyway, so anything we get from that angle is always gonna be a compliment. Basically keep the *NME* supplied with drugs and they'll write nice things about you, that's the order of the day.**”** **PETE (2002)**

“On the day you can't (turn media coverage to advantage) because you're just disheartened and saddened. But in the long term... there's that thing about there being no such thing as bad publicity. Actually there is such a thing as bad publicity. I know that now...” PETE (2005)

PETE DOHERTY *Talking*

"I mean you look in the paper and you see the bodies of mutilated people, and that's controversy. Controversy isn't saying something like 'Oh I've fucked Noel Gallagher' or something. Which I have."

PETE (2002)

"In some ways I'm not sure a lot of the things they are writing about me are really worth reading. Everyone seems to dwell on the far-fetched aspects of my life and the caricatures, lampooning, which is fair enough – fair enough in that world because you can exaggerate things and glorify things to suit a market or suit an idea, build a myth. In one way it's there, but in another way, it doesn't really exist because it's all artificial."

PETE (2004)

"You sit and talk about your hopes and your band's music and they say, 'Yeah, that's great. We're really gonna cover your band'. Then you read the *Mirror* and it's like, '£1,000 a day on crack and heroin.' So the five minutes you spent talking about drugs is the article." PETE (2004)

"This is the first time in years I've come on tour not being a heroin addict. It's a really positive vibe, a positive, exciting time. We're just here to play music." PETE (2005)

"That's the thing about a lot of the tabloid stuff. They keep using the word junkie. It's just not accurate." PETE (2005)

"My Dad reads this stuff in the papers. I don't know why he reads the *Daily Star* now. He never used to, and I don't know why he's interested now." PETE (2005)

"I'm not under the thumb, right, but I got a proper bollocking at the Ivor Novello thing because of speaking to people." PETE

"(Kate's) one of the most private people I've ever met. She doesn't speak to anyone. And me, I'm a right old fucking tart. I like the headlines, they make me laugh." PETE (2005)

" It's moved on to another level now. I can't go anywhere any more without my face staring back at me, without being photographed. The whole world's a circus, and I'm the ringmaster. **"** PETE (2005)

"I've become this cartoon character. I try not to follow it, but when you see pictures of yourself that have been Photoshopped to show you doing something you didn't... that's wrong. It's my worst nightmare – and being misquoted, too, especially as I'm so precious about words." PETE (2005)

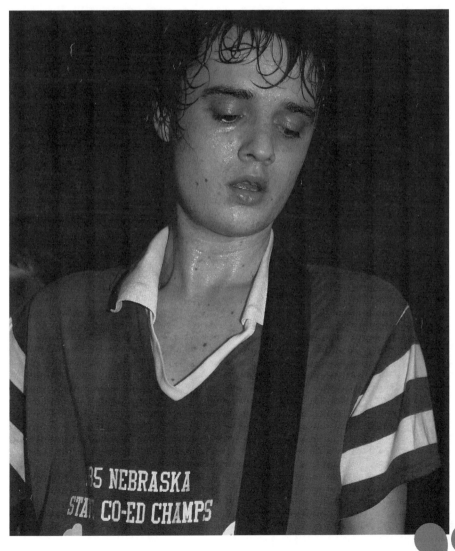

5 NEBRASKA STATE CO-ED CHAMPS

TAKING ON THE TABLOIDS

PETE DOHERTY *Talking*

Class&
Politics

"Well, it's just about bein' yourself... even when you're on the dole, it's about your leather jacket. Music is the last refuge of the working class, along with football... in fact, gigs and riots are the only things left that bring about that sense of spirit and community where you can let yourself go." **PETE (2004)**

"We don't give a fuck about anything. The Queen's a skanky old hag, but we don't even care about that." PETE (2002)

"I'd never say I wouldn't fight a war. In different ages I would have done. I'd have fought the Vikings." **PETE (2003)**

"I think that 'intellectual' is quite an exclusive word. I think it's just for anyone that has a thirst or a hunger to improve themselves, or a yearning to escape from somewhere to get to a better place." PETE (2002)

"Liberty is a heavy word so lightly thrown, as the song goes. It's in everything I say and do, the belief in liberty, not to bully or force people to do things they don't want to." **PETE (2005)**

"I'm obsessed by class. I spent two years at a school where 80 per cent of the kids were on meal tickets. Everything I know about morality and smoking I learnt there. Class is a fascinating thing. That was something that struck me about Carl when I met him –

here was this son of a factory worker who wanted to be Oscar Wilde. Personally, I just wanted to be the greatest songwriter of my generation.** PETE (2002)

What makes me angry? Injustice. Like, be a girl – try and be a girl for a day. Things happen to people you know, people who suffer because of their vulnerability. Oppression is overwhelming sometimes. To be raped or bullied or anything like that, where oppression is complete, and you're vulnerable and there's nothing you can do. PETE (2003)

For many people life is extreme. Getting up and digging holes, or pushing wheelbarrows into skips, that's extreme because you're really doing something you don't wanna do, but you do it because you know it's necessary. You can survive on the dole, but when you actually need to get a bit of money together you have to graft. But then the opportunity came along to make a bit of money doing what we do naturally. PETE (2003)

Just when you get really wound up, you turn a corner and you're somewhere else completely. You find an Arcadian glade – a glimpse of paradise in the middle of it all. And that's why you persevere. That's why you don't chuck yourself off a building or shoot yourself at the same time as someone else, like he (pointing at Carl) wanted us to. PETE (2003)

As a kid in school I was a bit of a blank canvas on certain issues. I was completely ignorant about drugs because it was such a taboo at home, and there was no education – you learnt things on the street or through experience. PETE (2004)

Bringing people together to fight capitalism – I'm into that. But I'm into learning as well. I need to know more of what it's about, and shape my own beliefs. A lot of the issues surrounding Third World debt and loans to countries involve keeping things as they are, rather than completely dismantling a system a majority of people find horrific. We need radical change. That's what I'm into and I think that's the only solution. PETE (2004)

CLASS & **POLITICS**

" PETE DOHERTY *Talking*

**"You have to replace capitalism because that's the only
thing it understands. It's like a disease or a fungus. You
can't tidy up the flower bed and restrain it a bit – you've got to
dig it out from the roots and replace it, otherwise it will keep
growing. That's the nature of capitalism. As far-fetched as it
seems, it can happen the way it's always happened in history,
and that's through a radical turnaround. Who really would have
thought in Russia in 1917 that that would happen? They were
coffee-shop philosophers who ended up in charge of the most
incredible revolution human history has seen." PETE (2004)**

"As well as being anti something, you've got to be pro something.
So you're anti racism, so what are you pro? You're pro community.
I would put my hand on my heart and I'd attach myself to socialist
ideas. Because I believe in society. And it's bollocks that black
people have any less worth in society than white people, which is
basically what people like the BNP say." **PETE (2004)**

**"I don't feel myself to be representative of a general feeling of
Englishness. I'm interested in William Blake, but there are less
spiritual, more practical people like Galton and Simpson, and Joe
Orton, who were interested in the fineries of everyday dialogue
and puns. In the same way that I immersed myself in the Smiths,
I did the same with a lot of aspects of English culture."** PETE (2004)

"I don't think you have to be a particularly developed human being
intellectually or spiritually to despise racism. It may be easy to be
complacent, but we need to encourage people to fight racism
whether with words or actions. I'll be there, fighting racism single-
handedly." **PETE (2005)**

**"I remember when I was four or five going to school and singing
racist songs but not realising what they meant. Things like 'Eeny-
meeny-miny-mo' and being told off but not knowing what for.
No one really explains anything, but (racism is) everywhere. It's
apparent in everyday life, in any place or industry and the music
industry is no different, it's like any other. As long as human
beings are involved, racism will be somewhere."** PETE (2004)

Trouble With The Law

"I kind of broke down. It's a stupid reaction, but I thought: 'I've jailed my friend.' But that's bollocks." **CARL BARAT (2004)**

"They (police) know I'm an addict, it's quite well publicised, but it's the dealers they want, don't they?" PETE (2005)

"I was pissed off at Peter's lack of self-worth. It was Peter once again crying out for attention and the only way he could do that was burgling his best friend. There were millions of people he could have done that to. He chose Carl." **GARY POWELL (2004)**

"Pentonville Prison was hell on earth. At night the noise was horrible and there is nothing more terrifying than the sound of a prison waking up. My cell stank of vomit and I felt the walls closing in. I thought I was going to die." PETE (2005)

On having a Libertines house party stopped by police

"It's been a pretty cool night, I don't really worry about the police. It's just great to play, y'know." **PETE (2003)**

After the tour bus was raided

"I kept thinking Jeremy Beadle was going to pop out. You should have seen the stuff they found under the mattress, it was like wall scrapings." PETE (2005)

PETE DOHERTY *Talking*

❝In the words of Dr Johnson, the law is a pain in the arse.**❞**

PETE (2005)

❝It's all a big mistake. Every day of this tour we have been told we are going to get raided and basically, they have found fuck all.❞

PETE (2005)

❝This fuckin' assistant hotel manager – jobsworth – shopped me and the Wolfman (his friend and occasional co-writer.) We had left blood on the walls and somehow they equated that to three grand's worth of damage.**❞ PETE (2005)**

❝It's like the police are waging a vendetta against me because young people look up to me and my music and want to make an example.❞ PETE (2005)

❝It's all been about police brutality. They had it in for me. I'm a bit worried about speaking out because the police will try and land something else on me.**❞ PETE (2005)**

❝Well, I'm not going back again (to Wandsworth Prison) that's for sure, not in a hurry anyway.❞

PETE (2003)

❝Wandsworth wasn't too bad, actually. There's so many people doing long sentences that you think yourself lucky, really.**❞**

PETE (2003)

❝I've penned a few songs and got a few tales to tell. (Prison) opened my eyes a bit, definitely. I thought I knew a thing or two, but no. I was well green in there.❞ PETE (2003)

"(Prison) opened my eyes to things. I think I lived a little bit blinkered. It made me want to sharpen myself up a bit. It wasn't a fun place to be. You're sat in a cell for 23 hours. Supposedly there's education and facilities, but in reality there's overcrowding and understaffing. You're sat in a cell and it's as boring as fuck. But alliances were forged, new worlds opened up, I did a lot of writing. There's a lot of unhappiness in prison, and I had some really unhappy moments. But there were people who reached out to me and helped me, and hopefully I helped a few people as well, in simple ways, like friendship." PETE (2004)

"Inside prison, I exchanged my phone credits for cigarettes so I didn't speak to anyone outside. When I came out, I rang the two people I love the most to tell them I'm OK – my mum and Kate."
PETE (2005)

"I felt like crying but the thought of Kate on the outside (of prison) kept me going. I was going through hell because of my heroin cold turkey." PETE (2005)

"I'd have made an escape attempt from the open prison if I'd been there much longer. People were running off all the time. I tried to arrange it with someone to bring a van down to the Isle of Sheppey." PETE (2005)

"One day I passed out in the dinner queue (of the open prison), fell unconscious and dropped forward. A fella caught me by the back of my shirt before I smashed my face in. I just lost consciousness through lack of nutrition because you don't get hardly anything to eat." PETE (2005)

"Carl came and met me, so the first thing I did was look shocked, because I was shocked. I'd kinda prepared in my mind for a life out of the Libertines, and I didn't have any fuckin' reason to go back to Carl. I felt completely betrayed, but I looked at it fairly and seen how I hurt him. I didn't not want to face it, I just wanted to get on, and I had so many songs waiting.

TROUBLE WITH THE LAW

I was just like, 'Give me a guitar!' And he was there. He embraced me. That certainly was a moment. Then we went to a pub in town just off Baker Street, I won't say what it's called... mainly because I can't remember! And we got ROYALLY fuckin' trashed! We got thrown out in the end, the pair of us; six cigars in mouth...** PETE (2004)

The screws don't turn a blind eye to drug use, and there's piss tests every five minutes. PETE (2005)

At the open prison my nan and sister came to visit, and Lisa with the baby but I couldn't wait to get back to the cell. I felt really ugly and dirty. PETE (2005)

I got a smack in the mouth in the first few days (at Wandsworth Prison) but then the fella who did it kind of embraced me, which was a bit strange. PETE (2005)

I shouldn't have been in Wandsworth because I was only a Category D prisoner and it's an A Category prison – but there were a lot more long-term hard-core criminals. PETE (2005)

I think I'll be really unlucky if I go back to prison, or stupid, but there are a lot of people who are in and out, in and out. Prison can make people hopeless, make them lose any sense of self-value.

PETE (2004)

Even like being in the dinner queue in the open prison was hard work; if another prisoner read this they'd think I was a complete fucking lunatic, but it was a real shock to the system. PETE (2005)

Time in Wandsworth Prison

Hundreds and hundreds of men in little rooms, all that food getting lobbed out of windows. They revel in their bad name, the overcrowding, the lack of positive outlets for people's energy. A lot of people can't read or write, or speak English, with no skills or training. PETE (2005)

On breaking into Carl Barat's house

❝I went to speak to Carlos about how I had a drummer and bass player living on my floor. They are on the dole and I needed to pay them because they are musicians. I was going down to Carlos's to say I can't pay them out of my own money and I found myself shouting at him and it turned out I was arguing with my reflection. When I realised, I booted the door in. I was engulfed by complete misery and despair. It wasn't revenge. It was more 'Why are you ignoring me?' – a cry from the darkness. I do feel remorse, I feel sick.❞

PETE (2003)

❝Alan McGee was the only person who said, 'You're gonna go to prison.' We ended up at my sister's house a week before the hearing and he just said, 'I think you'll go down.' I took what he said quite seriously, but [did not think] for a second that he might be right.❞ **PETE (2005)**

Arriving at Thames Magistrates Court

❝I'm free, to be whatever I, whatever I choose and I'll sing the blues if I want.❞ PETE (2005)

❝I had to take the guitar (to the Magistrates Court) because I had nowhere to leave it, and I didn't expect that kind of reception. I didn't really relate my arrival to the outcome of the case. I don't think it would have influenced it. I was under the impression that the magistrate was going to reply on the probation report and my arrival wouldn't influence him.❞ **PETE (2005)**

TROUBLE WITH THE LAW ❞

Albion –
My Country
& Me

>"I saw Mick Jones, Carl, John and Gary last night and I know I can mangle out all the creases and live out further my grandly Arcadian dreams and dear divine adventures all Albion's sons and daughters." PETE (2004)

>"At least we've got hot and cold running water here. We haven't got that at home. I have to flush my toilet with Evian (water). Only the best for the Albion rooms." **PETE (2003)**

>"The Albion is the name of the vessel. The band could have been called the Albion, but it's a shit name for a group." PETE (2002)

>"Anyone whose sofa I'd ever kipped on, who I'd ever scrounged a spliff off came to live at our new place, The Albion Rooms, 112a Teesdale Street, Bethnal Green." **PETE (2005)**

>"You know – Arcadia? The realm of the infinity? It's a poet's corner. This is the code by which we live our lives. This is the pact we've sworn all those years ago that turned us all from enemies into companions and wayfarers and travellers on the seas of Albion. It's not a cult or a religion – it's an awareness of your surroundings; you're not gonna force yourself on anyone and, equally, no-one's gonna force themselves on you.

PETE DOHERTY *Talking*

PETE DOHERTY *Talking*

And it's about community and pleasure. It came from a whisper
through the trees. It came from a crack in the pavement. It can
also come when you open a bag of crisps, or when you kick a
football against a goalpost. Even if I was winding you up, it
would still be true, because Arcadia and the Arcadian Dream is
so deep, is so true to our hearts... There have been Arcadian
gatherings over the years, but I think the best is yet to come.
It can be as powerful as your imagination can allow it to be.
But, it can also be as dark and twisted as your soul... Arcadia
encompasses the infinite, and that's why it comforts me.**"**

PETE (2002)

"The Albion is not reliant upon a certain four people being on a
poster together. It is for all our souls and imaginations. I embarked
upon this salty Arcadian venture before I met Carlos, or any of you,
and any of the other Libertines past (John, Gary) and present
(Max, Neil, Steve). It is reliant upon melody, not a dealer's number.
Upon trust, not citric acid. Upon strength and faith in adversity, not
a nice windbag full of bone on a summer's day belly down in the
yard with twin Polish birds rubbing coconut cream into me new
mermaid tattoo.**"** PETE (2003)

"I remember going to choose the place to live together. The
tension was there immediately deciding who was going to have
which room. Sadly my energy and positivity was matched by
Carl's paranoia and cautiousness.**"** PETE (2005)

"Albion is the good ship. It's the England we live in. The grey and
mundane. The glimpse of the clearing... Arcadia. It's important.
It's about melancholy and lust.**"** PETE (2005)

"It's what the Libertines are all about... capturing the Arcadian
Dream. The Arcadian Dream is a place in your imagination...
a communal imagination. A place where people can be
inspired by each other or even thrive off each others'
hatred.**"** PETE (2002)

The Future

“It's that mysterious thing called hype. I've looked under every rock, and I couldn't find out what it means. Certain people hear a certain melody, and they're attracted to it. I'm in love with that feeling. We're looking for fun and adventure and a bit of redemption and somewhere to live. Everything else is a blind venture into the unknown.” PETE (2003)

“**I don't know what the future holds any more, it's quite scary. I've got some kind of faith in optimism. I hope that friendship will out, above all else. Even if we never play again together, that would be nice.**” CARL (2005)

“Fair play to Michael Nyman for composing the song for Queens Park Rangers to come out on to the pitch but I've already written a song for when they win the FA Cup. He could do the B-side.”

PETE (2005)

“**Things aren't exactly perfect so maybe I'm painting a picture of doom and gloom – but God forbid that I would want to detract from the amazing times we had, round the piano with Mick (Jones), round the piano with John and Gary.**” PETE (2004)

“I'm gonna collaborate with Carl Barat. No I'm not (joking). I'm going to. Even if I have to kidnap him. We're gonna do a Christmas record. We always said we'd do a Christmas record. What better way to highlight the goodwill and forgiveness of man, than with a reunion?” PETE (2004)

PETE DOHERTY *Talking*

PETE DOHERTY *Talking*

"What I desire as a writer, or as an artist, is to stand alone and be seen as important and influential rather than be considered part of a group or part of a songwriting partnership." PETE (2005)

"Goodbye?... Hello?... I don't know really... I have a very bad relationship with the future... we don't get on. We just... ignore each other." PETE (2004)